HAWKER HURRICANE

A classic view of the MkIID in a banking turn.

Hawker
HURRICANE

Peter Jacobs

The Crowood Press

Acknowledgements

A book such as this could not have been written without help from many people. I have been fortunate to meet and correspond with many wonderful people and I thank all those who have helped me. In particular, I would like to thank Pat Wells for writing the foreword. Several years ago, I managed to track Pat down in South Africa and we have stayed in touch since. Thanks to him, for his contributions over the years. I would also like to thank my colleague and friend Sqn Ldr Clive Rowley for his contribution to the final chapter; although Clive and I have flown together in the Tornado F3 at RAF Coningsby, he has the advantage in that he flies the Hurricane of the Battle of Britain Memorial Flight in his spare time!

Not all those who contributed are men who flew the Hurricane; some have become associated with this great aircraft through a husband who flew it. In this context, thank you to Audrey Haw and Kristina Szczesny for providing me with material that I have managed to include. From the historical point of view, I thank the Air Historical Branch, the RAF Museum at Hendon, the Imperial War Museum, and the Public Record Office at Kew.

For the photographs, I thank Ken Delve, the Editor of *Flypast*, who provided me with many of them (most belong to the *Flypast* archives); Flt Lt Andy Thomas, and others, also contributed photographs.

Without continuous support and co-operation from these organizations and individuals, books such as mine would never be written.

My final thanks always go to my close friend Ken Delve who, during one cold and wet day in an office at RAF Finningley, started me on this seemingly never-ending road of writing.

Peter Jacobs

To Christopher and Matthew who, at the ages of just six and four, already know so much about the Hurricane and the Battle of Britain.

First published in 1998 by
The Crowood Press Ltd
Ramsbury, Marlborough
Wiltshire SN8 2HR

British Library Cataloguing in Publication Data

A catalogue record for this book is available from the British Library.

ISBN 1 86126 126 8

Typeset by Focus Publishing

Printed and bound in Great Britain by Butler & Tanner, Frome

Contents

Acknowledgements   4

Foreword by Sqn Ldr Pat Wells, DSO   6

Introduction   6

   1   DESIGN AND DEVELOPMENT   7
   2   THE FALL OF FRANCE   20
   3   BRITAIN ALONE – THE SUMMER OF 1940   33
   4   THE HURRICANE MARK II   51
   5   MALTA – THE FORTRESS ISLAND   68
   6   BENEDICT FORCE – MURMANSK, RUSSIA   76
   7   THE DESERT WAR   88
   8   THE FAR EAST – THE FORGOTTEN WAR   100
   9   EUROPE   113
  10   THE LAST OF THE MANY   136

Appendix A   Hurricane Production   144
Appendix B   Squadrons and Locations   146
Appendix C   Hurricane Order of Battle 1939-45   169
Appendix D   Squadron Codes   175
Appendix E   Hurricane Pilots Killed During the Battle of Britain   176
Appendix F   Hurricane Aces   181
Bibliography   188
Index   189

Foreword

As one who had a wild affair with the Hurricane it is a great privilege to be invited to write the foreword to this book. The Hurricane was built in several marks, some of which little is known of, and took part in air battles on every front, even the Battle of the Atlantic from the end of a catapult. It seems that every operational task was possible in a Hurricane and I believe that had the radiator not been where it was then she could have successfully carried a torpedo!

My first flight was in June 1940, having spent the previous eight days at a fighter OTU on Spitfires! There was little time to learn during the summer of 1940 but fortunately I survived and went on to complete nearly 300 operations on Mark Is and IIs; these included the Battle of Britain, fighter sweeps over northern France, flying off HMS *Ark Royal* for

service in Malta and then on to North Africa for the war in the desert. My final flight was from Malta back to Tunisia after attacking searchlights in Sicily which were causing problems to the airborne forces during that invasion.

An exceptionally sturdy aircraft, the Hurricane never ever let me down (except from battle damage) and how my aircraft stayed together after Adolf Galland's assault on me in 1940, with 132 machine-gun rounds and 64 cannon shells, is a mystery to me. Incidentally, I only ever had one mid-air collision. Whilst flying a Curtiss Mohawk at an OTU in the Middle East a pupil flying a Hurricane collided with me; the Mohawk was a wreck, but the Hurricane went on to complete the exercise!

Much has been written about the Hurricane over the years, but I believe that

Peter Jacobs has covered the most important aspects about this most famous aircraft. The fact that the Hurricane flew operationally on every day of the war, and in every theatre, is well made and he has spent much time researching the lesser-known marks and has covered the less documented theatres in which the Hurricane operated; the Battle of France, Malta, Russia, the Desert and the Far East are all covered as well as some detailed appendices which conclude his work. Most importantly, his work is well illustrated by some excellent photographs, many of which have not been seen before. I salute Peter Jacobs for writing such an excellent book on this most famous and well-loved aeroplane.

Squadron Leader Pat Wells DSO

Introduction

For as long as I can remember, my interest in the RAF's fighter pilots has had a major influence on my life: in my opinion, the heroics of the 'Few' during the summer of 1940 are second to none. I have always been equally fascinated by the Hurricane and Spitfire aircraft in which they flew. When I was younger, I could never have imagined how this fascination and admiration would prove to be so much more than just a passing interest.

I joined the RAF straight from college and have been lucky enough to serve on some of the most famous fighter squadrons. My interest in the history of those squadrons led me to writing and, when I was given the chance to write about the Hurricane, I jumped at the opportunity to learn more about this classic fighter. The experience has proved to be compelling; only the size of the book (and the inevitable deadline, now less than twelve

hours away) has stopped me writing more!

The Hurricane is one of the classic fighters of all time. It was designed and built for war and it played as big a part as any other aircraft in achieving final victory in 1945. A remarkable total of 14,533 Hurricanes were built and the aircraft served operationally on every day throughout hostilities. It was at the forefront of Britain's defence in 1939, and it helped to ensure final victory in the Far East in 1945. In between, it served in every operational theatre, and in every possible role, and this is covered in some detail in the book.

Many words have been written about the Hurricane; sixty years could hardly have passed without that happening! One of the most complete works on the subject is *The Hawker Hurricane* by Francis K Mason, while other excellent works include the *Hurricane at War* Parts 1 and 2 by Chaz Bowyer and Norman Franks.

Many others cover one particular theatre of operations or one specific campaign; excellent examples are *Twelve Days in May* by Brian Cull, Bruce Lander and Heinrich Weiss, and *The Battle of Britain* by Richard Townsend Bickers. This book covers the Hurricane's eighty years, from the origins of the single-seat fighter to the display of the Hurricane at air shows today. In between, it focuses mainly on the campaigns in which it fought, from the well-documented Battles of France and Britain, to the lesser-covered arenas, such as Malta and Russia. It also includes technical information about the aircraft, its systems and its armament, as well as details about some of the men who flew it. Finally, detailed Appendices cover specific aspects of the aircraft and the squadrons and men who flew it. Enjoy the book!

Peter Jacobs

CHAPTER ONE

Design and Development

Thomas Sopwith, one of the first manufacturers of aeroplanes; he formed the Sopwith Aviation Company in 1912, from which developed Hawker Aircraft Limited.

As with any classic aircraft, the Hawker Hurricane did not simply appear overnight. The origins of all the famous aircraft that made their name during the Second World War tend to go back to the first days of powered flight, and to the development of the aeroplane as a weapon during the First World War. The Hurricane is no exception. It was developed from a number of well-known aircraft built by Hawker Aircraft Limited during the late 1920s and early 1930s, but its true origins can be traced way back, to the Sopwith Tabloid single-seat aircraft which first arrived on the aviation scene in 1913.

The reason for beginning the story of the Hawker Hurricane so far back is because this most famous aircraft was the product of a famous designer who worked for a famous company during a period of post-war apathy following the end of the 'war to end all wars'. Although the First World War had seen the rapid progress of the aeroplane as a weapon of war, post-war Britain saw the aeroplane as more likely to succeed as a form of transportation rather than for any other purpose. After all, the very existence of the newly formed Royal Air Force was still being questioned.

In order to understand the Hurricane and how it came about, it is important to understand the people and the company that made this success story possible.

Origins

The Hurricane was built by Hawker Aircraft Limited. The company had its origins in the Sopwith Aviation Company, first formed by Thomas Sopwith at Kingston-upon-Thames, just outside London, in 1912. In common with many new companies at the time, they had plenty of new ideas, but their facilities during the early days were rather primitive – its first building had formerly housed Kingston's ice-skating rink.

Sopwith and Hawker

The life of Thomas Octave Murdoch Sopwith spanned many generations of air-craft design, from the first days of powered flight to the concept of vertical take-off and landing. He was born in 1888 and bought his first aeroplane in 1910. Within a couple of years he had proved himself as one of the country's finest pilots, before turning his attentions to the manufacture of aeroplanes.

One member of Sopwith's successful team during the early years was Harry Hawker, who became the company's test pilot. Born in Australia, Hawker was just a year younger than Thomas Sopwith. He moved to England to find work, and joined the Sopwith Company when it first formed, in 1912. He saved his money to fund flying lessons, and earned his flying licence within a couple of years. As the Sopwith Company's test pilot, he was involved in the design of every Sopwith aircraft during the First World War.

The Tabloid

The Sopwith Company's first aircraft was the single-seat biplane, the Sopwith Tabloid, which made an impressive public debut at Hendon in 1913. The following year the company achieved remarkable

The Sopwith Camel proved to be one of the most successful fighters on the Western Front during the final period of the First World War.

Sir Sydney Camm, the chief designer of the Hawker Hurricane, one of the best-known aircraft designers.

success by winning the coveted Schneider Trophy with a converted version of the Tabloid, which was fitted as a seaplane to meet the contest's requirements. Just a few months later, war broke out in Europe, and

the Tabloid entered service with the Royal Flying Corps and the Royal Naval Air Service. However, the Tabloid had not been built for war and it soon demonstrated that it had little potential in that role.

Sopwith Fighter Aircraft

The company adapted successfully to the new requirement of building aircraft for military use, developing its first true single-seat fighter, the Sopwith Pup, which entered service in 1916. It then found fame with one of the most success-ful fighters of the war, the Sopwith Camel, which arrived on the Western Front dur-ing the following year. After the Camel came the Sopwith Dolphin, a heavily armed single-seat fighter of high perfor-mance for that time. The Dolphin was followed by the Sopwith Snipe, a fighter that remained in service with the newly formed Royal Air Force after the war, and is remembered as the last of the great fight-ers built by the Sopwith Company.

Hawker Engineering

The end of the war in Europe put a stop to the demand for so many aircraft. In 1920, the Sopwith Company went into

voluntary liquidation and was re-formed under the name of H.G. Hawker Engi-neering Company Limited. Sadly, Harry Hawker never saw the benefits of the com-pany. While practising for an air display at Hendon in July 1921, his aircraft crashed, and the talented young aviator was killed.

The following year saw Captain 'Tommy' Thompson appointed as the Chief Designer at Hawker's but, after a couple of unsuccessful designs, he was soon replaced by W. George Carter. In Novem-ber 1923 a young draughtsman, Sydney Camm, arrived at the company, and began an association with the company that would last for forty-three years!

Sydney Camm

Undoubtedly one of the greatest aircraft designers of all time, Sydney Camm was born in Windsor in 1893. In common with almost all the early aircraft designers, his initial interest was in building model aircraft. He became an apprentice at Martinsyde at the outbreak of the First World War and was employed there for the next nine years, working his way up through the design department. In 1923, having been appointed as the head

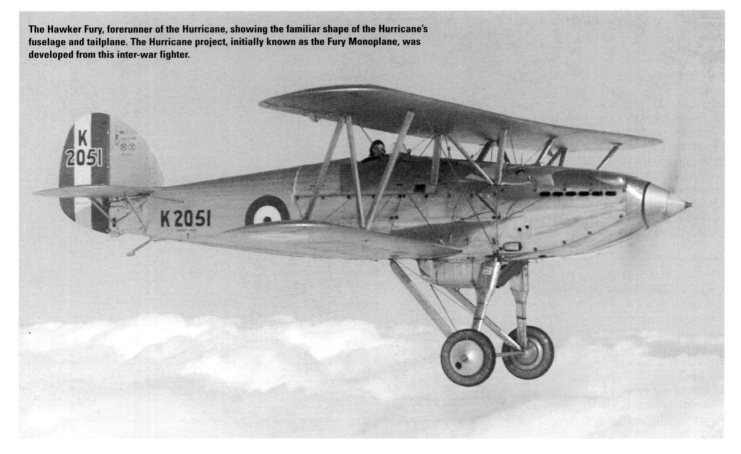

The Hawker Fury, forerunner of the Hurricane, showing the familiar shape of the Hurricane's fuselage and tailplane. The Hurricane project, initially known as the Fury Monoplane, was developed from this inter-war fighter.

K 2051

K 2051

The structure of the Hurricane's fuselage was a complicated arrangement of longerons, zig-zag construction struts and tie-rods.

draughtsman at Hawkers, he became immediately involved in the design of the Cygnet two-seat project. Two years later he was appointed as Hawker's chief designer, a remarkable achievement after just two years with the company.

The design of military aircraft became the prime task of Sydney Camm. He started with the Danecock, an adapted version of the Woodcock, for export to Denmark, and followed this with the Heron, the Horsley, the Hawfinch and the Harrier. None of these designs was particularly successful, but they all helped Camm build up his knowledge of aircraft design. In June 1928, the Hawker Hart light-bomber first appeared; this design proved to be an immediate success. It was the start of a new world in aircraft design and led to a similar design built as a fighter – this became the Hawker Fury, adopted by the RAF in 1930.

Hawker Fury

The specification for the Hawker Fury, originally named the Hornet, was issued in March 1930. It was designed as a competitor to the Bristol Bulldog, which had effectively been chosen as the RAF's standard fighter for the 1930s. Although the Fury proved to be more expensive than the Bulldog, it was faster. A limited number of twenty-four aircraft were ordered by the RAF, with the idea of equipping just one fighter squadron. In May 1931, the first aircraft were delivered

to 43 Squadron at Tangmere.

Flying exercises carried out during 1931 proved that the Fury was superior in performance to the Bulldog. Powered by a 525 hp Rolls-Royce Kestrel IIS engine, the Fury had a top speed of over 200mph (320kph) at 14,000 feet (4200m) and an operating ceiling of nearly 30,000 feet (9000m). It was armed with two 0.303in

Vickers machine-guns and had enough fuel to operate up to a range of 300 miles (480km).

As a result of the satisfactory exercises, forty-eight more aircraft were ordered, and two more squadrons – 1 Squadron, also at Tangmere, and 25 Squadron, at Hawkinge – were both equipped during February 1932.

The Prototype

The H.G. Hawker Engineering Company Limited became Hawker Aircraft Limited in 1933. In the same year, Camm decided that the future of aviation lay in a monoplane design and proposed the building of a low-wing monoplane fighter. This proposal was received with uncertainty by the Air Ministry (as were a number of other new ideas at the time). The situation in Europe was still stable, and many people felt there was no point in risking large sums of money on new and uncertain designs. Fortunately, the foresight of the private aircraft industry, and in particular people like Sydney Camm and Thomas Sopwith at Hawker, led to the project being funded by the company itself.

The Fury Monoplane

The project for the Hawker Hurricane effectively began during the spring of

Flown by Flt Lt 'George' Bulman, the Hurricane prototype (K5083) made its maiden flight from Brooklands on 6 November 1935

Fitted with tail struts, a slightly different hood design, and a retractable tail-wheel, the prototype (K5083) differed slightly from the production Hurricane.

The first production Hurricane (L1547), which made its maiden flight on 12 October 1937.

1933. The design office, led by Sydney Camm, worked on plans for a new aircraft, initially known as the Fury Monoplane. The early design proposed a similar fuselage to that of the existing Hawker Fury – a low-wing monoplane design of 28 feet (840cm) wingspan and a fixed undercarriage. The aircraft was to be powered by a single Rolls-Royce Goshawk engine, producing 660 hp, which would give it an estimated top speed of 280mph (450kph).

The project was given the name 'Hotspur', although this name was later dropped and used for another project.

Specification F.36/34

With increasing instability in Europe, the Air Ministry requirement for a new fighter became more urgent. Specification F.36/34 was issued in 1934. Known at Hawker simply as 'the Hawker monoplane fighter', building of the prototype (K5083) began in October 1934. In the same year, Rolls-Royce had come up with a new engine, the PV12, which produced an output of 1,050 hp at 15,000 feet (4500m). The PV12 later became the Merlin C, which was fitted to the prototype, and from it came the Merlin II, which would later be installed into the production Hurricanes.

For Sydney Camm and his design team there was one immediate question which had to be answered. Should the aircraft be designed along the lines of the team's experience – using aircraft structure techniques that were familiar – or should they try to explore unfamiliar territory, and design a fighter of a stressed-skin construction? The former was the more obvious answer and, in theory, would lead to a much quicker result. Designing a new construction would involve building new jigs and tools, which would probably lead to delays. The design team could ill afford to suffer any problems, so the more traditional method of using fabric covering won the day.

In the fuselage the longerons were made of circular-section steel tubes with the diagonal zig-zag struts running between top and bottom longerons made of duralumin. Bracing was by streamline tie-rods. As the primary structure of the fuselage was of rectangular section, it was necessary to add a secondary structure to give the rounded shape. This secondary structure was made of wooden formers and stringers, with the formers being attached to the longerons and the stringers carrying the fabric covering. The fabric covering extended from the stern to level with the pilot's seat; forward of this point, the fuselage was covered with light metal panels.

Immediately in front of the cockpit was the reserve fuel tank and, in front of that, between the fuel tank and the engine, was a fire-proof bulkhead. The Rolls-Royce Merlin engine was mounted on a steel tube structure in the nose of the fuselage, with large detachable panels ensuring easy access for maintenance. The radiator of the liquid-cooling system was mounted under the fuselage, with an oval air intake in front of the radiator and a rectangular opening behind it, inside which a hinged flap allowed the pilot to control the amount of cooling. The early Hurricanes were fitted with a twin-bladed wooden propeller. This was later changed on the MkI to a Rotol three-bladed constant-speed wooden propeller.

The wing structure was a mix of old concepts and new design. The depth of the wing, necessitated by the cantilever

The cockpit hood was a sliding arrangement of rectangular appearance.

Behind the cockpit hood was the distinctive aerial installation.

design, caused problems in the twisting stresses of the wing. The problem was solved by the drag members running zig-zag between the spars – the primary structure of the wing formed a frame, with the drag members stiffening the overall structure. Fabric was then placed over the wing and firmly attached to the wing ribs; the attachments to the ribs were tightened, causing the fabric to stretch tight. The portion of the inner wing was covered with light metal and was, therefore, strong enough for walking on. Metallic split trailing-edge flaps were fitted at the inner end of the wing, and

were operated hydraulically.

The centre section of the wing was a single unit attached to the fuselage at four points. It consisted of two continuous spars connected by ribs and drag bracing. Within the centre section of the wing were fitted the main fuel tanks and the retractable undercarriage. The undercarriage assembly consisted of two semi-cantilever shock-absorber struts hinged at the outboard ends of the centre-section front spar. It retracted inwards by a mechanism activated by Dowty hydraulic rams; these retracted the wheels into the centre-section spars, with the fairings

Balance tabs fitted to the rudder and elevators.

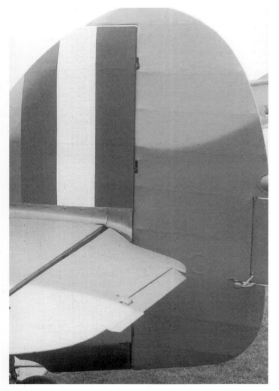

The tail section consisted of the tail, fabric-covered rudder and elevators.

Early production aircraft were fitted with fabric wings and ailerons, although these had been replaced by metal-clad wings by the outbreak of war.

leaving a smooth surface free of drag.

This inwardly retracting undercarriage was unlike that of the Hurricane's counterparts, the Spitfire and the Messerschmitt Bf 109. This design feature meant that the Hurricane had a wide wheel track – the distance between the two main wheels was wider than on others – and this made the Hurricane stable but easy to manoeuvre on the ground. The undercarriage was hydraulically operated, and there was a secondary method – a hydraulic hand pump – to lower the undercarriage in the event of an emergency.

The outer wing sections were also built on two spars, similar in construction to the centre section. Ailerons fitted on the trailing edge had a metal framework but were fabric-covered. The cantilever tail section also had a metal framework with fabric covering. The fin was built integral to the rear fuselage, and the original design provided for the tail-wheel to retract into a casing in the rear section of the fuselage.

First Flights and Trials

By late 1935, the prototype was finished. The first flight of K5083 was made from Brooklands on 6 November 1935; the overall silver appearance of the aircraft was a spectacular sight. The pilot was Flt

Lt P.W.S. 'George' Bulman and, according to his report, initial fears about the aircraft's handling qualities proved to be unfounded. In many ways, flying the low wing loading of the monoplane design was described as not dissimilar to flying the single-seat biplane fighters of the time. More flights of K5083 proved successful, with the aircraft achieving a top speed of 325mph (520kph) at 16,500 feet (4950m).

In February 1936, K5083 was delivered to the Aeroplane and Armament Experimental Establishment (A&AEE) at Martlesham Heath, where it went through more trials before the Hurricane could be accepted into RAF service.

There was only a handful of differences between K5083 and the airframe that would soon become the standard production variant. K5083 had tail struts fitted as a precaution against anticipated buffeting of the tail, but these were soon removed. It also had an early development of wheel fairings for the retractable main undercarriage, a retractable tail-wheel, and a slightly different cockpit hood design. It was powered by the Merlin C engine and had a twin-bladed fixed-pitch wooden propeller, which would later be modified to a controllable pitch design and, later, to a three-bladed design (with some variations being made of metal, and some of wood). The engine exhausts were also different on K5083, with more of a stub design; the production aircraft would later have flame-trap exhausts or ejector exhausts. Gentle dives showed that the aircraft was capable of 310mph (495kph) or 3,150 rpm, whichever came first.

The Hurricane MKI

Scheme F

The lack of stability in Europe led the Government to suggest that the military should present a series of expansion plans for rearming the armed forces, to assure the security of Britain's world-wide commitments. The first, Expansion Scheme A, approved in July 1934, proposed a maximum front-line strength, stated that the RAF would be ready for war in eight years' time, and identified Germany as the most likely opponent. The most important plan, Scheme F, approved in February 1936, indicated an overall increase in aircraft strength, and proposed that the RAF should have in service 500 Hurricanes and 300 Spitfires by March 1939. By coincidence, the scheme was announced in the same year as the RAF changed its structure. These changes led to the formation of Fighter Command, under Air Marshal Sir Hugh Dowding.

During 1934, Hawker Aircraft Limited bought Gloster Aircraft Company, which had one of the largest aircraft factories in the country, at Brockworth, near Gloucester. By June 1936, the name Hurricane had formally been given to the Hawker F.36/34 project. The company received an order for 600 Hurricanes and production began immediately. However, the decision to use an improved Merlin engine delayed the final completion of the first production aircraft (L1547) until the following year.

First Production Airframe

Completed during late 1937, L1547 was first flown by Hawker's test pilot Philip Lucas on 12 October 1937. This first production airframe differed only very slightly from the prototype; the main modification was to the engine – it was powered by the Merlin II engine in place of the Merlin C.

The Hurricane MkI was 31 feet (930cm) in length, just over 13 feet (390cm) in height and had a wingspan of 40 feet (12m). The fuselage had three parts, as follows:

The forward part of the fuselage – from the leading edge of the wing to the propeller – was purely the engine compartment that housed the Rolls-Royce Merlin.

The central part of the fuselage (essentially, the area above the wing) was all cockpit and equipment. The cockpit hood was a sliding arrangement of 'rectangular' appearance, providing one easy way of distinguishing the Hurricane from the Spitfire. The front windscreen was bullet-proof and on top of the hood was a rear-view mirror. Immediately in front of the pilot, and behind his seat, was armour-plating, to

The large glycol radiator and oil cooler can clearly be seen housed in a duct under the centre fuselage.

The carburettor air intake, located under the forward fuselage.

offer as much protection as possible. There was also a reinforced section of the upper fuselage immediately behind the cockpit, to help protect the pilot in the event of a crash landing. Behind this, on the upper surface of the fuselage, was the distinctive aerial installation, which carried the aerial from just behind the cockpit to the top of the tail-plane.

The rear part of the fuselage included the tail section, but housed little or no equipment. The tail section consisted of the tail itself, the rudder and the elevators. The rudder effectively took up the rear half of the tail section, with a rudder post passing vertically through the middle. The leading edges of the tail section were all metal, but the rudder was fabric; the taillight was mounted half way up the rudder. There were various fixed and balanced trim tabs, as well as a built-in mass balance at the top of the tail. Although the Hurricane was originally designed with a retractable tail-wheel, the production MkIs were fitted with a fixed Dowty tailwheel.

The wing section can be viewed as an outer section on each side, and a centre section that housed the retractable undercarriage. The upper surface of the inner part of the wing, which joined the

fuselage, was made of light metal sheeting. This was the area walked on by the pilot or ground crew. The rest of the wing was covered in fabric, except for the leading edges, which were metal. The split flaps were also made of light metal and were built on the underside of the wing, running from the radiator casing to the ailerons; the ailerons, however, were fabric-covered. The extreme tip of the outer wing section was detachable, a design feature which would help enormously when Hurricanes were crated up and shipped to other operational theatres. Aircraft lighting in the wing consisted of the landing lamps in the central area of the leading edge, and the aircraft's navigation lights located in the forward wing-tips.

Airframe Dimensions, Hurricane MkI	
LENGTH	31ft 0in
WINGSPAN	40ft 0in
HEIGHT	13ft 1in
PROPELLER DIAMETER	11 ft 0 in
WING AREA (TOTAL)	257 sq ft
TAILPLANE	20 sq ft

The Engine

The Rolls-Royce Merlin II engine and, later, the improved Merlin III engine, became the standard powerplant for the Hurricane MkI. Originally known as the Merlin G, the Merlin II engine was designed in 1937 and built at Derby. It was a 12-cylinder, upright-vee, ethylene glycol-cooled engine that produced 1,030 hp at 16,000 feet (4800m), at 3,000 rpm.

The installation of this modified Merlin necessitated a few changes to the design of the engine mounting (which led to a modification in the shape of the cowling), and also to the design of the radiator. The starting magnetos were fitted on the lower side of the engine, and the carburettor air intake was centrally mounted beneath the forward part of the fuselage. The large glycol radiator and oil cooler were housed in a duct under the central part of the fuselage; the oil cooler was sandwiched between the two elements of the glycol radiator.

The first propeller fitted to the early Hurricanes was fixed-pitch, twin-bladed and made of wood. In addition, stream-

Production Hurricanes were soon fitted with a fixed Dowty tail-wheel.

Hydraulically operated, the design of the main undercarriage later proved to be one of the Hurricane's strengths when operating from rugged airstrips overseas.

lined exhausts were fitted, and other modifications to the airframe made, including a change to the undercarriage leg fairings, and a more rounded windscreen.

The performance of the improved Merlin III, developed in 1939, was almost identical to that of the MkII, but the modified engine proved to be more reliable. One of the main differences was in the design of the propeller shaft, which meant that either a Rotol or a de Havilland propeller could be fitted. The engines were built by Rolls-Royce at Derby and Crewe.

The Controls

The throttle lever was situated on the left side of the cockpit. The airflow through the coolant radiator and oil cooler was controlled by a lever on the left side of the pilot's seat. The carburettor was controlled by a slow-running cut-out, operated by pulling out a knob on the right side of the cockpit. An external power supply for the starter motor was connected through a panel on the starboard engine cowling. Alternatively, two handles for hand-starting the engine were stowed in the undercarriage recess. Engine-starting was carried out by switching on the two ignition switches on the left side of the main instrument panel and using a starter push button and booster coil push button, both located next to the ignition switches.

The engine self-sealing oil tank, with a capacity of 9 gallons (40.5 litres), was built into the forward part of the port wing, just inboard from the fuselage, and protected by armour-plating. Oil was fed to the engine through a filter and cooler. Oil pressure and temperature gauges were fitted on the right side of the main instrument panel. Oil pressure was normally 60-80 p.s.i., with a minimum of 45 p.s.i. Oil temperature ranged between 59 degrees Fahrenheit (15 degrees centigrade), which was the minimum temperature for take-off, and 221 degrees Fahrenheit (105 degrees centigrade), the maximum permitted in combat.

Immediately behind the engine was located the header tank for the engine coolant, containing two gallons of glycol and air. Behind the header tank, and immediately in front of the cockpit, were a fire-proof bulkhead (for obvious reasons), the reserve fuel tank, and some armour-plating to protect the pilot. The coolant system was thermostatically controlled, the radiator being by-passed until the coolant reached the required temperature. Coolant temperature ranged between 140 degrees Fahrenheit (60 degrees centigrade), the minimum for take-off, and 275 degrees Fahrenheit (135 degrees centigrade), the maximum during combat. The airflow through the radiator was controlled by a flap lever on the left side of the cockpit.

Aircraft Systems

The Hurricane MkI used 100 octane fuel and was built with two main self-sealing fuel tanks, one on either side of the centre section of the fuselage, each holding 33 gallons (150 litres). In addition, there was a reserve tank of 28 gallons (127 litres) fitted between the fire-proof bulkhead and the instrument panel in the front section of the aircraft. These three tanks gave the Hurricane a total of 94 gallons (427 litres) of fuel. The fuel feed to the engine was by an engine-driven fuel pump. Normal operation was to use fuel from the main tanks before changing over to the reserve, although it was possible to use the fuel from the reserve tank first.

For the pilot, the operation of the fuel system was quite simple. The main fuel cock control was situated on the left side of the cockpit and was fitted with a spring-loaded safety plate, which prevented the fuel inadvertently being turned off. The fuel contents gauge was located on the right side of the instrument panel, above which was a gauge selector switch marked 'PORT-CENTRE-STBD'. By selecting any of the main or reserve tanks the pilot could see how much fuel remained in each. Next to the contents gauge was a fuel-pressure warning light. The normal operating pressure for the fuel system was 8-10 p.s.i. If the fuel-pressure warning light came on when operating at high altitude, nominally above 20,000 feet (6000m), showing that the pressure was below 6 p.s.i., the pilot was able to pressurize the main and reserve tanks by operating a fuel tank pressurizing cock, fitted to the left side of the cockpit and marked 'ATMOS-PHERE' and 'PRESSURE'.

The aircraft was fitted with a 12-volt generator that supplied the electrical services. The generator switch was fitted to the left side of the cockpit. A voltmeter

Performance figures for Merlin II/III Engines						
	Merlin II	Merlin III	Merlin II	Merlin III	Merlin II	Merlin III
RPM	3,000	3,000	2,600	2,600	2,200	2,200
BHP	1,225	1,100	980	960	700	690
BOOST	+ 10	+ 9.8	+ 6.2	+ 5.9	+ 2.5	+ 2.1

An early Hurricane MkI, showing the two-bladed propeller and machine-gun ports.

was fitted to the rear of the left side of the cockpit and there was a red power failure warning light on the left side of the main instrument panel, marked 'POWER FAIL-URE', which came on when the generator was not charging the accumulator.

Apart from the various aircraft instruments, gauges and aircraft services selectors, electrical power was provided to many different switches. Working around the cockpit, from left to right, electrical power was provided to the following: radio master switch, cockpit lighting, landing lamps, weapon switches, heated clothing socket, navigation lights, windscreen de-icing pump, and IFF ('identification friend-or-foe') switches.

Hydraulic pressure was used to operate the Hurricane's undercarriage and flaps; an engine-driven hydraulic pump provided the correct operating pressure. A hand pump was located on the right side of the cockpit for use in an emergency should the hydraulic system pressure fail (in the case of an engine failure or a hydraulic pump failure). For the pilot the system was easy – straightforward operation of the under-

carriage selector and flap lever was sufficient to operate it. The lever was situated on the right side of the cockpit and had a neutral position for both undercarriage and flaps. To operate the flaps, the selector lever was moved to the outboard position and the flap indicator, situated below the selector lever, showed the position of the flaps, marked 'UP' and 'DOWN'. Next to the lever was an undercarriage selector safety catch, designed to prevent inadvertent selection of 'wheels up' while the aircraft was on the ground. The catch had to be turned clockwise before the selector lever could be moved into the wheels up position.

The undercarriage position indicator was located on the top left part of the main instrument panel. It was electrically powered and consisted of two pairs of lights: green to show that each main wheel was in the down and locked position, and red to show that the main wheels were up and locked. There was a dimmer switch in the centre of the indicator for night flying. When the wheels were up, the pilot could see them through two small windows in

the bottom of the cockpit. There was also a red undercarriage warning light on the instrument panel; this came on whenever the throttle was less than one-third open, and the wheels were not down and locked.

The emergency undercarriage-lowering system was activated by selecting 'undercarriage down' in the normal way, and then by operating the hydraulic hand pump. If this did not work, the pilot could operate a red-painted foot pedal; this released the wheel lock, and the undercarriage could fall and lock down under its own weight.

The wheel brakes and the gun-firing mechanism were operated pneumatically. Air was stored in a cylinder, at a maximum pressure of 300 p.s.i., and provided to the services by an engine-driven compressor. The wheel brake lever was located on the control column, with a catch to retain the brakes on for parking. A triple pressure gauge forward of the control column showed the air pressure in the pneumatic system and at each brake.

The Hurricane was fitted with oxygen, which allowed it to operate at all altitudes. The oxygen bottle was located just aft of the pilot's position on the starboard side of

L1582 was one of the first batch of 600 MkIs built by Hawker, and entered service during 1938.

the aircraft. The oxygen supply cock was situated on the left side of the cockpit and the oxygen regulator just to the left side of the main instrument panel.

The prototype Hurricane had been designed with an all-up weight of 5,700lb (2590kg). The bare weight of the production Hurricane MkI was just over 4,900lb (2230kg), and more than 650lb (295kg) of equipment gave the basic weight of the aircraft at nearly 5,600lb (2545kg). Armed with eight 0.303in Browning machine-guns (see Chapter 4), the all-up weight of

a combat-capable MkI increased to 6,600lb (3000kg).

Flying the Hurricane

The main instrument panel on the Hurricane MkI was located centrally and consisted of the six basic flight instruments, three on top and three beneath. The top row included (from left to right): an airspeed indicator, artificial horizon, and a climb and descent indicator. The bottom row (from left to right) included: an altimeter, direction indicator (compass), and a turn and slip indicator.

The Hurricane was designed as a longitudinally stable aircraft. The control column was a spade-like design and incorporated the gun-firing push button and the parking-brake lever. The rudder bar was standard and adjustable. The elevator-trimming tab was controlled by a hand

wheel on the left side of the cockpit, with an associated indicator next to it. Rudder balance was controlled by a small control wheel, also situated on the left side of the cockpit. The flying controls could be locked by attaching a bracket to the control column – just below the spade grip, for locking the aileron controls, and two struts, for locking the rudder bar and control column.

As with any tail-wheeled aircraft, in order to taxi the pilot needed to be able to see around the nose of the aircraft, so the seat of the Hurricane had to be as high as possible. As little time as possible was spent on the ground, particularly in hot climates, to avoid any chance of the engine over-heating.

Once the aircraft was ready, the seat was re-positioned, the trim set, the fuel mixture set to rich, the throttle friction tightened, the pitch set to fine, the flaps tested, and the radiator half-closed.

During the first part of the take-off run, the aircraft would occasionally swing, but

Weights of the Hurricane MkI (in lb/kg)	
BARE WEIGHT (EMPTY)	4,910/2232
EQUIPMENT	670/305
PILOT AND FLYING EQUIPMENT	200/90
AMMUNITION	160/73
FUEL AND OIL	660/300
TOTAL WEIGHT	6,600/3000

this was never a problem. As soon as the aircraft was off the ground, the undercarriage was raised. In order to carry out this slightly awkward technique, the pilot's left hand would have to come off the throttle to hold the control column, while the right hand transferred to the undercarriage selector lever. To avoid any chance of too many revs in fine pitch, the preferred technique was to throttle back while maintaining a slightly steep climb before raising the undercarriage, after which the hands could once again swap position, to change the pitch and reduce the boost. For some pilots on their first solo, and for a few trips after, the undercarriage safety catch certainly caused problems, and it was not unusual to see the aircraft 'dip' down at this point! (This slightly complicated technique was not necessary on the later variants of Hurricane, which had constant-speed propellers; the rpm was set, and left during the selection of 'undercarriage up'.)

After take-off, the hood was closed and the seat re-positioned once again. The all-round view out of the cockpit was described as extremely good. At cruising speed the controls felt comfortable and stable; the ailerons remained light and very responsive. During hard manoeuvring, however, it was easy for the pilot to be too aggressive and pull more 'G' either than he was used to, or was comfortably able to take.

For landing, the speed was initially reduced to 150mph (240kph) when the wheels were lowered. The final approach was carried out at about 90mph (145kph), with the propeller in fine pitch and the flaps selected 'down'. Although the stalling speed was not much less than the approach speed, typically about 70mph (110kph), the Hurricane was described by some as relatively simple to land, although care had to be taken not to lose too much speed during the final approach, due to the drag of the aircraft.

If the pilot had to abandon the aircraft in flight, the recommended procedure was to decrease speed and then dive over the side. It was important for the pilot not to stand on the seat before jumping, as this would result in him hitting the aircraft's tail-plane. Of course, it was not always possible for the pilot to follow this recommended procedure!

For a rapid ground exit, there was an emergency detachable panel on the starboard side of the cockpit. To jettison the

panel the hood had to be fully opened and the release lever, located on the right side of the cockpit, moved aft and upwards. If it was necessary to jettison the hood, there was a hood lever on the left side of the cockpit; this had to be operated sharply forwards and upwards. If necessary, the pilot could further assist the hood by pushing it upwards. The pilot's notes for the Hurricane also advise the pilot to lower his head in the case of hood jettisoning, to avoid any possible injury!

If the pilot had to make a forced landing on the ground, the recommended procedure was to move the propeller speed control fully aft and gliding at about 130mph (208kph). With the undercarriage and flaps up the gliding speed was between 120-140mph (190-225kph), with a very flat glide angle. Over the sea it was recommended that the pilot should abandon the aircraft rather than trying to ditch. However, if ditching was the only answer, the cockpit hood should be jettisoned and the

Best range and speeds at various altitudes, Hurricane MkI		
HEIGHT (FT/M)	RANGE IN MILES/KM	SPEED (MPH/KPH)
5,000/1500	830/1330	168/269
10,000/3000	800/1280	180/288
15,000/4500	775/1240	196/314
20,000/6000	730/1170	213/341
25,000/7500	695/1112	232/371

Time to altitude, Hurricane MkI	
FROM TAKE-OFF TO ALTITUDE (FT/M)	TIME
5,000/1500	2 mins
10,000/3000	4 mins 30 secs
15,000/4500	6 mins 30 secs
20,000/6000	9 mins 30 secs
25,000/7500	13 mins

Ceilings and rate of climb, Hurricane MkI	
SERVICE CEILING	35,000ft/10500m
ABSOLUTE CEILING	36,000ft/10800m
MAX RATE OF CLIMB	2,420ft/min at 11,000ft/ 725m/min at 3300m

flaps lowered to reduce the speed as much as possible; the undercarriage, however, should remain up. The attitude of the aircraft on ditching should be tail-down in a banked turn, to prevent the radiator filling

Hurricanes of 56 Squadron before the war. At that time, the aircraft's identification letter was not painted on the rear fuselage, but is just visible under the exhaust manifold.

with water too early. Then it was a matter of vacating the aircraft as quickly as possible. There was also a first aid kit located on the inside of the detachable panel, and a crow bar stowed to the right of the pilot's seat.

Into Service

The first Hurricanes to enter service with the RAF were delivered to 111 Squadron at Northolt; the first four airframes (L1548-L1551) arrived just before Christmas 1937, with the remainder being delivered during early 1938. On 10 February 1938, the squadron's commanding officer, Sqn Ldr John Gillan, flew the 325 miles (520kph) from Turnhouse, Edinburgh, back to Northolt in 48 minutes – a most impressive average ground speed of 410mph (655kph)! The squadron's Gloster Gauntlets were soon replaced, and within a couple of months 'Treble One' Squadron was fully equipped with sixteen Hurricanes. The second squadron to be equipped with the new Hurricane was 3 Squadron at Kenley, under the command of Sqn Ldr Hugh Lester, with the first aircraft arriving during March. The third squadron to equip was 56 Squadron at North Weald, under the command of Sqn Ldr Charles Lea-Cox, which began to take delivery of its first Hurricanes just a few weeks later.

By the time the third squadron had been equipped, some fifty Hurricanes had been delivered to the RAF and a number of changes to the basic MkI had

Pilots of 87 Squadron carrying out a 'briefing' for the camera.

taken place. The tail-wheel had been fixed, having originally been designed to retract. This was to ease the design of the aircraft and remove the risk of the tail-wheel failing to lower; the main undercarriage legs, for example, could lower under gravity if the hydraulic system had completely failed. There was also the addition of the fin to the lower side of the fuselage at the rear, designed to prevent the aircraft from spinning. The engine exhausts were also further modified and, eventually, the two-bladed propeller was replaced by a three-bladed constant-speed propeller, 11 feet in diameter, built by either Rotol or de Havilland.

The most significant modification to the structural design of the aircraft was to replace the fabric-covered wings with all-metal ones. The first Hurricane to be fitted with metal-clad wings was L1877, which first flew on 28 April 1938. The new wing was not only stronger than the original but also lighter.

These modifications improved the overall performance of the MkI, increasing its top speed to 335mph at 17,500 feet. However, it would be some time before many production aircraft were fitted with the new wings, and most of the early aircraft were completed with fabric wings.

When the order for Hurricanes increased, work was sub-contracted to the Gloster Aircraft Company at Brockworth. This MkI (V6635) was built at Brockworth, and served with 249 Squadron during the Battle of Britain.

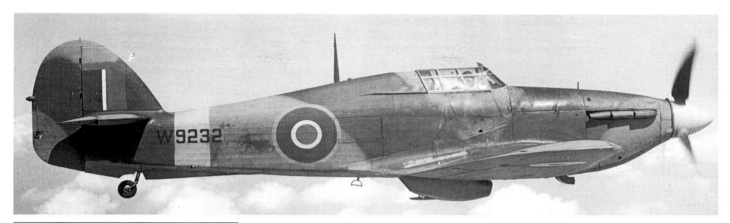

Overseas Contracts

Canada

The initial order for 600 Hurricanes had saturated the Hawker production lines at Kingston-upon-Thames, Brooklands and Langley. When another order came in during 1938, for a further 1,000 Hurricanes, Hawker sub-contracted the work out to its other company, Gloster Aircraft Company at Brockworth, near Gloucester. Hurricanes were also built in Canada by the Canadian Car and Foundry Company of Montreal. Twenty Hurricanes from the first batch of aircraft built by Hawker were shipped to Canada, some for use as pattern aircraft for the production variant, and the others as trainers for the RCAF.

The first aircraft built in Canada was P5170, which began construction in February 1939 and was completed by the end of the year. It made its first flight from St Hubert airport on 10 January 1940. The production rate in Canada was most impressive, and a total of more than 1,400 Hurricanes were built in Canada before the end of the war. In common with other British aircraft built under licence in Canada, the Canadian-built Hurricanes were designated as Hurricane MkXs. These aircraft were powered by Merlins built under licence in the United States by the Packard Motor Corporation; the engines were sent both to Britain and Canada for installation in various aircraft, including the Hurricane and the Lancaster. (Packard had been granted a licence to produce Merlins in anticipation of a likely shortage of capacity at Rolls-Royce, although, in the event, this never proved to be a problem.)

Europe

As the Second World War approached, many European countries recognized the

need for more capable combat aircraft. Belgium ordered twenty Hurricanes in March 1939, the first aircraft being delivered the following month. In addition, a contract was set up for a further eighty aircraft to be built under licence by Avions Fairey in Belgium.

In 1938, Yugoslavia had placed an initial order with Hawker for twelve Hurricane MkIs, with the first two aircraft (L1751 and L1752) being delivered to Belgrade in December 1938. This was followed by a second order for improved MkIs to be delivered during 1940. In addition, some fifteen Hurricanes were built under licence in Belgrade and Zemun, giving the Yugoslav Air Force about forty Hurricanes by the time it entered the war.

Further Afield

Hawker also received orders for Hurricanes from the Eastern Mediterranean and the Middle East. Persia ordered eighteen aircraft, to be modified with tropical air filters. However, the filter modification had not been fully adapted by the outbreak of war, and only one aircraft (L2079) was delivered before the end of 1939. Turkey received fifteen unmodified Hurricanes in September 1939. Hurricanes were also sent to Finland, Romania and South Africa, although few of these early examples saw action during the war. Poland ordered one Hurricane for evaluation; this aircraft was delivered just before the German invasion.

In February 1939, George Bulman had established a new speed record for the Hurricane in L1606. This aircraft carried the civil registration of G-AFKX and had been fitted with an improved Merlin III engine (with a constant speed unit and Rotol constant-speed propeller). Fitted with ballast to represent a full weapon load, the aircraft had an all-up weight of 6,400lb (2910kg) and achieved a level

W9232, another Gloster-built MkI.

speed of 345mph (552kph) at 15,000 feet (4500m).

The second half of 1939 was spent equipping as many of Fighter Command's squadrons as possible with the Hurricane and Spitfire, in preparation for war with Germany. By the end of September 1939, the last aircraft of the first batch of 600 Hurricanes ordered had been completed, although only some 300 had been delivered to the seventeen Fighter Command squadrons so far equipped. The others had either been delivered overseas or were at various training and maintenance units in the UK. Although Fighter Command was still some way from its preferred strength, the effort made by the production lines in meeting the demand for the Hurricane represented a remarkable achievement.

RAF Hurricane Squadrons and locations 1 September 1939	
SQUADRON	**LOCATION**
1 Squadron	Tangmere
3 Squadron	Biggin Hill
17 Squadron	North Weald
32 Squadron	Biggin Hill
43 Squadron	Henlow
46 Squadron	Digby
56 Squadron	North Weald
73 Squadron	Digby
79 Squadron	Biggin Hill
85 Squadron	Debden
87 Squadron	Debden
111 Squadron	Northolt
151 Squadron	North Weald
213 Squadron	Wittering
501 Squadron	Filton
504 Squadron	Digby
605 Squadron	Tangmere

CHAPTER TWO

The Fall of France

Background

At the outbreak of the Second World War, the RAF had just over 1,500 front-line combat aircraft, with up to another 2,000 in reserve. The figures may sound impressive, but just over 500 were front-line fighters, with around 300 more in reserve, while the Luftwaffe potentially had some 9,000 aircraft available; in this context, the situation can be seen to be far more serious. The production rate of Hurricanes was steady, but the entire fighter reinforcement programme was still a few months behind schedule. Some 600 Hurricanes had been completed, but only half were serving with Fighter Command's front-line squadrons. Considering the fact that the Hurricane was Britain's front-line fighter at the outbreak of war, and that only seventeen fighter squadrons had so far been equipped, the RAF was still some way short of full strength. It had been assessed before the war that the RAF

would need fifty fighter squadrons if it was to stand a chance of defending Britain against a German attack, and that figure had been assessed to meet the threat coming from Germany. Should France and the Low Countries be invaded, then fifty squadrons would be a bare minimum, as the threat would be that much closer, so it was vital that France should not fall.

When Prime Minister Neville Chamberlain made the decision to send the British Expeditionary Force (BEF) to France, it consisted mainly of Fairey Battle and Bristol Blenheim light bombers. They were assigned to an organization known as the Advanced Air Striking Force (AASF), under the command of the Air Officer Commanding (AOC) AASF, Air Vice-Marshal P.H.B. Playfair, CB CVO MC. These aircraft would be no match for any German fighters, so four squadrons of Hurricanes, a total of ninety-six aircraft, were sent to provide fighter protection as part of

an organization known as the Air Component, under the command of the AOC, Air Vice-Marshal C.H.B. Blount, OBE MC. The overall command of these two air organizations was given to Air Marshal A.S. Barratt, CB CMG MC.

To France

The first four Hurricane squadrons all arrived in France on 9 September 1939. The original intention of all four squadrons forming the Air Component was unsound, as the AASF had no fighter squadrons attached to it. Therefore, it was decided that two Hurricane squadrons (1 and 73 Squadrons) would be attached to the AASF, under the control of 67 Wing, while the other two squadrons remained as the Air Component, under the control of 60 Wing based in the Rouen-Boos area. To replace the two Hurricane squadrons transferred from the Air Component, two Gladiator squadrons (607 and 615 Squadrons) were sent to France, under the control of 61 Wing.

The two Hurricane squadrons attached to the AASF (1 and 73 Squadrons) were located at Octeville with 85 and 87 Squadrons, both part of the Air Component, based at Rouen. All four squadrons were as experienced as any other in the RAF at the time; all had formed during the rapid build-up programme of 1938, and had spent a year to eighteen months gaining experience with the Hurricane, and developing tactics in preparation for war. When the order came for the squadrons to deploy to France, 1 Squadron (commanded by Sqn Ldr 'Bull' Halahan) had been one of two Hurricane squadrons at Tangmere. Based there since 1928, it had operated the Hawker Fury as part of the fighter defence for the UK throughout the mid-1930s, before converting to the Hurricane in October 1938. Based at Digby, 73 Squadron (commanded by Sqn Ldr J.W. More) had been equipped with Gloster Gladiators before converting to

A practice scramble for the pilots of 87 Squadron at Lille Seclin, November 1939.

Pilots and ground crews with a souvenir of an early success, Lille Seclin, November 1939.

Hurricane deployment to France, 9 September 1939		
ORGANIZATION	SQUADRONS	LOCATION
AASF	1 and 73 Squadrons	Octeville
Air Component	85 and 87 Squadrons	Rouen

the Hurricane, in July 1938. Similarly, the two Debden squadrons, 85 and 87 Squadrons (commanded by Sqn Ldrs J.O. Oliver and J.S. Dewar respectively) had both been equipped with Gladiators, converting to the Hurricane throughout the summer of 1938.

Early Days

The 'Phoney War'

Following the German advance through Poland it was unclear exactly what would happen next. The French felt reasonably secure with the Maginot Line and Britain's contribution of sending the BEF and four squadrons of Hurricanes was as much political as military; these British forces were intended to supplement the French forces, which consisted of about 3,000 aircraft of all types.

The first Hurricanes to be sent to France were very early MkIs, which were fabric-covered and had two-bladed propellers. Considering its short period in service, the Hurricane proved a most reliable fighter at that time. It was stable in flight and

showed itself well capable of operating from less than perfect strips, the under-carriage proving an ideal design for such operations. However, there was little air activity during the early months of the war

as both sides prepared for the onslaught that would later come. This period, later known as the 'Phoney War', gave the pilots valuable time in the air to get to know the Hurricane better and to find out what its limitations might later be in combat. Most flying carried out by the squadrons in France consisted of formation tactics, with the occasional patrol against any reported enemy activity.

First Encounters

Even during the 'Phoney War', there was the occasional early encounter between the Hurricane pilots and the Luftwaffe. The RAF's first fighter claim of the war came on 30 October 1939, when Plt Off Peter 'Boy' Mould of 1 Squadron destroyed a reconnaissance Dornier Do 17, flying Hurricane L1842 from Vassincourt. The engagement took place to the west of the town of Toul and, such was the high profile of this first success, Mould received an immediate award of the Distinguished Flying Cross (DFC). He went on to serve with the squadron throughout the Battle of France and was eventually credited with seven confirmed kills before returning to the UK.

Another young Hurricane pilot to make an early impact in France was Fg Off 'Cobber' Kain of 73 Squadron. He became the RAF's first 'ace' (five confirmed kills) of the war.

The first victory for 85 Squadron was achieved on 21 November, when Fg Off

Hurricanes of 85 Squadron pictured at Lille Seclin during an inspection by King George VI, December 1939.

Sgt 'Dinky' Howell suffered from early political problems, when he force-landed his Hurricane in Belgium in December 1939, and had to retreat hastily across the French border.

Pilots of 73 Squadron were among the first involved in the air fighting over France towards the end of 1939. All three of these pilots achieved fame during the campaign: (left to right) Fg Off 'Ginger' Paul, Fg Off 'Fanny' Orton, and the legendary Fg Off 'Cobber' Kain.

Dickie Lee destroyed a He 111 near Boulogne. Educated at Charterhouse, Richard Hugh Anthony Lee had always been destined for a career in the RAF, having Lord Trenchard as a godfather! He joined the RAF in 1935 at the age of just eighteen and was among the first to arrive in France in September. The number of kills achieved by Lee over France is un certain, but is believed to have been nine; he was awarded the DFC in March 1940, followed by a Distinguished Service Order (DSO) in May. Sadly, for Lee, the war proved to be a relatively short one; he was last seen chasing three Bf 110s out to sea on 18 August 1940.

Conditions in France

For the pilots and ground crews of the Hurricane squadrons the first few months were busy, not because of extensive air activity but because of the number of moves the squadrons made. For 73 Squadron, after its first arrival in France at Le Havre, there were moves to Octeville, to Norrent Fontes at the end of September, and then to Rouvres on 9 October. At the same time, 1 Squadron also left Octeville for Norrent Fontes, before moving on to

Vassincourt a few days later. The two squadrons initially based at Rouen, 85 and 87 Squadrons, were both re-located to Merville at the end of September, and then on to Lille at the beginning of November.

Accommodation and working conditions for the pilots and ground crews serving in France varied from extremely lavish to very basic (wooden huts), depending on the location. Most of the airfields were of poor quality, and deteriorated to nothing more than muddy

fields during the winter months.

There was a general wish not to risk too many front-line Hurricane squadrons in France, so the four Hurricane squadrons were supplemented by two squadrons of Gladiator MkIs (607 and 615 Squadrons), which moved to Merville on 15 November to reinforce the Air Component of the BEF. A month later, both squadrons moved to Vitry-en-Artois, where they would remain until re-equipping with Hurricanes during March and April 1940.

As the year came to an end, the period

L1767 at Martlesham Heath during the 'Phoney War'.

Hurricanes of 87 Squadron at Lille Seclin, March 1940, during a practice air attack.

of the 'Phoney War' proved politically 'petty' to the military. RAF bomber crews were not allowed to bomb targets on German soil, for fear of reprisals against the French. In addition, neighbouring countries such as Belgium, still neutral at that stage, did not want to be seen to be involving themselves; in one incident, Sqn Ldr W. Coope of 87 Squadron had to force-land his Hurricane on a main road in Belgium early in November, and the aircraft was interned by the Belgians. This turned out to be the first of many examples of Hurricanes being interned. (Of course, the situation was later to change! Indeed, Britain supplied the Belgian Air Force with some Hurricanes early in the war, and more – eventually about forty in total – were built under licence in Belgium.)

Identifying Aircraft

There had been increasing problems of identification during the early months of the war, so the rudders of the RAF Hurricanes were painted in full red, white and blue vertical stripes. There had been several occasions when French gunners on

the ground had been unsure of an aircraft's identity and had taken shots at it anyway. This had also happened in the air, with nervous pilots mis-identifying aircraft. In fact, this problem was not just associated with France; it would continue to be a problem during the early stages of the Battle of Britain, and, indeed, would never go away throughout the war (and never really has!). However, painting the rudders seemed to put the Hurricane pilots more at their ease.

The other ways of identifying the individual Hurricane squadrons was by the code letters painted on the fuselage to the left of the roundel; for example, VY identified an aircraft of 85 Squadron and

RAF Hurricane Squadrons and locations in France, February 1940	
SQUADRON	**LOCATION**
1 Squadron	Vassincourt
73 Squadron	Rouvres
85 Squadron	Lille/Seclin
87 Squadron	Lille/Seclin

LK an aircraft of 87 Squadron. The third letter, painted on the right side of the roundel, identified an individual aircraft of that squadron. The Hurricane squadrons in France also had unit markings on the tail; an aircraft of 85 Squadron had a white hexagon, and an aircraft of 87 Squadron a white arrow.

The Battle of France, May 1940

10 May 1940

For the RAF in France the situation changed on 10 May 1940, when the main air war began.

With hindsight, the 'Phoney War' could have been better used with respect to the reinforcement of Hurricanes to France. Vital information gained from reconnaissance sorties and intelligence during the first week of May had failed to convince certain powers that a German invasion of the Low Countries was imminent. The 'sudden' German advance during the first hours of daylight on Friday, 10 May seemed to catch many by surprise. On paper, the French Armée de l'Air numbered some 600 fighters, many of which were almost obsolete. Nevertheless, those that were not obsolete looked to be a capable force, when combined with the RAF reinforcements. As part of the French 2nd Regiment, Escadrille 2/1/2 had on its strength eleven Hurricanes that were the survivors from Belgium.

The Low Countries

The main German advance through the Low Countries began at about 4.00 a.m. On that day there were six Hurricane squadrons available to meet the onslaught: 1 Squadron was based at Vassincourt to the west of Nancy, 73 Squadron at Rouvres, 85 Squadron at Lille, 87 Squadron at Senon, 607 Squadron at Vitry-en-Artois, and 615 Squadron was operating in two flights from Merville and Abbeville.

As dawn broke, and the German advance began, Hurricanes were immediately scrambled to meet the air threat over Belgium and northern France. The first Hurricanes to engage the enemy were those of 73 Squadron, which had been scrambled from Rouvres to meet a group of enemy bombers attacking the airfield.

Hurricanes of 85 Squadron and 607 Squadron had also been scrambled to meet the first wave of attack. The former scrambled from Lille to meet a group of Hs 126s and Ju 88s. Leading Red Section was Flt Lt Bob Boothby, who destroyed a Ju 88 near Mons. Also scrambled, to patrol the sector of the Maginot Line, was 1 Squadron at Vassincourt; they had to wait an hour before sighting the enemy. Leading the section, Flt Lt Prosser Hanks shot down a Do 17. At the same time, another section of 73 Squadron had been scrambled to meet more Do 17s approaching Rouvres.

Temporarily based at Senon, 87 Squadron was also in action during the first two hours of the battle. The squadron's first victory of the day was credited to Fg Off Harry Mitchell, who shot down a Do 17 to the south-west of Senon at 4.30 a.m. Less than half an hour later, two more Hurricanes of 73 Squadron were scrambled from Rouvres. Fg Off 'Cobber' Kain destroyed a Do 17 to the east of Metz, his sixth confirmed kill of the war. Shortly afterwards, the squadron achieved its second kill of the morning when its commanding officer, Sqn Ldr J.W.C. More, destroyed a reconnaissance He 111 near

Thionville. The same bombers were also intercepted by four Hurricanes of 87 Squadron; one Do 17 was shot down by Harry Mitchell, bringing the second kill of the morning, both for the squadron and for Mitchell.

Northern France

The same air battle over northern France during the early hours of 10 May saw five Hurricanes of 1 Squadron scrambled from Vassincourt to patrol the Metz area. They soon encountered a lone Do 17 on a reconnaissance sortie, and promptly shot it down near Dun-sur-Meuse. At Vitry-en-Artois the story had been similar for 607 Squadron; operating in sections of three, the pilots met anything from a single reconnaissance aircraft to a force of forty bombers. Down to the south-east, near the border with Luxembourg, two sections of Hurricanes, one each from 87 Squadron and 607 Squadron, had joined forces to attack two reconnaissance HS 126s; during the following few minutes both were shot down, both were credited to Sgt Gareth Nowell.

The first hours of daylight had been a frantic period for the Hurricane squadrons,

Pilots of 56 Squadron at North Weald during spring 1940. Pictured left to right are Fg Off Holden, S/L Knowles (OC 56 Squadron), F/L Coghlan, Plt Off Wicks, Plt Off Sutton and Plt Off Dryden. This squadron was heavily involved in the air fighting over France and detached across the Channel on a regular basis.

South African ace Plt Off Albert Lewis, of 85 Squadron, who achieved seven kills in France during the week 12-19 May.

with much confusion and uncertainty. All across northern France, as far as the Belgian and Luxembourg borders, Hurricanes from each squadron had been scrambled to meet the first waves of the German attack. By 8.00 a.m. things had become relatively quiet and the Air Staff back in England began to put into action a reinforcement plan. Three more Hurricane squadrons were immediately sent to France. During the early afternoon, 67 Wing was strengthened at Betheniville by the arrival of sixteen Hurricanes of 501 Squadron from Tangmere. The squadron was immediately in action and by the late afternoon had claimed its first kill – a Do 17 north of Vouziers, shot down by Fg Off Derrick Pickup. The other two squadrons, 3 and 79 Squadrons, were sent to reinforce Merville. In addition, flights were also moved around within the sector, 1 Squadron providing aircraft to Berry-au-Bac, and 87 Squadron moving to Lille to reinforce the central area.

The pattern during the afternoon of 10 May was very much the same as during the first hours; Hurricanes being scrambled, engaging the enemy and then landing, refuelling and scrambling again. It had, in fact, also been a bitter day of fighting for the French, Belgian and Dutch pilots. For the Hurricane pilots, darkness brought to an end a day that none would ever forget. Large sections of the French, Dutch and Belgian air forces had already been

destroyed. More than 200 Hurricane sorties had been flown; forty-two enemy aircraft were confirmed as destroyed, for the loss of seven Hurricanes.

11 May 1940

The following day, more Hurricanes became involved in the air battle. Twelve Hurricanes of 32 Squadron, based at Biggin Hill, were sent to Ypenburg in

Belgium. More patrols were flown, by Hurricanes of 56 Squadron, which had been moved from its base at North Weald to Gravesend, and of 17 Squadron, which had been detached from Debden to Martlesham Heath. Although a No 11 Group asset, and not formally assigned to either the AASF or Air Component, the Hurricane pilots of 17 Squadron were very much in the thick of the action, particularly during the late afternoon, when they became caught up with Bf 109s patrolling the Dutch sector. The result of the fierce air battle which followed was three Bf 109s and two HS 126s destroyed; the Bf 109 kills were credited to Sqn Ldr George Tomlinson, Fg Off Dickie Meredith and Sgt Charles Pavey, with the two HS 126s being destroyed by Fg Off Jerrard Jeffries and Sgt Wynn. The squadron also suffered, however, with four Hurricanes shot down; two pilots, Flt Lt Michael Donne and Plt Off George Slee, were killed, and the other two were taken as prisoners of war.

Throughout 11 May the Luftwaffe had continued attacks against French airfields from first light, and across the border in Belgium the story was much the same. For the Hurricane pilots the day progressed in very much the same way as the previous day. This time, however, there seemed to be no particular pattern to the waves. Unlike the first day, which had seen a lull following the dawn attack, there was no rest on 11 May, with attacks by Do17s and

Hurricane operating bases, northern France.

Plt Off K. Dryden with parachute at Dover rail station.

He 111s throughout the day. This time, there was more fighter escort evident, with the bombers being backed up by Bf 110s, with Bf 109s carrying out various sector patrols. The day ended with the Hurricane pilots claiming more than fifty enemy aircraft destroyed during the day, for the loss of thirteen Hurricanes.

Sgt Gareth Nowell

It had been a busy day for the pilots of 87 Squadron, and in particular for Sgt Gareth Nowell. Born in Cheshire, 27-year-old Nowell was one of the Squadron's older pilots. He had already claimed his first victim two days earlier when he shot down a Bf 110 near Longwy, followed the next day by two HS 126s and a Do 17 confirmed, and a further Do 17 shared. The squadron records were subsequently lost during the later evacuation from France, but he is believed to have shot down at least four more Do 17s on 11 May. He was awarded an immediate Distinguished Flying Medal (DFM) and bar, with a citation stating that

he had destroyed twelve enemy aircraft during the week. It has become impossible to confirm or deny this claim – some of the successes were probably shared with other pilots – but Nowell's was undoubtedly a remarkable achievement, and such numbers also emphasize the ferocity of the air war over France.

Nowell was later seriously wounded and burnt during an engagement in June. After a long period of recovery, he returned to operational flying and was eventually credited with ten individual kills, although this figure may have been as high as sixteen.

12 May 1940

By 12 May the German advance was beginning to make significant progress into Holland and through Belgium. Hurricanes of 151 Squadron had also entered the arena, having detached from North Weald to Martlesham Heath. It made sense to carry out patrols from bases in southern England, as the German air effort was very much against French and Belgian airfields. The Hurricane was an ideal

aircraft for these patrols – it was only a short distance to the area, and the Hurricane's fuel economy meant that it was able to patrol for some considerable time. There was no threat to the pilots once they were on the ground, and they were able to rest undisturbed before returning across the Channel.

Orders were issued to reinforce the RAF contingent in France further, with four more Hurricane squadrons. The plan was for the first unit to arrive that same day, and 504 Squadron was sent immediately to Vitry-en-Artois. Three more squadrons would follow across the Channel during the following six days – 151 Squadron also to Vitry-en-Artois, and 213 and 601 Squadrons to Merville. With the German advance reaching new heights, these extra reinforcements brought the total number of Hurricane squadrons based on French soil to nineteen, the highest number of Hurricane squadrons in France at any one time during this first period of the war. The squadrons were not all located together, as detachments and flights were operated from different bases on several occasions. This served two purposes: it split the assets across a larger area, and also reduced losses resulting from the frequent attacks by the Germans on those French airfields from which the Hurricanes were operating.

Other Contributions

The Hurricanes of the AASF and Air Component undoubtedly bore the brunt of the battle in May 1940 – the pilots had little or no reaction time before meeting any number of enemy aircraft, and were given little or no rest between sorties – but many more squadrons were involved from across the Channel. Many sorties were flown across the Channel by other Hurricane units, as well as by Spitfires, Battles and Blenheims. There was also the contribution by squadrons from Bomber Command, both in France and at home, with night bombing of German positions carried out by Whitleys and Hampdens. This contribution from other units towards the defence of the Low Countries and northern France cannot be underestimated.

The first two Victoria Crosses of the Second World War were won in France during the morning of 12 May. Five Fairey Battles of 12 Squadron based at Amifontaine were tasked with attacking vital road bridges over the Albert Canal at Vroenhaven and Veldwezelt, in an

Fg Off Roland Beamont served with 87 Squadron during the Battle of France and later became chief test pilot with English Electric, where he flew the Canberra, Lightning, TSR 2 and Tornado prototypes.

Plt Off Ken Tait, a New Zealander serving with No 87 Sqn, was successful in France and later during the Battle of Britain before he was killed in action during August 1941.

attempt to halt advancing units of the German Army. Led by Sqn Ldr 'Bull' Halahan, eight Hurricanes of 1 Squadron, based at Berry-au-Bac, provided fighter cover for the attack. The opposition encountered by the attacking force was fierce, with a large number of Bf 109s in the air and heavy ground fire in the target area. Despite the heroic action of the pilots of 1 Squadron in helping the Battle crews get to the target area, the two Battles in the first section were soon shot down by Bf 109s. Led by Fg Off Donald Garland, the three Battles in the second section carried out their attack, but, against overwhelming odds, two were shot down by ground fire and one was forced down soon after. The attack by Garland's aircraft had caused significant damage to the western end of the Veldwezelt bridge; as a result, both he and his observer, Sgt Thomas Gray, were posthumously awarded the Victoria Cross.

The mission proved suicidal, with none of the five Battles surviving. The Hurricanes of 1 Squadron did not fare much better. Plt Off Ray Lewis managed to bale out, having been shot down by one of the Bf 109s. Sqn Ldr Halahan and Sgt Frank Soper had to force-land their Hurricanes, having also been overcome by the superior numbers of the Bf 109s. Of the other five Hurricanes, two were severely damaged, although both pilots recovered their aircraft to base and were unhurt.

With 1 Squadron providing fighter cover for the Battle attack during the morning, the pilots of 501 Squadron at Betheniville bore the brunt of 67 Wing's involvement in the air fighting over northern France. For 501 Squadron, the first main encounter of the day had been at 7.00 a.m., when it had been scrambled to intercept a force of He 111s being escorted by Bf 110s. In the hard fight that followed, four of the He 111s were shot down. The squadron was in action again later during the day when more fighting took place to the north-east of Betheniville, in the area of Sedan.

Although two Do 17s were shot down, the squadron lost its second pilot of the day when Fg Off Michael Smith was killed, shot down by a Bf 110 to the north of Sedan.

Hurricane Losses

The day had seen several air battles between the RAF Hurricanes and a continued onslaught from the Luftwaffe. The increasing number of enemy fighters entering the orbat shows how difficult the RAF Hurricanes and the other European air force pilots were making it for the Germans. As far as the Hurricane pilots were concerned they were doing as much as could possibly be expected. The increasing number of Messerschmitts was starting to tell. During the next two days, thirty-three Hurricanes were shot down by enemy fighters. Although more than fifty enemy aircraft had been shot down by the Hurricanes, the Luftwaffe could afford to lose a few bombers and fighters; the RAF could not. More Hurricanes and pilots were sent across the Channel in an attempt to help the situation, but the Luftwaffe's superior numbers would eventually win the day.

There was an increasing number of heroic actions by the Hurricane pilots in France. In one battle during the morning of 14 May, Hurricanes of 607 Squadron came across an attacking force of fifteen HS 123s escorted by more than forty Bf 109s near Louvain. During the air battle that followed, ten enemy aircraft were shot down, including four by Fg Off Ian Russell, an Australian pilot attached to the squadron from 245 Squadron. However, four of the squadron's Hurricanes were also shot down, with all four pilots killed.

Another gallant young Australian fighter pilot lost as a result of the action on 14 May was Fg Off Leslie Clisby of 1 Squadron. As in many cases, the exact circumstances of his death, and the number of kills he achieved, are unclear. He was heavily involved with the air fighting during April and the first two weeks of May, achieving up to sixteen confirmed kills, all but two of which he shot down during the five-day period leading up to his death. During the morning of 14 May, six aircraft were scrambled to intercept a large formation of Bf 110s near the airfield of Berry-au-Bac. During the following action, three of 1 Squadron's Hurricanes were shot down, including Leslie Clisby, who was seen on fire spiralling to earth to the south of Sedan.

Plt Off Watty Watson, 87 Squadron.

Early Aces

There were several pilots from 1 Squadron who distinguished themselves during these few days. Fg Off 'Iggy' Kilmartin from Ireland brought his personal score to eleven; Canadian Fg Off 'Hilly' Brown achieved eight kills during the week; Sgt Frank Soper scored six kills during the same week; there were five kills in four days for Fg Off Paul Richey, Flt Lt Prosser Hanks, and Fg Off 'Boy' Mould; and Sgt Arthur Clowes also became an 'ace' during the same week.

The achievements of 1 Squadron were undoubtedly amazing, but pilots of the other Hurricane squadrons involved in the air fighting over France at the time were no less heroic. Among the high achievers of 73 Squadron during the same period were Fg Off 'Cobber' Kain; Flt Lt John Scoular, who brought his personal tally to nine; and Fg Off 'Fanny' Orton, who scored seven confirmed kills. From other squadrons, the South African Plt Off 'Lew' Lewis of 85 Squadron achieved seven kills in one week, while Plt Off Dennis David and Sgt Gareth Nowell, both of 87 Squadron, scored at least eight kills each during the week.

A number of pilots first made their mark in France and later went on to achieve great fame as top-scoring Hurricane pilots

during the war. The second-highest score of the war was achieved by Hurricane pilot Frank Carey, who served with 3 Squadron during the campaign over France. He shot down four He 111s on 10 May, and added nine more kills to his tally during the following four days; he was awarded a DFC and bar, to add to his DFM gained with 43 Squadron earlier in the war. Carey was eventually credited with twenty-five Hurricane kills before the end of the war.

The man who went on to be the RAF's top-scoring pilot of the Battle of Britain also first made his mark in France. Sgt 'Ginger' Lacey was also an ace by the end of the Battle of France, having achieved five kills while serving with 501 Squadron over France. Ginger Lacey went on to become the third top-scoring Hurricane pilot of the war, with twenty-three confirmed kills.

The Hon. Max Aitken became an ace in just two days in France. Serving with 601 Squadron, he destroyed three He 111s, two Ju 87s and a Bf 110 in a period of just over twenty-four hours between 18-19 May. Aitken went on to achieve fourteen confirmed kills (seven in Hurricanes) before the end of the war.

At no other time in the war did so many aces emerge in such a short period of time. Before the Battle of France was over, the RAF had at least forty confirmed aces, and several more unconfirmed. All the pilots gained valuable combat experience in the

Fg Off Roddy Rayner achieved five kills while serving with 87 Squadron during the Battle of

air war over France, which would stand both them and Fighter Command in good stead for the Battle of Britain. The young pilots who went to France without any combat experience would return to England as combat veterans.

The commanding officer of a remarkable group of fighter pilots – 1 Squadron – during the campaign in France. S/L 'Bull' Halahan (sixth from left) is surrounded by aces from the Battle of France, including Fg Off Leslie Clisby (second from left), F/L Prosser Hanks (fourth from left), Fg Off 'Boy' Mould (fifth from left), Fg Off Paul Richey (fourth from right), and Fg Off Iggy Kilmartin (third from right).

This Hurricane of 85 Squadron shows a distinctive white hexagon, following its return from France in June 1940.

An impossible situation

During the two-day period of 15-16 May, the Germans broke through the defences of Sedan in the east and forced the Allies to withdraw to the River Escaut in the

north. The Hurricane squadrons were forced to move back towards the coast and it was only a matter of time before the Allies were defeated. The bitter aerial war in the skies over France during this period brought further appeals from France. On 16 May, Winston Churchill flew to Paris for further talks, but the RAF was already down to its minimum squadron strength if Britain was to stand any chance of opposing the Luftwaffe, should France fall.

Winston Churchill was committed to saving France, but RAF Fighter Command's Commander-in-Chief Sir Hugh Dowding stood firm. Dowding felt that he simply could not afford to send any more fighter squadrons across the Channel. He was working on the assumption that the RAF needed at least fifty squadrons if it was to stand any chance of defeating an assault on Britain by the Luftwaffe. Fighter Command was already down to two-thirds of that number. According to Dowding it was, simply, impossible for the RAF to do any more. In a letter to the Air Council, dated 16 May, Dowding wrote:

> I must point out that within the last few days the equivalent of 10 squadrons have been sent to France, that the Hurricane squadrons remaining in this country are seriously depleted, and that the more squadrons which are sent to

S/L Johnnie Dewar, awarded the DSO and DFC for his outstanding leadership while commanding 87 Squadron during the Battle of France; sadly, he was soon to lose his life during the Battle of Britain.

RAF Hurricane squadrons and locations – 18 May 1940	
SQUADRON	**LOCATION**
1	Anglure
3	Merville
17	Lille/Marcq and Merville
32	Abbeville and Merville
56	Lille/Seclin/Norrent-Fontes
73	Gaye
79	Merville
85	Lille/Seclin
87	Lille/Marcq and Merville
111	Lille/Marcq/Abbeville/Vitry-en-Artois
145 detachment	Merville
151	Abbeville and Vitry-en-Artois
213	Abbeville/Lille/Marcq/Merville
253	Vitry-en-Artois/Lille/Marcq
501	Anglure
504	Lille and Norrent-Fontes
601	Merville/Abbeville
607	Norrent Fontes
615	Moorseele

Fg Off 'Cobber' Kain of 73 Squadron was the RAF's first ace of the war, and achieved seventeen confirmed kills before his death on 6 June 1940.

Fg Off 'Cobber' Kain, DFC (73 Squadron)

One young Hurricane pilot who made an early impact in France was 21-year-old Fg Off 'Cobber' Kain. Born in New Zealand, Edgar James Kain joined the RAF in 1936. After training he was posted to 73 Squadron, and flew Gladiators before converting to the Hurricane in the summer of 1938. In September 1939 he accompanied the squadron to France. He claimed his first victory, a Dornier Do 17 near Metz, on 8 November, followed by a second Do 17 later in the month. He was awarded the DFC in January 1940 and by the end of March he was the RAF's first ace of the war, having claimed three Messerschmitt Bf 109Es during the month; two in one combat near Saarlautern on 26 March.

Kain served with 73 Squadron throughout the Battle of France, the only squadron pilot to do so. During the main air battles over northern France between 10-21 May 1940, he shot down eight aircraft, including three in one day, on 19 May. Three more confirmed kills between 25-27 May brought his total to seventeen. Kain's squadron remained in France after the main withdrawal of Hurricane squadrons on 20 May, but he was ordered back to England for a rest. On 6 June, he took off from Echemines and began a low slow roll. The wing-tip of his Hurricane hit the ground and the aircraft crashed, killing the courageous young 'Cobber'.

No pilot contributed more than Fg Off 'Cobber' Kain during the Battle of France, and he will be remembered as the RAF's first ace of the war. With seventeen kills and the experience gained in France, who knows what he might have achieved during the Battle of Britain? Sadly, we will never know.

northern France during 17 and 18 May resulted in the British withdrawing further towards the coast.

By the end of 18 May, the German forces had reached the areas of Cambrai and beyond, and little stood between them and the vital ports. This area, which had witnessed such terrible fighting little more than twenty years before, was once again to be the scene of devastation. This time, however, there was no chance of defending towns such as St Quentin and Arras, as the Germans rolled through the Somme. The airfields at Lille were abandoned, as the Hurricane squadrons moved to what was left of the French airfields and the coast. The squadrons moved daily, sometimes two or three times in the same day, as the surviving Hurricane pilots in France made a last stand. Although no more aircraft were to be sent to France, Hurricanes of No 11 Group based across the Channel did take part in some of the desperate air battles in the skies over northern France.

The air fighting during the three days of 17-19 May resulted in about 150 enemy aircraft destroyed, for the loss of about eighty Hurricanes; fifteen Hurricane pilots were killed, with a further twenty or more either wounded or taken prisoner of war.

Evacuation

By 20 May, the situation in France had become impossible. The airfields at Merville, Moorsele and Norrent-Fontes were evacuated, and all the Hurricanes capable of flying returned across the Channel, leaving just three squadrons assigned to the AASF remaining in France: 1 and 501 Squadrons at Anglure, and 73 Squadron at Gaye.

Returning the Hurricanes

The evacuation of the RAF from France in May 1940 brought many tales of heroics and improvisation. The serviceable Hurricanes had flown back across the Channel, but it had not been possible to recover all the ground equipment and spares; this resulted in much being lost during the retreat. More importantly, however, every Hurricane would become vital to the defence of Britain in the air battle that was to follow. Where possible, the remaining Hurricanes were fixed up just enough to enable them to get back across the Channel.

Engineering support was sent hastily to

France the higher will be the wastage and the more insistent the demands for reinforcements. I must therefore request that on a matter of paramount urgency the Air Ministry will consider and decide what level of strength is to be left to Fighter Command for the defence of this country, and will ensure me that when this level has been reached, not one fighter will be sent across the Channel however urgent and insistent the appeals for help may be. If the Home Defence Force is drained away in desperate attempts to remedy the situation in France, defeat in France will involve the final, complete and irremediable defeat of this country.

Dowding's letter was too late to stop the arrival of 213 and 601 Squadrons at Merville on 17 May, or the arrival of 151 Squadron at Vitry-en-Artois less than twenty-four hours later. It did, however, bring to an end the sending to France of Hurricane squadrons, although a number of aircraft did fly across the Channel during the day, returning at night; examples of this 'compromise' were contributions from 56 and 111 Squadrons, which detached Hurricanes from their home base to Lille and Abbeville respectively. The German advance through the centre sector of

RAF Hurricane squadrons and locations, June 1940		
SQUADRON	**LOCATION**	**DATE**
1 Squadron	Chateaudun	3-14 June
	Nantes/Chateau Bougon	14-17 June
	St Nazaire	17-18 June
17 Squadron	Le Mans	8-17 June
73 Squadron	Echemines	3-7 June
	Raudin	7-15 June
	Nantes	15-18 June
242 Squadron (detachment)	Chateaudun	8-14 June
	Ancenis	14-16 June
	Chateau Bougon	16 June
501 Squadron	Le Mans	2-11 June
	Dinard	11-17 June

France in any available aircraft. One remarkable incident involved Plt Off Louis Strange, DSO MC DFC, a former pilot with the Royal Flying Corps, who was sent to Merville to organize the recovery of straggling Hurricanes. He found himself with just one partly service-able Hurricane left, with no one to fly it back to England. Just short of his fiftieth birthday, and never having flown a Hurricane before, he considered that he had no alternative but to take the controls. The journey home was hectic; he was attacked and chased by a number of Bf 109s, which he managed to shake off, before finally landing at Manston. For this remarkable action Louis Strange was awarded a well-deserved bar to his First World War DFC.

Operation Dynamo

The RAF ground crews were left to get back to England by any possible means. They joined the thousands of retreating British and French forces towards the coast and the eventual evacuation port at Dunkirk. Although the majority of the Hurricanes had withdrawn to England, it was still necessary to provide vital air cover over the Channel ports if the evacuation of the men was to be possible. This vital air support was flown from the fighter airfields in southern England and amounted to some 200 sorties per day.

Under Operation Dynamo, the evacuation of the British forces at Dunkirk began on 26 May, and during the following week nearly 350,000 troops were evacuated from the beaches and port. RAF fighters flew nearly 3,000 sorties in support of the evacuation during the period, most in the area of Dunkirk itself, destroying nearly 200 enemy aircraft, for the loss of more than 100 RAF fighters. Although this

contribution from the fighter squadrons has often come under criticism, the pilots did all that was possible considering the operating range from their home airfields and the overwhelming numbers of the Luftwaffe bombers. The loss of Hurricanes and Spitfires during May was devastating in terms of the forthcoming defence of Britain, and the loss of experienced pilots was even more disastrous; nearly 100

fighter pilots from the AASF, Air Component and Fighter Command were either killed or taken prisoner of war during just a few weeks.

The Remaining Squadrons

Not all the RAF Hurricanes were withdrawn across the Channel. Three squadrons remained in France following the evacuation from French airfields on 20 May – the two original Hurricane units of the AASF, 1 and 73 Squadrons, based at Anglure and Gaye respectively – with 501 Squadron, also based at Anglure, continuing to fight a rearguard action until mid-June.

This move to keep Hurricanes in France right up to the bitter end was political, rather than representing a significant contribution to the effort. For France, the situation became more impossible with every day that passed. As the German advance continued during early June, the three squadrons withdrew to airfields nearer the coast. They were briefly reinforced by the arrival of 17 Squadron from England, and a detachment of 242

Plt Off (later Gp Capt) Dennis David, CBE DFC and bar AFC - 87 Squadron

Born in Surrey on 25 July 1918, Dennis David joined the RAFVR in 1937. After training he was posted to 87 Squadron, and was among the first to be sent to France following the outbreak of war. Although he did not achieve his first confirmed kill until 10 May 1940 (an He 111 in the area of Senon), he enjoyed remarkable success throughout the following nine days of intense air fighting. He destroyed a Do 17 on the same day, another Do 17 and a Ju 87 during the following day, and a He 111 on 12 May, making him an ace in just three days. By 19 May, his personal score had risen to eight, although the citation to his DFC and bar credits him with eleven kills.

David enjoyed more success with 87 Squadron during the Battle of Britain and, by the end, brought his total to fifteen; the last kill was with 213 Squadron after his posting as a flight commander in mid-October. After a brief spell flying Spitfires with 152 Squadron he was rested from operational flying and became an instructor, during which time he was awarded the AFC and promoted to the rank of Squadron Leader.

After a period in the Middle East, David was promoted to the rank of Wing Commander in July 1943 and given command of 89 Squadron in Ceylon, where he flew Beaufighters. The following year he commanded Minneriya and Kankesanteran, after which he was promoted to the rank of Group Captain. At the end of the war he remained in the Far East until returning to the UK in 1946. Dennis David remained in the post-war RAF, retiring from the service in 1967.

Plt Off Dennis David was one of the most successful pilots to have served with 87 Squadron; he achieved at least eight kills during the Battle of France and was eventually credited with fifteen kills, for which he was awarded the DFC and bar. David remained in the RAF after the war and retired as a group captain in 1967.

Squadron Hurricanes during June. The former joined 501 Squadron at forward operating bases at Le Mans and Dinard for a few days between 8 and 17 June. The detachment from 242 Squadron operated from three different locations during its eight days in France. The Hurricanes were able to provide some vital air support around the Channel ports of Le Havre, Cherbourg and Brest, while more British forces managed to evacuate from French soil.

Finally, the situation became impossible and both 17 and 242 Squadrons flew back to England during 16-17 June. Somewhat appropriately, the last two units to leave France were those that had been the first two to arrive. By 18 June, 1 and 73 Squadrons were operating out of St Nazaire and Nantes respectively, when the orders came for the last Hurricanes to fly back to England.

Further North

The attack on France and the Low Countries was not the only concentration of German effort. Elsewhere in northern Europe, they had made further progress. On 9 April 1940, the German advance swept through Denmark and attacked southern Norway. Captured Norwegian airfields could be used by German bombers to carry out attacks against northern England, and the Norwegian ports would give the German Navy vital access to the North Sea and the Atlantic.

Determined to stop a move northwards through central Norway, the British prepared an expeditionary force to sail north, with the aim of denying the German Navy the northern port of Narvik. One squadron of Gladiators (263 Squadron) and Hurricanes of 46 Squadron were embarked on HMS *Glorious*, setting sail on 9 May, and arriving at Harstad in Norway soon after. It took several days to prepare a landing ground for the Hurricanes and finally, on 26 May, the aircraft were flown off HMS Glorious, landing at Skaanland and Bardufoss, just 50 miles (80km) from Narvik. Two days later, Fg Off Lydall scored the first kill, when he shot down a Ju 88. A handful more kills for the squadron followed during the next few days, as the unescorted German bombers proved good targets for the Hurricane pilots.

The inevitable German advance northwards meant, however, that German

A most remarkable story involved First World War fighter ace Louis Strange, DSO MC DFC, who was put in charge of recovering Hurricanes during the evacuation of France in May 1940. With no pilots left, and having never flown a Hurricane before, he promptly climbed into the cockpit of a Hurricane and flew it back to England, during which he fought off a number of enemy fighters, bringing him a well-earned bar to his First World War DFC!

bombers began to be escorted by fighters, and the situation in Norway soon became hopeless. The Hurricane detachment of 46 Squadron had been in northern Norway for less than two weeks before the order came to embark on to HMS *Glorious* for the journey home. The last Hurricanes left Norway on 8 June. Tragically, within a few hours, *HMS Glorious* was sunk by the German warships *Scharnhorst* and *Gneisenau*, and the surviving Hurricanes from Norway were lost, along with all but two of the squadron's pilots.

Final tally to June 1940

The Battle of France continued until the French surrendered on 22 June. By this time, the RAF had lost the best part of a thousand aircraft, half of which were fighters. Indeed, during the month before the evacuation at Dunkirk, the RAF had lost the equivalent of forty fighter squadrons during the defeats in Norway and France. Since September 1939, more than 450 Hurricanes had been sent to France, and

less than seventy returned. Records and sources vary, but the Hurricane pilots made 500 claims of enemy aircraft destroyed during the twelve-day period of 10-21 May alone; well over 100 more were claimed as 'probably' destroyed during the same period.

One of the first squadrons to arrive in France, 1 Squadron alone had lost nearly forty Hurricanes during the Battle of France. In return, it was credited with about eighty enemy aircraft destroyed, and produced no fewer than ten confirmed aces. This squadron, and 73 Squadron, the two original Hurricane units of the AASF, remained in France and fought the final air battles, before being the last Hurricanes to leave, on 18 June. The loss of pilots was probably more critical than the loss of aircraft; more than 400 had either been killed, wounded or taken prisoner of war. Nevertheless, the heroics during the evacuation of Dunkirk had ensured that the British had lived to fight another day, albeit to fight it alone.

CHAPTER THREE

Britain Alone

The Summer of 1940

Let us therefore brace ourselves to our duties, and so bear ourselves that, if the British Empire and its Commonwealth last for a thousand years, men will still say, 'This was their finest hour'. (Winston Churchill, 18 June 1940)

The fall of France meant that Britain now stood alone. There is not the time in this book to deal with each day of the Battle of Britain in detail. However, it would be incomplete without study of this enormously significant air battle, so each phase is covered in some detail. The Hurricane, after all, did play a major part in the survival of Britain. The battle also changed the lives of so many of the young men who fought it. Many became famous names in history, while many others became the unfortunate and tragic statistics of air warfare; those Hurricane pilots killed in the battle are commemorated in Appendix E.

The Battle of Britain

The Situation

The French surrender on 22 June 1940 meant that the situation for Britain was now straightforward. The questions of whether or not more Hurricanes should be sent across the Channel, and whether or not Europe would falter against the German advance, were now answered. Quite simply, at the end of June, Britain stood alone. For Air Chief Marshal Hugh Dowding, at the head of Fighter Command, this position was far from ideal. He had established the number of fighters that would be needed to defend Britain. However, the loss of so many of Britain's main fighter assets in France, and of so many of the experienced pilots, meant that the situation was desperate. What Fighter Command and Britain needed was time.

Fortunately, that much-needed time actually became available. The German advance stopped at the Channel, as Hitler

Pilots of 56 Squadron at North Weald, just before the opening phase of the Battle of Britain: (left to right) Plt Off Dryden, Flt Lt Coghlan and Fg Off Brooker.

An early-morning scene typical of any fighter airfield along the south coast as a Hurricane pilot prepares for yet another patrol.

Plt Off Francois Xavier Egenoff de Spirlet escaped from Belgium and served with 87 Squadron throughout the Battle of Britain.

still felt that there might be a peaceful solution to the war in the West, and that he might need to concentrate on Russia in the East. However, it soon became obvious that Britain would not give in and German preparations for a landing by sea were put in motion during early July; the aim was to make an invasion of England possible within two months. First, however, it was necessary for the Luftwaffe to gain air superiority over the Channel to minimize losses during any such invasion. These vital few weeks gave Britain's aircraft production lines the chance to turn out more fighters, and gave Fighter Command the chance to train new pilots and to rebuild its squadrons.

The full Hurricane order of battle for the opening day is shown in Appendix C. It essentially consisted of 31 Hurricane squadrons, which made up some 60 per cent of Fighter Command's squadrons at the time. The remainder were equipped mainly with Spitfires, supplemented by a handful of Blenheim and Defiant squadrons. Dowding now had the minimum fifty-plus fighter squadrons that he had felt were essential if Britain was to stand any chance of survival.

Command and Organization

Fighter Command, under Dowding, was divided into four groups, each commanded by an Air Vice-Marshal (AVM) as its Air Officer Commanding (AOC); each group was divided into a number of sectors. These sectors, established geographically, eased the command and control of the fighter bases and squadrons within it. The organization was quite straightforward. No 11 Group's area of responsibility extended from Norwich southwards across the Thames to Dover, along the south coast as far as Southampton, and northwards to the north-west of London. Its main task was to protect London and the south-east and it would, therefore, be in the forefront of the action. The area from mid-Hampshire to the West Country, and as far north as the southern Midlands, was the responsibility of No 10 Group. The Midlands was covered by No 12 Group, with the far north of England and Scotland being covered by No 13 Group.

For the time being, the organization of the Hurricane squadrons was stable: fourteen squadrons in No 11 Group, seven in No 12 Group, six in No 13 Group, and four in No 10 Group. Squadron strength varied between ten and fifteen Hurricanes, but averaged about twelve aircraft at any one time, most of which were serviceable. The majority of the fighter squadrons came under the control of No 11 Group in the south-east, including fourteen Hurricane squadrons – four at Tangmere, two each at North Weald, Croydon and Debden, and one squadron each at Biggin Hill, Hawkinge, Northolt and Kenley.

The number of serviceable aircraft would become the key factor during the following months and the figure available for combat would vary from day to day. Fortunately, the Hurricane proved to be a robust aircraft in combat, and there would be many occasions when aircraft could be recovered to base and repaired within a matter of hours, or days, so that they could rejoin the battle. It could also operate from the most basic of airfields and this, again, would prove to be most valuable as RAF airfields became badly damaged.

Some of the squadrons that had recently returned from France were sent north for a well-deserved rest. Among the last to return had been 73 Squadron, which was sent to Church Fenton in Yorkshire. There, it flew night fighter patrols, in response to thoughts of German air attacks from occupied airfields in Norway. Other squadrons were not so lucky, including 1 Squadron; on its late return in June, it was sent to Northolt to defend London, only moving to the Midlands in September. However, before long the squadrons and pilots were being moved around as if in a giant game of chess. The organizational structure meant that, as squadrons became

Sergeant pilots of 56 Squadron at North Weald. The defence of the country was the responsibility of gallant young men of Fighter Command such as these.

Pilots of 'A' Flight, 87 Squadron: (left to right) Fg Off Watty Watson, Sgt Rubber Thorogood, unknown, Flt Lt Ian Gleed, Plt Off Ken Tait and Fg Off Roddy Rayner.

Plt Off Andrew McLure of 87 Squadron destroyed a Bf 109 off Portland on 11 August.

tired or depleted, they could be replaced by more aircraft and fresher pilots. The idea was that, with luck, Dowding would never have to commit all his front-line squadrons at the same time. The concept was sound and Dowding was largely able to keep to the plan.

Phase One, 10 July – 10 August

According to the history books, the Battle of Britain opened on Wednesday, 10 July 1940. From both the British and German point of view, this date does not mark any specific event in the battle. Indeed, since the evacuation from France, a number of aerial combats had taken place over the Channel and southern England. However, the air fighting over the British convoy Bread, during the early afternoon, officially started the most famous air battle in history.

The day started with miserable weather and heavy rain showers spreading from the south-west. The first casualty occurred before a shot had been fired, when Sgt Ian Clenshaw, flying a Hurricane of 253 Squadron based at Kirton-in-Lindsey in Lincolnshire, crashed in bad weather during a dawn patrol. The first success of the battle went to the Spitfires of 66 Squadron, based at Coltishall in Norfolk, following an engagement with a reconnaissance Dornier Do 17.

By lunch-time the weather had improved and the first heavy build-up of enemy aircraft was detected just after 1.00 p.m. The first fighters on the scene were Hurricanes of 32 Squadron from Biggin Hill and 111 Squadron based at Croydon, soon joined by Spitfires of 74 Squadron and Hurricanes of 56 Squadron from North Weald. The combat soon deteriorated into a free-for-all, from which the RAF's fighter pilots soon learnt that pre-war textbook tactics would not always work against such large numbers and with so little reaction time. One of the 32 Squadron pilots to enjoy success on this opening day was Fg Off John Humpherson, a veteran of the campaign in France, who destroyed a Do 17 over Dungeness. The

Fighter Command structure showing groups, sectors and Hurricane squadrons – 10 July 1940			
AIR CHIEF MARSHAL SIR HUGH DOWDING			
10 GROUP	**11 GROUP**	**12 GROUP**	**13 GROUP**
AVM Sir Quintin Brand	AVM K.R. Park	AVM T.L. Leigh-Mallory	AVM R.E. Saul
Middle Wallop - 238, 501	Debden - 17, 85	Coltishall - 242	Catterick
Filton - 87, 213	North Weald - 56, 151	Duxford - 310	Usworth - 607
	Hornchurch	Wittering - 229	Acklington
	Biggin Hill - 32, 79	Digby - 46	Turnhouse - 245, 605
	Kenley -111, 615, 1(RCAF)	Kirton-in-Lindsey - 253	Dyce - 263
	Tangmere - 1, 43, 145, 601	Church Fenton - 73, 249	Wick - 3, 504
	Northolt - 257		

One of many Australian airmen to distinguish himself was Fg Off John Cock of 87 Squadron, who destroyed two aircraft during the fighting over Portland on 11 August. By the end of the Battle of Britain, his personal score was ten, for which he was awarded the DFC.

Hurricanes of 56 Squadron also enjoyed success. One of the flight commanders, Flt Lt 'Jumbo' Gracie, destroyed a Bf 110 near Dover, while Sgt Clifford Whitehead scored his fourth kill when he also destroyed a Bf 110 in the same area.

The Hurricanes of 111 Squadron, led by Sqn Ldr John Thompson, became engaged with Messerschmitt Bf 109s of JG3 and JG51 escorting Dornier Do 17s of KG2 to the south of Folkestone. Fg Off Henry Ferris, already an ace with six victories, claimed his seventh victim when he destroyed a Bf 109 over Folkestone and shared in the destruction of a Do 17. Another of the first Hurricane successes of the battle was achieved in sad circumstances, when Fg Off Tom Higgs lost a wing after colliding with a Do 17 at 6,000 feet (1800m), sending both aircraft into the sea.

There were a number of early successes and the RAF's advantage in operating close to home, and in the role of defence rather than attack, was evident from the very first day. Further along the coast, a large number of German bombers had made further attacks with limited success in Cornwall and South Wales. The overall result at the end of the first day was thirteen enemy aircraft destroyed, for the loss of six RAF fighters.

The following few days saw a similar pattern to the opening day; it would be some time before the Battle of Britain reached its height. There were several reasons for this. First, the weather was generally unfavourable; early-morning fog and low cloud made targeting for the German bombers difficult. Second, the Luftwaffe bomber force was not quite ready for an all-out assault against the RAF. The problem of attacking well-defended targets in daylight, over a prolonged period, against a well-trained and most determined opposition was an entirely different challenge to the quick defeats of Poland, France and the Low Countries. The third, and most important, reason was that Hitler had not yet decided on exactly when and how he would finally attempt to defeat Britain.

The Luftwaffe's main target during the opening two weeks of the battle was shipping in the Channel, off the ports of Portland and Dover. The weather had been variable, with rain showers precluding much air interaction, although there were inevitably clashes between the two sides, with associated losses. The first two days of the phase, 10-11 July, had resulted in more than thirty enemy aircraft destroyed, for the loss of just ten RAF fighters, including six Hurricanes. Probably the most famous

Flt Lt Ian Gleed and ground crew of 87 Squadron.

fighter pilot scored his first success in a Hurricane on 11 July; leading 242 Squadron from Coltishall, Sqn Ldr Douglas Bader destroyed a reconnaissance Do 17 near Cromer on the Norfolk coast.

The next week resulted in twenty-eight enemy aircraft destroyed, for the loss of eighteen RAF fighters (twelve Hurricanes), and the following week fifty enemy aircraft for the loss of twenty-seven RAF fighters (eighteen Hurricanes). With the exception of the opening two days, when the RAF had enjoyed undisputed success, these first two weeks of the battle had seen both sides locked in a stalemate. Although the overall score was in favour of the RAF, the Luftwaffe could afford to lose aircraft at the current ratio of three to two.

The air battle had started to take shape and many early lessons had been learnt on both sides of the Channel, mainly that air combat was hard and that the superior aircraft generally won each engagement. The previously successful Junkers Ju 87 Stuka was completely outclassed by the Hurricane and Spitfire; similarly, although much had been expected of the RAF's Boulton Paul Defiant, it soon became obvious that it was no match for the Messerschmitt Bf 109. In one encounter, on 19 July, six Defiants from 141 Squadron were shot down over the Channel by Bf 109s of JG51. In a matter of minutes, ten of the squadron's pilots and gunners were dead. Only the arrival of the Hurricanes of 111 Squadron prevented a total massacre, enabling three Defiants to recover to Hawkinge.

During July, 302 and 303 Squadrons were formed, at Leconfield and Northolt respectively, both made up of Polish personnel evacuated from France. The experience level of 303 Squadron was such that it became operational before the end of the month, when it was literally thrown into battle, with little preparation. It was several weeks before 302 Squadron moved south to join the battle. The vital contribution of such units cannot be underestimated – many Polish, Czech and other overseas personnel would give their life before the battle was over. Another new Hurricane squadron was 232 Squadron, which formed during July at Sumburgh, where its Hurricanes flew on defensive duties in the north of Scotland. These three squadrons were the only additions to the Hurricane orbat, bringing the maximum number of operational Hurricane units at any one time during the battle to thirty-four.

Pilots of 249 Squadron at Boscombe Down relax with 'pipes various' during August. Pictured left to right are: Plt Off George Barclay, Plt Off Percy Burton, Fg Off Pat Wells, and Plt Off Bryan Meaker. Tragically, of those pictured, only Pat Wells would survive the war.

The Luftwaffe continued its attacks against the Channel convoys throughout the rest of the month. One of the heaviest attacks was made against a large convoy off Dover on 25 July. The weather had been fine all day and many attacks were carried out by Ju 87s, escorted by Bf 109s. Despite being heavily outnumbered, the RAF destroyed twenty enemy aircraft, for the loss of nine fighters, just one of which was

a Hurricane, of 87 Squadron. However, a number of ships in the convoy were either lost or severely damaged. It was a similar story three days later, when more attacks were made against shipping off Dover, and the same again the following day. By now, the good weather was proving favourable to the RAF, with the pilots able to use the sun and height to gain the advantage. In the last four days of July the RAF destroyed thirty-five enemy aircraft for the loss of just eleven, including seven Hurricanes.

Although the Hurricanes damaged in the air could land back at base (or almost anywhere, if necessary), where they could be repaired and put back into the air in a relatively short period of time, the loss of pilots could not be so readily accepted. It took time to train young pilots and the training units struggled to turn out new pilots at the rate at which the RAF was starting to lose them. By the end of July, after just three weeks of the battle, twenty-five Hurricane pilots had lost their lives, with many more recovering from wounds or injuries.

By the beginning of August, the good weather had become settled, although it was cloudy at times. Whenever possible, the Luftwaffe continued its attacks against shipping in the Channel, extending its area of operations by night to the Midlands, the north of England, South Wales and Norfolk. There were few exchanges during the first week of August, but this all changed on the 8th, when the convoy CW9, codenamed Peewit, was attacked several times during the day off the Isle of

Hurricanes of 'A' Flight of No 87 Squadron.

Above: **Flt Lt Ian Gleed in 'LK-A' of 87 Squadron.**

Left: **Australian S/L Terence Lovell-Gregg was commanding 87 Squadron at Exeter when he was killed, following an engagement with Bf 109s over Portland on 15 August.**

Wight. This day saw the heaviest air fighting to date, with a new record figure of thirty-one enemy aircraft destroyed. It was, however, a particularly bad day for the Hurricane squadrons – twelve of the RAF's twenty fighters lost were Hurricanes, with the loss of all the pilots.

One Hurricane squadron caught up in the heaviest combats of the day was 145 Squadron from Westhampnett, which lost five Hurricanes during the day – two during an encounter with Bf 109s of JG27, shortly after 9.00 a.m., and three more

during the late afternoon while engaging Bf 110s and Ju 87s. Also lost in the same afternoon action were two Hurricanes of 43 Squadron, while 257 Squadron lost three Hurricanes in similar circumstances at midday. However, several of 145 Squadron's pilots did manage to achieve success. It was a significant day for one of the flight commanders, Flt Lt 'Ginger' Boyd, who destroyed five aircraft south of the Isle of Wight in three hectic sorties during the day. The heroics of some of the squadron's youngest pilots were also notable on this day. Two young men, both 'veterans' who had served during the Battle of France, were once again thrown into the heat of battle. Nineteen-year-old Plt Off 'Jas' Storrar destroyed two Ju 87s just off the Needles, bringing his personal score to eight. Just a year older, Plt Off Peter Parrott destroyed a Bf 109 and a Ju 87 over the Channel, bringing his personal total to four. Fg Off Witold Urbanowicz had escaped from Poland and had only been serving with the squadron for just four days when he claimed his first kill with the RAF, a Bf 109 over the Channel. One of the squadron's Hurricane pilots lost in the

afternoon action was Fg Off Lord Kay-Shuttleworth, of the well-known family.

It was certainly a mixed day for 145 Squadron. It had destroyed at least ten enemy aircraft but had lost five Hurricanes and, more importantly, had suffered the sad loss of many pilots who could not easily be replaced. Within a few days, the squadron was withdrawn to Scotland for a well-deserved rest.

Phase Two, 11 August – 6 September

The battle entered a new phase during mid-August as the German high command changed its priorities to attacking the vital airfields of Fighter Command. However, it would not be until 13 August before the Luftwaffe launched its new offensive. Following two relatively quiet days, the fighting intensified once again on 11 August, when shipping and the ports of Dover, Portland and Weymouth were heavily attacked. The first main action of the day occurred off the Dorset coast soon after 10.30 a.m., when Hurricanes of 87, 145, 213, 238 and 601 Squadrons engaged large numbers of Ju 88s and Bf 110s, with the Hurricanes of 87 and 213 Squadrons being caught up in some of the heaviest action. During a fierce engagement over Portland Bill there were

Hurricanes of 85 Squadron were among the 150 RAF fighters which intercepted a mass raid against the airfields of North Weald and Hornchurch on 18 August.

two kills each for Plt Offs John Cock and Dennis David of 87 Squadron, bringing their personal scores to eight and ten respectively. Among the successful pilots of 213 Squadron, there were kills for Plt Off Bill Sizer, Sgt Reg Llewellyn and a first kill for Fg Off James Strickland. One lucky pilot of 213 Squadron was Belgian Plt Off Jacques Philippart. Having shot down a Ju 88 over Portland, Philippart's aircraft had become severely damaged but he managed to nurse the aircraft back to Exeter with damage to the wings, the oil tank and engine.

Two of the squadron's more experienced pilots were not so lucky. Flt Lt Ron Wight, one of the flight commanders, was shot down and killed while leading three Hurricanes into a formation of Bf 110s; also killed during the same combat was Sgt Sam Butterfield. Both men had served over France, both had been credited with five kills for which both had been decorated; these were, indeed, sad losses for the squadron.

During the afternoon, the second main action took place, when Hurricanes of 111 Squadron were involved in heavy air fighting over Margate. A new record figure of thirty-eight enemy aircraft were destroyed, but the number of RAF fighters lost highlights the ferocity of the air action. A total of twenty-two Hurricanes were lost, with twenty of the pilots killed in action. Four of these pilots were from 238 Squadron

and four more were from 601 Squadron; all eight being tragically shot down and killed during ten minutes of fighting over Portland and Weymouth. Four more were from 111 Squadron, lost during the afternoon action over Margate.

Hitler's objectives had become much clearer when he issued his Fuhrerdirectiv No 17 on 1 August, which ordered the destruction of the RAF as quickly as possible. Goering had also personally briefed his commanders about the nature of his expected victory with a new offensive, Adlertag ('Eagle Day'), beginning on 13 August. With the new offensive just twenty-four hours away, the Luftwaffe changed tactics with attacks against the four radar stations at Dover, Dunkirk, Rye and Ventnor in an attempt to take the early-warning 'eyes' away from the RAF. These were followed by attacks against the airfields at Manston, Lympne and Hawkinge resulting in some of the heaviest air fighting to date. Honours were about even at the end of the day, with each side losing more than twenty aircraft.

Tuesday 13 August – Adlertag

Goering's Adlertag was launched in some confusion early on Tuesday 13 August demonstrating that communications in any operational command is vital. The operation had been planned for some time but when the weather forecast predicted low cloud and drizzle, Goering himself gave the order to postpone Adlertag. However, the order of postponement did

Leading 85 Squadron during the summer of 1940 was S/L Peter Townsend. Shown here with his ground crew, Townsend destroyed three enemy aircraft on 18 August and by the end of the month had brought his total to eight, for which he was awarded the DFC and bar, followed by the DSO.

Flt Lt Jumbo Gracie, 56 Squadron, destroyed five aircraft during the Battle of Britain, including a Bf 110 on the opening day and another over Ashford on 18 August.

The ground crews proved to be the unsung heroes of the battle.

not reach all units and, shortly after 5.00 a.m., Do 17s of KG2, escorted by Bf 110s of ZG26, took off to attack targets at Sheerness and Eastchurch. The Bf 110s received the message to cancel the operation soon after and turned back, but the Do 17s did not, and pressed on alone. Due to the weather over the targets, the attack had to be carried out below the cloud, at heights of little more than 1,000 feet (300m). For the Luftwaffe, the result of the attack was good, but several of the Do 17s were shot down after being intercepted over the Thames Estuary by Hurricanes of 111 and 151 Squadrons and Spitfires of 74 Squadron at 7.00 a.m. One of the Hurricanes of 151 Squadron was a 20mm cannon-armed experimental variant, flown on this occasion by Flt Lt Rod Smith. Although this aircraft was described by the pilot as less manoeuvrable, the firepower was significantly better, and this was soon proved when Smith shot down one of the Do 17s at a range of some 300 yards.

Goering was furious at the confusion and, anticipating an improvement in the weather, ordered Adlertag to commence properly during the mid-afternoon. The first mass raid, some 300 aircraft, crossed the Channel at 3.30 p.m. Sweeping ahead of the main force were Bf 109s of JG53, followed by more Bf 109s from JG27 and Bf 110s, escorting Ju 88s of KG54 and LG1, with Ju 87s from StG2 and StG77. One of the targets was the port of Southampton and it was over the Solent that the Hurricanes of 43 and 257 Squadrons first encountered the enemy. Heavily outnumbered, distracting the bomb-aimers was about as much as the Hurricane pilots could do.

An hour later, more Ju 87s, escorted by Bf 110s, were detailed to attack Rochester but were successfully turned back by Hurricanes of 56 Squadron. There were further attacks by Ju 87s on the airfield at Detling, which had mistakenly, been

identified by German intelligence as a Fighter Command operating airfield. Although there were a number of casualties on the ground, Detling was not considered to be a priority airfield, and Fighter Command escaped relatively unscathed.

The opening day of Adlertag had ended in favour of the RAF. The day had started in confusion and ended with the loss of another new record of forty-five enemy aircraft, for the loss of just thirteen RAF fighters, twelve of which were Hurricanes. As the day ended, the night offensive began, with a number of raids against targets all over the country.

Thursday, 15 August

Two days later, on 15 August, the story was much the same. As dawn broke, it was obvious to the defending pilots that a fine day was in store; no one, however, could have forecast the ferocity of the air

Hurricane squadrons and locations, Adlertag, 13 August 1940			
10 GROUP	**11 GROUP**	**12 GROUP**	**13 GROUP**
Exeter - 87, 213	Biggin Hill - 32	Church Fenton - 73, 249	Acklington - 79
Middle Wallop - 238	Croydon - 111, 1(RCAF)	Coltishall - 242	Aldergrove - 245
	Debden - 17, 85	Digby - 46	Castletown - 504
	Gravesend - 501	Duxford - 310	Drem - 605
	Kenley - 615	Leconfield - 302	Grangemouth - 263
	Northolt - 1 , 257, 303	Wittering - 229	Sumburgh - 232
	North Weald - 56, 151		Turnhouse - 253
	Tangmere - 43, 601		Usworth - 607
	Westhampnett - 145		Wick - 3

fighting which would take place. Hitler had dictated that the destruction of the RAF was to be completed by 15 September, so an all-out effort by the Luftwaffe was made, with *Luftflotte* 5 also taking part, operating from bases in Scandinavia.

The basic plan was for the Luftwaffe to carry out an attack over a wide front, with the main targets being the radar stations and airfields of Fighter Command. The first raids were carried out during the late morning by Ju 87s and Bf 110s, escorted by Bf 109s, and were directed against the radar sites at Dover and the fighter airfields in Kent. Hurricanes of 615 Squadron at Kenley and 501 Squadron at

down another Ju 87; fortunately, he did so successfully.

Early in the afternoon, *Luftflotte* 5 carried out attacks from bases in Scandinavia against targets in the north-east of England. The main targets were airfields in north Yorkshire and the industrial areas of Newcastle and Sunderland. The raid was detected well out to sea, giving the RAF fighters time to intercept. Lacking any fighter cover, and underestimating the numbers of RAF fighters in the north, several German bombers were shot down. Hurricanes of 605 Squadron from Drem were among the fighters scrambled; they intercepted more than 60 He 111s from

Hurricanes and Spitfires of 10 and 11 Groups carried out patrols and were scrambled to meet the ever-increasing numbers of German aircraft; some 150 RAF fighters were involved, the largest number to date. In the south-east, there were further raids at about 3.00 p.m. against airfields at Martlesham Heath and Hawkinge, as well as attacks against Rochester and Eastchurch. Among the fighters meeting these raids were Hurricanes from 1 Squadron at Northolt, 17 Squadron from Debden, 32 Squadron from Biggin Hill, 111 Squadron from Croydon and 151 Squadron from North Weald.

Leading 111 Squadron from the front, Sqn Ldr John Thompson shot down two of the raiders, a Do 17 over the Thames and a Bf 110 attacking Croydon airfield. His efforts were matched by Sgt Tom Wallace, a South African who had travelled to the UK to join the RAF and had just arrived on the squadron; he shot down two Bf 110s for his first kills of the war. Throughout the afternoon there were other successes for the other squadron pilots, including two kills each for Flt Lt Stanley Connors (bringing his personal score to eleven), and for Sgt Bill Dymond (bringing his total number of kills to eight). Sadly, neither of these young men would survive the Battle of Britain: Connors was shot down and killed over Kenley just three days later; Dymond was shot down over the Thames on 2 September, at the age of just twenty-three.

Further to the west, there were raids against airfields at Middle Wallop and Worthy Down, as well as further raids against Portland. The two Exeter-based Hurricane squadrons, 87 and 213, were scrambled. Just before 5.00 p.m., they found themselves in the thick of the action again, after intercepting Ju 87s, escorted by Bf 110s, at 15,000 feet (4500m), south of Portland. In the mass combat that followed, four of 213 Squadron's pilots each shot down three enemy aircraft; Sgt Reg Llewellyn and Plt Off Jacques Philippart each destroyed three Bf 110s, while Flt Lt Jackie Sing and Plt Off Joseph Laricheliere each destroyed two Bf 110s and a Ju 87. These kills brought Laricheliere's personal total to six, all of which were achieved in two days of action. Sadly, the Canadian was killed in action over the Isle of Wight the following day. There were also two further kills each for Fg Off James Strickland and Plt Off Bill Sizer.

A section of 87 Squadron relaxing between sorties at Exeter, late August 1940. Pictured left to right are Fg Off Roddy Rayner, Plt Off Roger Malengreau and S/L Johnnie Dewar. Belgian Malengreau escaped to England after the fall of France, and joined the squadron just before this picture was taken; sadly, Dewar was killed on a routine sortie days later.

Gravesend were scrambled to intercept the raid. The result was successful for the raiders, with the radar stations at Dover, Rye and Foreness being put out of action for several hours. However, the pilots of 501 Squadron had a particularly successful morning after intercepting Ju 87s attacking the airfield at Hawkinge. Sgts Donald McKay and Paul Farnes each shot down two Ju 87s, bringing their personal scores to four and five respectively. Two Poles who had both just joined the squadron after evacuating Europe also scored their first successes: Fg Off Stefan Witorzenc shot down two Ju 87s, while Sgt Toni Glowacki destroyed another. Flt Lt Johnny Gibson was forced to bale out of his damaged Hurricane after shooting

KG26 to the south-east of Newcastle just after 2.00 p.m. One of the flight commanders, Flt Lt Archie McKellar, claimed four Heinkel He 111s, shot down into the sea to the south-east of Newcastle, although only one of them could be verified; two more He 111s were shot down by Plt Off 'Bunny' Currant. Slightly further down the coast, 79 Squadron from Acklington intercepted more He 111s off Middlesborough, three of which were promptly shot down by Plt Off Bill Millington.

In just ten minutes of combat, the RAF had shot down more than twenty bombers. The losses suffered by Luftflotte 5 were too great and it would make no further mass daylight raids during the battle.

Throughout the long afternoon, the

Flt Lt (later Wg Cdr) James Nicolson, VC DFC – 249 Squadron

Of the thirty-two Victoria Crosses awarded to air crew during the Second World War, it is surprising that just one was awarded to a fighter pilot. That award was made to Flt Lt Eric James Brindley Nicolson, following his heroic action over Southampton on 16 August 1940.

James Nicolson was born in Hampstead on 29 April 1917. He joined the RAF in 1936 and, after training, was posted to 72 Squadron at Church Fenton flying Gloster Gladiators. By the beginning of the war the squadron had converted to Spitfires and moved to Leconfield. Following several moves with the squadron, Nicolson was posted to 249 Squadron at Leconfield as a flight commander in May 1940. It was then that he converted to the Hurricane, with the squadron being moved south to Boscombe Down on 15 August to join in the defence of southern England. On 16 August, Nicolson took off from Boscombe Down in Hurricane P3576 'GN-A' as leader of three Hurricanes detailed to patrol near the Southampton area. The citation for Nicolson's VC reads:

During an engagement with the enemy near Southampton, Flt Lt Nicolson's aircraft was hit by four cannon shells, two of which wounded him, whilst another set fire to the gravity tank. When about to abandon the aircraft, owing to flames in the cockpit, he sighted an enemy fighter, which he attacked and shot down, although as a result of staying in his burning aircraft he sustained serious burns to his hands, face and, neck and legs. Flt Lt Nicolson has always displayed great enthusiasm for air fighting and this incident shows that he possesses courage and determination of a high order. By continuing to engage the enemy after he had been wounded and his aircraft set on fire, he displayed exceptional gallantry and disregard for his own life.

As a result of the damage to his aircraft, Nicolson was forced to bale out. He was rushed to Southampton hospital, where he fought for his life. The announcement of the award of the VC was made on 15 November. However, he was not fit to return to operational flying and he carried out instructional duties after which he was posted to staff duties in the Far East. Finally, Nicolson was posted to command 27 Squadron in August 1943 to fly Mosquitos. For the next year he led the squadron during the campaign in the Far East for which he was awarded the DFC. On promotion to wing commander, he was appointed to staff duties at RAF Burma HQ. On 2 May 1945 he flew on a Liberator of 335 Squadron based at Salbani, Bengal. Soon after take-off, the aircraft crashed into the sea, and Nicolson was killed.

Flt Lt Ian Gleed, OC 'A' Flight 87 Squadron, showing off 'Figaro' painted on the side of his cockpit.

The lead section from 87 Squadron was led by Flt Lt Ian Gleed, who shot down two of the escorting Bf 110s. Soon after, the second section intercepted more Ju 87s, escorted by Bf 109s, over Portland. Two of the Ju 87s were shot down by Plt Off Dudley Jay, who then found himself in combat with the escorting Bf 109s. During the action his aircraft was damaged and he was forced to make an emergency landing in a farmer's field. The squadron commander, Sqn Ldr Terence Lovell-Gregg, was not so lucky; following his clash with Bf 109s, he was killed after crashing into a wood at Abbotsbury, while attempting to reach Warmwell.

More attacks continued into the early evening, with further raids across Kent to attack the airfields at Biggin Hill and Kenley. However, a combination of mis-identification of the different airfields, and good work by the Hurricanes of 32 Squadron at Biggin Hill, meant that the raiders bombed Croydon and West Malling instead. There has always been confusion and uncertainty about exactly what happened.

Thursday 15 August proved to be the most hectic day during the Battle of Britain. The Luftwaffe flew more than 2,000 sorties against England, while Fighter Command flew nearly 1,000. The German losses that day were the heaviest of the entire Battle of Britain: a total of seventy-five aircraft, of which just seven were Bf 109s; the rest were bombers and fighter-bombers. Neither did the RAF suffer lightly: thirty-four fighters were lost,

including nineteen Hurricanes. There was also significant damage to many airfields, and a number of casualties on the ground.

Friday, 16 August

The pattern was much the same the following day, with further heavy attacks against airfields in Kent and Sussex as well as further attacks against the radar site at Ventnor on the Isle of Wight. It was a particularly good day in the air for 43 Squadron from Tangmere, with three of the squadron's pilots each destroying three Ju 87s off Selsey Bill. The commanding officer, Sqn Ldr 'Tubby' Badger, brought his total to seven, for which he was awarded the DFC. Sgt 'Darkie' Hallowes had become known earlier in the war for 'scoring' the first enemy aircraft to come down on English soil; his three kills on 16 August brought his total to twelve. Plt Off Hamilton Upton shot down three Stukas before he was forced to crash-land on Selsey beach with oil system problems. Although it had been a good day in the air, 43 Squadron had lost a total of eight Hurricanes. Four were destroyed on the ground during an air attack at Tangmere, two more were shot down (both pilots safe), and two crash-landed.

This particular day has its own place in history for another reason. On 16 August, the only Victoria Cross won by a pilot of Fighter Command during the Battle of Britain, and indeed throughout the entire war, was awarded. There has been much discussion as to why this should be the case, but this book is not the place to

continue that debate. For more information about its recipient, Flt Lt James Nicolson, serving with 249 Squadron at Boscombe Down, see page 42.

The total number of German aircraft destroyed during 16 August was forty-five, with the loss of twenty-four RAF fighters, sixteen of which were Hurricanes. Despite fine weather the following day, there was little air activity. Presumably, the Luftwaffe was recovering from the fierce fighting on 15 and 16 August.

Sunday, 18 August

The brief rest on 17 August was over the next day, when the Luftwaffe once again launched mass attacks against Fighter Command's airfields and the radar sites; the Battle of Britain now reached its peak.

The weather on Sunday 18 August was initially hazy, but this soon lifted to reveal another fine day. Soon after midday, the first mass raid of 100 bombers, escorted by 150 fighters, crossed the Channel to carry out attacks against Kenley and Biggin Hill. Five squadrons of fighters were scrambled to patrol the Canterbury-Margate area to meet the raid, including Hurricanes of 17, 56 and 501 Squadrons, while four squadrons, including Hurricanes of 32 and 615 Squadrons, patrolled overhead the Kent airfields. More than 100 RAF

Above: **Flt Lt Derek Ward of 87 Squadron was one of many New Zealanders to serve with the RAF during the war. In the Battle of Britain he was OC 'B' Flight, and claimed his third victim during a night patrol on 3 September. He was later awarded the DFC and bar but, sadly, was killed in North Africa during 1942.**

Below: **Pilots of 56 Squadron at Boscombe Down during early September 1940, modelling characteristic flying clothing: No 1s, scarves and 'Mae Wests'. On the left is Pole, Plt Off Marian Chelmecki, who was posted to 56 Squadron at the end of August after escaping from Poland, and went on to serve with 17 Squadron at Debden.**

Phase 3 opened on 7 September, with a devastating attack against London.

fighters were airborne to meet the raid, and two-thirds of them were Hurricanes. The main bomber force passed to the west of the patrol at 1.00 p.m., directed towards the airfields of Biggin Hill and Kenley. The only squadron to become engaged initially was 501 Squadron, which was bounced by Bf 109s of JG26 over Canterbury. The following combat was devastating and resulted in four Hurricanes being shot down in just two minutes by Oberleutnant Gerhard Schoepfel.

A beam attack was executed on a group of Do 17s heading towards Kenley airfield by 111 Squadron, which had also been scrambled from Croydon to intercept the raid. For several minutes the Hurricanes chased the Dorniers but, one by one, they either ran out of fuel or ammunition and had to turn for home. It was a costly encounter. Several claims were made, but the Hurricane squadron lost three aircraft in the five minutes of combat.

Kenley was home to 615 Squadron; some of its Hurricanes were not able to get off the ground before the attack struck, and three aircraft were destroyed on the ground. High above the airfields, the Hurricanes of 615 Squadron were heavily engaged with the Bf 109 escort. The

squadron managed to tie up the escort long enough to allow the Hurricanes of 32 Squadron to attack the main force. Leading the front section was Sqn Ldr Mike Crossley, who destroyed a Ju 88 near Ashford. Another Ju 88 was shot down, by Plt Off Boleslaw Wlasnowolski, to the southeast of Biggin Hill. Leading the second flight was Flt Lt Peter Brothers, who destroyed a Do 17 attacking Biggin Hill.

As the force began to withdraw southwards towards the Channel it was the turn of the Hurricanes of 56 Squadron to engage the enemy. Overhead Ashford, the squadron first intercepted a group of Bf 110s of ZG26. Fg Off Percy Weaver shot down one, another was destroyed by Flt Lt 'Jumbo' Gracie, while Fg Off Innes West-macott, Plt Off Maurice Mounsdon and Sgt Clifford Whitehead each shared in the destruction of others. Meanwhile, the Hurricanes of 1 Squadron had been waiting between Ashford and Dover when they caught sight of the Bf 110s. Plt Off George Goodman was still only nineteen, but was already an experienced combat pilot, having served with the squadron during the campaign in France. He sighted a straggling Do 17, which he and his section finished off over Dungeness. He then spotted one of the Bf 110s coasting out at low level, and immediately carried out his attack, shooting it down into the

sea before he was 'jumped' by a Bf 109 and had to turn for home.

The Hurricanes of 17 Squadron had also been waiting for the egressing bombers and had joined the fight from the east. Leading the attack was Sqn Ldr Cedric Williams, who claimed his first victim of the war, a Do 17 to the south-east of Dover. His section was then attacked by a group of Bf 109s making their way back across the Channel, and all three Hurricanes scattered for home; Plt Off Neville Solomon was not seen again. Sadly, Williams too was killed in action, just a week later.

The attack was over; the raid had lasted less than an hour. The airfield at Kenley had been heavily hit, with a number of aircraft destroyed on the ground and significant damage to all the hangars. Biggin Hill had, however, suffered little damage and all aircraft had managed to get off the ground before the attack took place. West Malling had suffered damage to the hangars, and a group of Bf 110s had attacked Manston on the way home, destroying a number of Spitfires on the ground.

No sooner had the aircraft landed from the first mass raid than the second was starting to build. This time it was the turn of the Stukas, with more than 100 Ju 87s of StG77, escorted by 150 Bf 109s, detailed to attack the airfields at Thorney Island, Gosport and Ford, and the radar station at Poling along the Sussex coast. Having detected the raid, the ground controllers believed that the targets would once again be the airfields. Hurricanes of 601 Squadron were patrolling their base at Tangmere, 43 Squadron was patrolling Thorney Island and 213 Squadron was patrolling over St Catherine's Point. In addition, there were four squadrons of Spitfires covering the area from Portsmouth to the south of the Isle of Wight, and the airfields at Westhampnett and Middle Wallop.

The attack began at about 2.30 p.m. Before the Stukas could reach Thorney Island they were attacked by the Hurricanes of 43 and 601 Squadrons. Leading 43 Squadron was Flt Lt Frank Carey, already one of the RAF's leading aces with eighteen confirmed kills. He promptly shot down a Ju 87 and was attacking a second when he was hit by an escorting Bf 109, and forced to crash-land near Pulborough. Three more Ju 87s were shot down by Sgt 'Darkie' Hallowes of 43 Squadron, who thereby achieved his eighth kill of the week, making his personal total fifteen, and won a bar to his DFM. It had been a devastating blow for the Stukas of 1 Gruppe, with some ten aircraft shot down. However, despite the success of 43 and 601 Squadrons, the majority of the Stukas reached their targets and carried out a number of successful attacks. The naval airfield at Ford had been virtually destroyed, there was significant damage to the radar station at Poling, and serious damage had been caused to the airfields at Thorney Island and Gosport. There had also been a number of casualties on the ground.

There then followed a couple of hours of calm before the third mass raid crossed the Channel at about 5.00 p.m. This time, about 100 enemy bombers, escorted by 150 Bf 109s and Bf 110s, were detailed to attack the airfields at North Weald and Hornchurch. To meet the attack were about 150 fighters, two-thirds of which were Hurricanes from 32, 46, 56, 85, 151, 257 and 501 Squadrons. The first unit to engage was 56 Squadron, which intercepted the He 111s just off the Essex coast heading for North Weald. While half the squadron became engaged with the fighter escort, two sections were able to attack the bombers. Meanwhile, to the south, the Hurricanes of 32 and 501 Squadrons were

trying to attack the bombers heading for Hornchurch, but large numbers of Bf 109s made the task almost impossible. Two of the Bf 109s were shot down by two Polish pilots serving with 501 Squadron – Fg Off Stefan Witorzenc and Plt Off Pawel Zenker. The pilots of 32 Squadron were also heavily involved in the dogfight, where honours seemed to turn out even. Sqn Ldr Michael Crossley shot down a Bf 109 before successfully baling out, having been shot down by another. Two others were shot down by Plt Off Alan Eckford and by another Polish pilot, Plt Off Karol Pniak.

Back up to the north, over the North Weald area, the Hurricanes of 46, 85 151 and 257 Squadrons had all joined the fight. The following activity was chaotic and many kills were claimed by either side. Leading 85 Squadron was Sqn Ldr Peter Townsend, who destroyed two Bf 109s. However, there were mixed fortunes for the other pilots of 85 Squadron. One of the He 111s was shot down by Canadian

Flt Lt 'Hammy' Hamilton, but the squadron was saddened by the loss of one of its most popular members, Fg Off Dickie Lee who was last seen chasing three Bf 110s out to sea. The cloud over southeast England had made it impossible for the Germans to bomb the airfields and many ditched their bombs over towns instead; among the worst hit were Shoeburyness and Deal.

Sunday 18 August had proved to be a hectic day. The Luftwaffe had launched 1,000 sorties and had lost seventy aircraft. Fighter Command had flown 900 sorties and had lost about thirty aircraft, twenty-six of which were Hurricanes, plus three more destroyed on the ground. Most importantly, from the twenty-six Hurricanes shot down, seventeen pilots were saved. For the time being it was probably

Right: **A former schoolmaster, Fg Off Richard Brooker served with 56 Squadron during the Battle of Britain. He later served in the Far East and Europe (for which he was awarded the DSO and bar, and DFC and bar), but was killed just two weeks from the end of the war.**

Below: **It was not uncommon for pilots to fly up to six or seven sorties a day during the height of the battle; in between, they had to take every possible opportunity to relax and share a joke.**

Sgt Josef Frantisek of 303 Squadron. This gallant Czech pilot destroyed seventeen aircraft during September, before being killed on 8 October.

as much as the Germans could take. In the past eleven days, the Luftwaffe had lost more than 360 aircraft, while the RAF had lost half that number. Although the Battle of Britain was far from over, the losses suffered by the Luftwaffe during the two days of fighting on 15 and 18 August were far greater than had been anticipated.

19 August – 6 September

The build-up of weather seen on 18 August led to some cloudy and wet conditions over the following days. It would not be until 24 August that the weather became fine enough for the Luftwaffe to launch another large attack. The raids against the airfields of North Weald, Hornchurch and Manston continued, as well as attacks against Dover, Ramsgate and Portsmouth. Among the successful Hurricane pilots on that day was Sgt Toni Glowacki, who destroyed three Bf 109s and two Ju 88s in his four sorties during the day, earning the award of the Virtuti Militari.

The heavy attacks of 24 August marked the start of a new and more determined series of raids against Fighter Command's airfields, which stretched the pilots and ground crews of No 11 Group to the limits. That night, the first large number of bombs fell on London, which led to a revenge attack on Berlin by Bomber Command the following night. The following days were much the same, with honours ending almost even.

It was during this period that Dowding and his group commanders began to feel drained. True, the gallant young fighter pilots were shooting down large numbers of German aircraft, but RAF losses were also high and there had been significant damage to the airfields of No 11 Group. Although the fighter production lines were working hard to maintain the balance between aircraft shot down and new aircraft produced, improvements to the Hurricane were being made locally at the squadrons. The fitting of armoured plate behind the seat, and the addition of a rear-view mirror were examples of improvisation intended to help increase the pilot's chance of survival. The ground crews were undoubtedly the unsung heroes of the battle, working all hours to repair damaged aircraft and to refuel and rearm each Hurricane, despite the airfield being under attack.

However, the decrease in the number of pilots was beginning to tell. It is true that many were escaping with their life, but a high proportion of the survivors were either badly burned or wounded, and unable to return immediately to the front line. They were replaced by more young men, with very few flying hours in single-engine fighters, who were thrown straight into the 'lion's den'. Until now, Dowding had been able to send squadrons and crews north for a well-earned rest from battle but, as the losses mounted, this was becoming less of an option. The only new Hurricane unit to form during this period was 312 Squadron at Duxford, made up of Czech personnel. As soon as it received its Hurricanes, it was sent to Speke to defend Merseyside.

In the afternoon of 29 August, the Luftwaffe massed a raid of more than 600 fighters in an attempt to tempt the RAF into a fighter-fighter battle, but the plan

---

Flt Lt (later Wg Cdr) Ian 'The Widge' Gleed, DSO DFC – 87 Squadron

Ian Richard Gleed was born in London on 3 July 1916. He joined the RAF in 1936 and after training was posted to 46 Squadron, where he flew Gauntlets and then Hurricanes. Known as 'The Widge' (due to his size), he was flying Spitfires with 266 Squadron at the outbreak of war. In May 1940, he was posted as a flight commander to 87 Squadron in France and within his first week had destroyed five enemy aircraft.

During the Battle of Britain, Gleed led the squadron on numerous occasions, during which time he destroyed a further four enemy aircraft, for which he was awarded the DFC. In December 1940, he was promoted to the rank of squadron leader and given command of the squadron, then based at Charmy Down. In November 1941, he was promoted to the rank of wing commander and returned to the Spitfire, leading the Middle Wallop and Ibsley Wings on numerous occasions, for which he was awarded the DSO. In January 1943, Gleed was posted to North Africa where he commanded No 244 Wing. On 16 April, he led a patrol over the Cap Bon area, and failed to return.

The extensive damage to the tail section of this Hurricane shows the skill of Fg Off John Cock in force-landing his aircraft following a mid-air collision with Plt Off Dudley Jay on 24 October; sadly, Jay was not so lucky, and went down with his aircraft.

failed as the RAF fighters were ordered to keep clear. This apparent avoidance of air combat suggested to the Germans that the Luftwaffe now had air superiority over the Channel. This led to another significant German attack against the airfields on 30 August; Fighter Command flew more than 1,000 sorties and proved that it was by no means beaten.

The raids during the last two days of August had, however, stretched No 11 Group to the limit. The system of air defence worked because of the overall effort and co-ordination shown by all personnel, communicating from the radar sites and the observation posts of the Observer Corps to the Sector Operations Centres, and then from the Unit Operations to the squadrons. Unsurprisingly, the ever-increasing number of attacks and the subsequent damage had led to a reduction in the effectiveness of this system.

Throughout the first week of September, the weather remained fine. Large numbers of aircraft carried out daylight attacks against the airfields, while maintaining the night offensive against cities in the Midlands and the North. The attacks against the airfields were proving most costly and, had they continued for much longer, the only option for Dowding would have been to withdraw the fighters further north. He wished to avoid this at all costs – in the event of an invasion, his fighters would be too far away from the fight and the RAF would suffer the disadvantages currently being suffered by the Luftwaffe. Fighter Command needed a break from the attacks against the airfields and, as if by a miracle, that much-needed rest soon came.

Phase Three, 7–30 September

The opening day of this new phase started quietly, with no mass raid detected before mid-afternoon. This raid, consisting of nearly 1,000 aircraft, proved to be the largest ever by the Luftwaffe.

At first, the ground controllers assumed that it was an all-out effort to destroy No 11 Group, and twenty squadrons of fighters were scrambled to defend the airfields. It was then that the main force unexpectedly turned for London. The fact that the RAF were defending the airfields meant that the German bombers reached London unscathed; by the time the ground controllers realized what was happening, it

One of the most successful fighter pilots of the war was Sqn Ldr Bob Stanford Tuck, who commanded 257 Squadron at North Weald during the Battle of Britain. He was eventually credited with twenty-seven kills (mostly while flying Spitfires), for which he was awarded the DSO and the DFC with two bars.

was too late to stop them. The fighters then headed for the bombers, but the escorting Bf 109s and Bf 110s did a good job of intercepting them, and the bombing attack proved so successful that a second attack that evening saw London burning from many miles away. A total of forty German aircraft were lost during the day, of which just fourteen were bombers. The RAF lost thirty fighters, sixteen of which were Hurricanes. Despite the losses, this turn against London gave the airfields of Fighter Command the rest they so desperately needed.

Although the weather was fine during the next couple of days, it was a relatively quiet period by daylight, although the offensive against London by night continued. Having taken over command of 253 Squadron at Kenley on 5 September, Sqn Ldr Gerry Edge made an immediate impact. During fighting over the Thames on 7 September, he shot down two He 111s; he followed this up on the 9th by shooting down four Ju 88s just outside London. He then shot down two more He 111s and a Bf 109 on the 11th, bringing his total for his first week in command of the squadron to nine. Flt Lt Archie McKellar of 605 Squadron was also in the thick of the action on 9 September when he shot down three He 111s and a Bf 109 over Farnborough. It appears that his three He 111 kills came about from shooting down

one, which blew up and took out two more on either side of it.

The German invasion date had been fixed for 20 September and time was now running short. Hitler decided that he would delay until the following week the announcement as to whether or not the invasion would take place. The increasing number in fighter escort meant that it was becoming increasingly harder for Fighter Command to stop the bombers reaching London. On 11 September the RAF scrambled late and, caught out during the climb, suffered higher losses than the Luftwaffe; nineteen Hurricanes were lost during the day, with the loss of eight pilots. It was a bad day for Fighter Command.

Sunday, 15 September

Bad weather over the next three days meant little air activity. This gave Fighter Command a bit of a rest before the next major onslaught, which was launched on 15 September, the day which subsequently became known as Battle of Britain Day. Although this date saw the largest number of enemy aircraft attacking London, it was not the most successful day in terms of enemy aircraft shot down. However, the RAF's famous victory in the air on 15 September did mark the beginning of the end of the Battle of Britain.

The day started quietly, but a mass raid destined for London started building up

Sgt (later Sqn Ldr) 'Ginger' Lacey, DFM and bar – 501 Squadron

James Harry Lacey was born in Wetherby, Yorkshire on 1 February 1917. Following a period as an apprentice pharmacist, Lacey joined the RAFVR in 1937. He was called up following the outbreak of war and posted as a sergeant pilot to 501 Squadron at Filton to fly Hurricanes. He went to France in May 1940 for a few hectic weeks of action before the squadron was withdrawn back across the Channel. During his time in France, Lacey destroyed five enemy aircraft, for which the French awarded him the Croix de Guerre; he went on to became famous as the top-scoring RAF fighter pilot during the Battle of Britain. By the end of August 1940, his personal score had reached eleven and he had been awarded the DFM. During September and October, Lacey destroyed a further twelve enemy aircraft, bringing his score during the Battle of Britain to eighteen, and his overall total to twenty-three, for which he was awarded a bar to his DFM.

Commissioned in January 1941, Lacey remained with 501 Squadron converting to Spitfires soon after. As a flight commander he gained his first kill while flying a Spitfire on 10 July 1941, followed soon after by three more kills. He was rested from operations the following month and posted to instructional duties. He briefly returned to operational flying in March 1942 with 602 Squadron, before returning to various non-operational duties. He was finally posted to the Far East and gained his final kill of the war while flying Spitfires with 17 Squadron over Burma.

After the war, Lacey remained in the RAF and eventually became a fighter controller. He retired from the RAF as a squadron leader in 1967 and returned to Yorkshire. 'Ginger' Lacey died from cancer in 1989.

soon after 11.00 a.m. The first wave consisted of 100 Do 17s of KG3 and KG76, escorted by a similar number of Bf 109s, which crossed the Channel soon after. Spitfires were the first fighters to intercept the raid, followed soon after by the Duxford Wing, led by Sqn Ldr Douglas Bader, which consisted of three squadrons of Hurricanes (242, 302 and 310 Squadrons) and two squadrons of Spitfires. The Duxford Wing intercepted the raid as it approached the outskirts of London, where they were joined by Hurricane squadrons from North Weald (46 and 249 Squadrons), as well as 17 and 73 Squadrons from Debden, 253 and 501 Squadrons from Kenley, 605 Squadron from Croydon, 504 Squadron from Hendon, and 229, 303 and 1 (RCAF) Squadrons from Northolt.

With London as the target, the Luftwaffe fighters had to escort the bombers over a greater distance than usual; by the time the bomber force reached the capital, the fighter escort was already on its way home. This gave the RAF fighters the chance to wait and choose their areas of interception. The RAF also enjoyed the advantage of larger numbers and was able to get ready in formation in good time; this gave them the further advantage of extra height. The overall result was success for the RAF fighters, with many of the German bombers being shot down. Many ditched their bombs, resulting in widespread damage across the south-east, but nothing of significance was destroyed. Within minutes, the German force was running for home.

Just two hours later, a second raid against London took place. No sooner had the Hurricanes landed, refuelled and rearmed than they were scrambled again. There were two other raids, against Portland and Woolston. The scene over southern England during the afternoon of 15 September appears to have been total confusion. Many Hurricane pilots enjoyed success during the day and the mass raids meant that many of the aces were able to add to their scores. The 23-year-old Yorkshireman Sgt 'Ginger' Lacey of 501 Squadron destroyed two Bf 109s and a He 111 during the day, bringing his personal total to nineteen. 'Ginger' Lacey became famous as the highest-scoring RAF pilot during the Battle of Britain, with a total of eighteen kills. He had also destroyed five aircraft in France and later went on to achieve five more kills while flying Spitfires, bringing his overall total for the war to twenty-eight.

Another pilot who became famous for his heroics during the Battle of Britain also added to his score on 15 September. The Czech pilot Sgt Josef Frantisek destroyed a Bf 110 to the south of London. Frantisek had served with the Czech Air Force before the German occupation, when he escaped to Poland. He then served with the Polish Air Force before German occupation once again forced him to flee the country. After flying during the Battle of France, he ended up in England and was posted to the newly formed 303 Squadron at Northolt. Including his kill on 15 September, Frantisek had destroyed eleven enemy aircraft during the first two weeks of September. He went on to shoot down six more before the end of the month, bringing his total to an impressive seventeen for the month of September; he was the highest-scoring pilot during the height of the battle, and the highest-scoring Czech fighter pilot of the war. Sadly, Frantisek's amazing success was short-lived, as he was killed during a routine patrol on 8 October.

At the end of the day, both sides were left to count the cost. The RAF believed that it had shot down more aircraft than on any other day, and the BBC announced the total for the 24-hour period to be more than 180 German aircraft destroyed. In fact, the real number was just one-third of that. The exaggerated total was not untypical; the scores for both sides were usually inflated. This is particularly understandable, considering the confusion on 15 September, when several pilots made claims which, with the benefit of more than fifty years of analysis and research, have often proved to be against the same aircraft.

The importance of the RAF's victory on 15 September cannot be over-emphasized. However, it was not without cost. Twenty-three Hurricanes and seven Spitfires were destroyed during the day, with, sadly, nine Hurricane pilots killed. The battle of 15 September was not just about the number of enemy aircraft destroyed; it proved to be about the difference between the two sides on either side of the Channel. For the RAF there was the sense of victory. However, the morale of the German air crew was in a different state and within forty-eight hours Hitler had cancelled his planned invasion of England – indefinitely.

Ground crew find a moment to relax against the tail of one of the squadron's aircraft.

16–30 September

The weather turned to showers again for the next few days, preventing all daylight activity, except a small raid against London on 18 September. However, night raids against London continued. Across the Channel, the invasion barges were being dispersed and Britain was safe from invasion, for that year at least. During the last week of September the weather improved. The Germans modified their tactics to add other sites to their list of daylight targets, including Southampton, Merseyside, Bristol and Plymouth.

The biggest raid for nearly two weeks took place on 27 September. During the morning a number of incursions across southern England were made, as well as an attack by Luftflotte 3 against the Bristol Aeroplane Company at Filton. To meet this raid, Hurricanes of No 504 Squadron, which had moved to Filton only the day before, were scrambled. Among the first into the fray was Flt Lt Tony Rook, who engaged a Bf 110 at 12,000 feet (3600m) over Filton and shot it down, causing it to crash into a hillside 15 miles (24km) north of Poole. Rook's cousin, Plt Off Michael Rook, also shot down a Bf 110, to the south of Cerne Abbas, while Sgt 'Wag' Haw claimed his first victim of the war during the same combat, also destroying one of the Bf 110s. Haw's aircraft was damaged during the action, and he was forced

Flt Lt James Nicolson, 249 Squadron, following the award of the Victoria Cross.

to land in a cornfield at Kilmington near Axminster. The damage to the cornfield clearly upset the farm labourer, and Haw was sent on his way carrying his parachute. He caught a lift to Taunton, where the driver bought him lunch. They were soon joined by some grateful onlookers, and all enjoyed a beer together before Haw caught a train back to Bristol and his squadron!

The action over Filton had seen 504 Squadron destroy six Bf 110s, with only Haw's aircraft damaged. In appreciation, the workforce at Filton presented the squadron with a commemorative ashtray machined out of a highly polished cylinder head, and treated them to lunch!

The most remarkable effort on 27 September was by a young South African, Plt Off 'Day' Lewis of 249 Squadron at North Weald, who destroyed six aircraft in four sorties during the day. First, he destroyed two Bf 110s and claimed another as 'probable' near Redhill. He then destroyed a Bf 109 near Canterbury and later destroyed a Ju 88 and two more Bf 109s near London. These six kills

brought his personal total to eighteen, for which he was awarded a bar to his DFC. These proved to be Lewis's final kills of the war, as he was shot down the next day. Although he managed to bale out, he suffered serious burns and did not return to flying until the following May. He was then sent to serve in the Far East, in command of 261 Squadron in Ceylon, but was shot down and wounded again, after which he returned to the UK and took part in no further operational flying.

Overall, the Luftwaffe lost more than fifty aircraft on 27 September; thirteen Hurricanes were lost during the day, with the loss of nine pilots.

Although any thoughts of a German invasion had gone, the Battle of Britain was not yet over, and the last few days of September saw several losses, particularly for the Hurricane squadrons. The last major daylight raids, involving more than 200 aircraft, took place on 30 September, with attacks against London and the Westland factory at Yeovil. During the day, Fg Off Witold Urbanowicz of 303 Squadron at Northolt destroyed four enemy aircraft, bringing his total to fifteen, for which he received a well-

Ginger Lacey was the highest-scoring RAF pilot of the Battle of Britain, with an overall total of twenty-three, for which he was awarded the DFM and bar.

earned DFC. German losses were high – nearly fifty aircraft – for the loss of just twenty RAF fighters, including fourteen Hurricanes. One squadron to suffer was 56 Squadron at Boscombe Down. During the day it lost five Hurricanes, two during combat with Bf 109s and Bf 110s over Bournemouth in the morning, and three more during an attack against Do 215s and Bf 110s over Portland at 5.00 p.m. Fortunately, all of the pilots survived.

Phase Four, 1–31 October

The final phase of the battle began with another change in Luftwaffe tactics. Although the night raids against London and the other large cities would continue for several months, the mass daylight raids against London were over. This last period witnessed many small daylight incursions against southern England by modified Bf 109s, capable of carrying either long-range fuel tanks or a single 250-kg bomb. These proved to be nothing more than a nuisance, their main aim being to keep the defences split over a large area, with the idea of continuing the offensive during the following spring. Many of these raids were carried out by small numbers of Ju 88s, escorted by Bf 109s, at a high level, where the Hurricane was not at its best; much of the defending was left to the Spitfire squadrons.

The first week of October was mainly showery, with limited activity. On 7 October, a heavier raid was carried out by Ju 88s against the Westland factory at Yeovil; German losses were high, with more than twenty aircraft destroyed during the day. One successful pilot was Sqn Ldr Archie McKellar, who had just taken over command of 605 Squadron at Croydon. During the day he destroyed five Bf 109s, four in one engagement over the

Flt Lt Ian 'The Widge' Gleed was eventually credited with thirteen kills and awarded the DSO and DFC before his death in April 1943.

Westerham-Maidstone area. This brought McKellar's total to fourteen, for which he was awarded a bar to his DFC. McKellar would destroy three more Bf 109s before the end of the month. Sadly, the gallant Scot was killed on 1 November, following an engagement with Bf 109s over Maidstone, after which came the announcement of the award of a DSO.

There was more rain during the second week and Hitler formally announced that the planned invasion of Britain would take place during the following spring. The Luftwaffe now concentrated all their efforts on the Blitz against London, with the numbers of bombers continuing to increase. The night of 15 October saw the heaviest raid on London, with more than 400 aircraft taking part.

The increasingly bad weather became a major factor, leading to less daylight activity. When the weather was good, though, the Hurricane squadrons continued to be involved in scrambles and combats, with the number of sorties never easing. However, for the first time, it was possible to think about reinforcing theatres elsewhere. As a result, 73 Squadron was withdrawn from operations in preparation for a move to the Middle East.

By the end of October, there were still thirty-four operational Hurricane squadrons in the UK, with two more Polish units (306 and 308 Squadrons) working up. For the historians, the Battle of Britain ended on 31 October, but the incursions across southern England and the night raids on London continued for several months. The cost in aircraft and lives was devastating, but Britain's safety had been achieved, at least for the time being, meaning that valuable support could now be given elsewhere.

Never in the field of human conflict was so much owed by so many to so few. (Winston Churchill, 20 August 1940)

Top-scoring Hurricane squadrons of the Battle of Britain (various sources)	
SQUADRON	NUMBER OF KILLS
303	127
501	93
213	81
249	75
601	74
32	71
43/238	70
242	69
17	68
56	60

Hurricane squadrons and locations, 30 October 1940			
10 GROUP	**11 GROUP**	**12 GROUP**	**13 GROUP**
Boscombe Down - 56	Croydon - 605	Digby - 151	Acklington - 32
Chilbolton - 238	Kenley - 253, 501	Duxford - 242, 310	Aldergrove - 245
Exeter - 87, 601	Martlesham Heath - 17	Kirton-in-Lindsey - 85	Castletown - 3
Filton - 504	Northolt - 229, 302, 615	Leconfield - 303	Drem - 232, 263
	North Weald - 249, 257	Pembrey - 79	Montrose - 111
	Stapleford Tawney - 46	Speke - 312	Prestwick - 1(RCAF)
	Tangmere - 145, 213	Wittering - 1	Turnhouse - 607
			Usworth - 43

The Hurricane Mk II

Introduction of the Mk II

As the Battle of Britain was being fought, and won, a modified variant of the Hurricane was introduced into service. Indeed, a cannon-armed Hurricane first saw action during August 1940 with 151 Squadron. There were significant advances in the design of the Hurricane MkII over the earlier MkI. The basic Hurricane characteristics remained unchanged, but there were changes in the aircraft's powerplant and significant improvements in its overall combat capability. The standard 0.303in Brownings were replaced by more potent cannons and underwing hardpoints gave the Hurricane the capability to carry bombs, rocket projectiles or external fuel tanks. These significant improvements in design were the reason why the Hurricane proved to be so versatile, and contributed to its success in every operational theatre throughout the war.

Design Improvements

Engine

The prototype Hurricane MkIIA (P3269) made its first flight on 11 June 1940. As with the MkI, the MkIIA first entered operational service with 111 Squadron at Dyce in October 1940. Essentially, there was no change in the basic airframe dimensions (although the MkIIC and MkIID were just over 12in (30cm) more in length than the MkI and the earlier MkIIs). The first of the MkIIAs were

Engine performance figures for Merlin XX engine			
RPM	3,000	2,600	2,200
BHP	1,370	1,050	750
BOOST	+ 11.4	+ 7	+ 2.9

powered by an improved Rolls-Royce Merlin III liquid-cooled V-type 12-cylinder engine, which developed a maximum of 1,030 hp at 3,000 rpm at 16,000 feet (4800m). This gave the Hurricane a top speed of more than 330mph (530kph) at 18,000 feet (5400m) and a service ceiling of 35,000 feet (10500m).

The later MkIIAs and all other MkII variants were further improved, with a Merlin XX series engine developed from the Merlin X in 1940 and fitted with a

The Hurricane MkIIA Z3451.

Engine limitations for Merlin XX engine				
	RPM	BOOST (P.S.I.)	COOLANT TEMP (DEG C)	OIL TEMP (DEG C)
MAX TAKE-OFF (TO 1,000FT/300M)	3,000	+ 12	-	-
MAX CLIMB (MAX 1 HOUR)	2,800	+ 9	125	90
MAX RICH CONTINUOUS	2,650	+ 7	105	90
MAX WEAK CONTINUOUS	2,650	+ 4	105	90
COMBAT (MAX 5 MINS)	3,000	+ 16	135	105

A MkIIC (Z2905) shown fitted with two large drop tanks; these large tanks (88 gallons each) would be used for long-range transits only.

two-speed supercharger. With the low-gear supercharge the Merlin XX gave a maximum power of 1,260 hp at 12,000 feet (3600m) and with high-gear supercharge it produced 1,175 hp at 21,000 feet (6100m). Engine boost control and mixture control was automatic. Propeller control was by a speed control lever, on the left side of the cockpit, which varied the governed rpm, from 3,000 down to 1,800 rpm. The supercharger was controlled by a push-pull control fitted to the left side of the instrument panel; pushing in was for low (M) and pulling out was for high (S). With the Merlin XX series engine the aircraft was capable of a service ceiling of a remarkable 41,000 feet (12300m).

Additional Tanks

Two additional fuel tanks could be fitted to the Hurricane, one under each wing, when the aircraft was not fitted with external armament. There were two types of auxiliary fuel tank – fixed or drop – and two sizes of drop tank. The fixed tanks each held 44 gallons, and the drop tanks either 44 or 88 gallons each. Fuel from the fixed tanks was fed from the external tanks to the engine by electrically driven pumps,

and fuel from the drop tanks was fed direct to the engine-driven pump by air pressure.

When fitted with fixed external tanks the pilot switched on the electrically driven pump using a switch on the left side of the cockpit. The procedure was to use the main tanks first, in the normal manner. When the level in the main tanks was down to 5 gallons, the pilot switched on the auxiliary fuel pumps, which transferred fuel to the main tanks. When the

contents of the main tanks was 25 gallons, the pilot switched off the pump and carried on as normal until, once again, the fuel level in the main tanks was down to 5 gallons. This procedure was followed until the auxiliary tanks were empty.

For the external drop tanks, the controls were on the right side of the cockpit – a fuel cock marked OFF-PORT-STBD and a jettison lever. The fuel cock for the drop tanks had to be in the OFF position before the jettison lever could be operated. The procedure was to use the main tanks, as normal, for take-off and, when at a safe

Fuel tank capacities for the Hurricane MkII	
TANK FIT	**TOTAL FUEL CAPACITY**
Main and reserve tanks (internal)	94
Internal + 2 x fixed external tanks or 2 x small drop tanks	182
Internal + 2 x large drop tanks	270

Fuel consumption in weak mixture. Figures in gallons per hour			
BOOST (P.S.I.)	**RPM**		
	2,650	2,300	2,000
+4	56	50	46
+2	52	46	42
0	47	42	38
-2	42	37	34
-4	37	33	30

height, to change over to one of the drop tanks, pressurizing the system and turning off the supply from the main tanks. When the first drop tank was empty, the pilot selected the second drop tank. When this was empty, the pilot reverted to the main tanks and operated the system in the normal way.

These fuel tanks gave the Hurricane a total fuel capacity of 94 gallons internally, 182 gallons, with fixed external tanks, or 182 gallons or 270 gallons, with external drop tanks. The external tanks significantly improved the combat capability of the Hurricane, particularly in theatres such as North Africa or the Far East when the aircraft operated far away from its home airfield.

When the large external drop tanks were fitted to the Hurricane, an additional auxiliary oil tank of four gallons was fitted behind the pilot's seat, with the cock control fitted to the left side of the seat. An oil dilution push button was also fitted to the left side of the cockpit. When flying long-range missions with external fuel tanks, it was necessary for the pilot to turn on the cock for the auxiliary oil tank after about three and a half hours; once turned on, the supply could not be turned off. On long ferry missions, for example, when flying the aircraft for maximum range with reduced power settings, it was not necessary to switch on the auxiliary supply until after five hours of flight.

Right: **An identification feature of the forward part of the MkII is the longer propeller spinner.**

Below: **The six-stub exhaust manifold.**

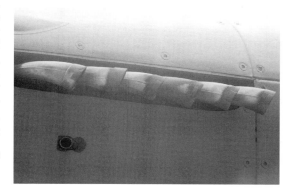

Above: **The right side of the cockpit.**

Left: **The left side of the cockpit.**

Aircraft Handling

Without external stores the Hurricane was essentially longitudinally stable. However, when fitted with the large external fuel tanks, the aircraft became longitudinally unstable and a minimum speed of 190mph (305kph) was necessary. When carrying bombs, however, the stability was unaffected. With the undercarriage and flaps down, the pilot had to trim the aircraft nose down. Aerobatics and violent manoeuvres had to be avoided when carrying 90-gallon drop tanks, bombs or rocket projectiles. Spinning of MkIID and MkIV aircraft was prohibited, as was spinning of all other MkIIs when carrying 90-gallon drop tanks, bombs and rocket projectiles.

When operating at all-up weights in excess of 8,750lb (3980kg), it was necessary to take care with the Hurricane during ground handling; the aircraft was only supposed to take off from runways of concrete, or equivalent. To start the engine, the pilot selected the fuel cock to the main tanks, 'cracked' the throttle half an inch open, selected the propeller control fully forward, set the supercharger to 'moderate', and opened the radiator

Fuel consumption in rich mixture. Figures in gallons per hour		
BOOST (P.S.I.)	RPM	CONSUMPTION
+12	3,000	115
+9	2,850	95
+7	2,650	80

This picture shows the underside of a MkIIB (BE485) fitted with bomb racks and a pair of 250-lb GP bombs.

shutter. He then switched on the ignition and pressed the starter and booster coil push buttons; the engine would start within a few seconds. The throttle was advanced to about 1,000 rpm to allow the engine to warm up, and during this time the pilot checked the temperatures and pressures, while carrying out functional checks of the hydraulics by lowering and raising the flaps.

After warming up, the pilot opened up to + 4 p.s.i. boost and checked the supercharger and constant speed propeller, as well as checking that the generator was charging. With the propeller control fully forward, he then opened the throttle to +12 p.s.i. boost to check that the rpm was at 3,000. He then throttled back to + 9 p.s.i. boost and checked each magneto in turn. He then checked that the brake pressure and pneumatic pressure were both good before proceeding to taxi the aircraft. From the pilot's notes for the Hurricane MkII, the pre-take-off checks were as follows:

◆ Trimming tabs – rudder to fully right

and elevator to neutral
◆ Propeller control – fully forward
◆ Fuel – check contents, main tanks ON, auxiliary tanks OFF, pressurizing cock to ATMOSPHERE
◆ Flaps – UP (or 28 deg down for shortest take-off run)
◆ Supercharger control – MODERATE
◆ Radiator shutter – fully open

For take-off, the throttle was advanced to the gate, with any aircraft swing countered by rudder. After leaving the ground, the undercarriage was raised and

the aircraft trimmed nose heavy; at 140mph (225kph) a climb could be initiated. The aircraft was generally climbed at 2,850 rpm and + 9 p.s.i. boost at 140mph (225kph) for the maximum rate of climb. Once at the required cruising altitude, the aircraft was flown at a maximum of + 4 p.s.i. boost and the required speed set, nominally 160mph (255kph) for maximum range, with the corresponding rpm being at about 1,800 to 2,000.

For landing, the checks were as follows:

◆ Brake pressure – minimum of 100 p.s.i.

Airframe speeds and limitations, Hurricane MkII	
CONFIGURATION	INDICATED AIR SPEED (MPH/KPH)
Max rate of climb (clean)	140/225
Max rate of climb (external stores)	155/250
Max range (clean)	160/255
Max range (external stores)	175/ 280
Stall (u/c + flaps down)	60-75/95-120
Diving	390 (max)/625
Undercarriage and flaps down	120 (max)/190
Approach speed	95/150

- ◆ Speed – reduce to 120mph (190kph)
- ◆ Hood – check locked open
- ◆ Undercarriage – DOWN (check two green lights)
- ◆ Propeller control – fully forward
- ◆ Supercharger control – MODERATE
- ◆ Flaps – DOWN

The approach speed for landing was 95mph (150kph) if clean, but with external stores it was increased to 110mph (175kph). Once the aircraft was back on the ground, the flaps were raised. To stop the engine, the throttle was set to idle (800-900 rpm) for about thirty seconds, and then the slow-running cut-out was pulled until the engine stopped. The fuel cock was then turned off and the ignition switched off.

Without external stores, the MkII was capable of top speeds up to 340mph (545kph) at 21,000 feet (6300m). With external stores, and fully armed, the Hurricane MkII's all-up weight was increased to about 8,250lb (3750kg), compared with 6,000lb (2725kg) for the basic MkI.

In certain theatres, such as the Middle East, the MkIIs had to be 'tropicalized'. This was done by adapting the radiator and fitting an air-filtered intake to protect against the sand. Even at the maximum all-up weight, and with a tropicalized air filter, as well as the increased drag of external stores, the Hurricane MkII was still capable of achieving top speeds of more than 300mph (480kph). It also retained its good manoeuvrability throughout. Its most impressive feature, though, was its impressive operational range of some 1,500 miles (2400km) when fitted with external fuel tanks.

Hurricane Variants

The MkIIB – 'Hurri-Bomber'

The RAF's need for a capable fighter-bomber led to the development of the Hurricane MkIIB, known as the 'Hurri-bomber'. The wings were stressed to carry extra weight and bomb racks were fitted underneath the wing, outboard of the undercarriage. Initially, the MkIIB could only carry a single 250-lb bomb under each wing, but by the end of 1941 it could carry the 500-lb bomb. These hardpoints could also be used to carry either the 44- or 88-gallon external fuel tanks.

The MkIIB entered RAF service at the end of 1940 and was initially fitted with twelve 0.303in Browning machine-guns, without bombs, and used for intruder missions across the Channel. It was some time before the MkIIB carried out its first bombing attack and this finally occurred on 30 October 1941 when two aircraft of 607 Squadron at Manston attacked a power station at Tingry.

The range of the MkIIB was about the same as that of a standard MkI. When it was fitted with bombs, the number of Browning machine-guns was usually reduced to ten. Attacks were generally carried out at low level, to increase bombing accuracy, but could be higher (up to about 12,000 feet/3600m), depending on the target defences. The Hurri-bomber was generally a daylight bomber, although some attacks against shipping at night are

A Hurricane MkIIC of 245 Squadron during the summer of 1942.

Originally designated the MkIIE, the Hurricane MkIV was developed with an improved wing, known as the 'universal' wing, and increased armour. Although the prototype was fitted with a four-bladed propeller, production MkIVs retained the three-bladed propeller for the Merlin 20 series engine.

known to have happened. A total of 3,100 Hurricane MkIIBs were built.

Note: the following table includes only RAF operational squadrons that operated the MkIIB for more than three months during the periods shown. It does not include squadrons of the SAAF or IAF, which also operated the MkIIB in North Africa and the Far East. The table does not include detachments of periods

of less than three months, nor does it show training or reconnaissance squadrons which may occasionally have operated the MkIIB. For this table, squadrons based on Malta have been included under the North African heading. As always, sources vary and there were often many cases when a squadron operated different marks of Hurricane at the same time.

The MkIIC

The origins of the Hurricane MkIIC can be traced back to before the war when the need for a single-seat cannon-armed fighter was first recognized. It was also stated that the aircraft should be capable of operating by day and night although, at that stage, there was no suitable cannon available. A contract was awarded to Westland for the development of the Whirlwind, so, for the time being, Hawker concentrated on Hurricanes armed with machine-guns.

Hawker first experimented with a cannon-armed Hurricane as early as May 1939, when a MkI (L1750) was modified to carry an Oerlikon 20mm cannon in a fairing under each wing. Operational trials were carried out by 151 Squadron at North Weald during the summer of 1940 using a Hurricane MkI (P2640) fitted with two internally mounted Hispano-Suiza cannons. The first production MkIIC was powered by a Merlin XX engine and first flew on 6 February 1941. It was armed with four 20mm cannons, two internally mounted in each wing, made obvious by the protrusion forward of the leading edge of the wing. More than 4,700 MkIICs were built, the highest number produced of any Hurricane variant, and they were sent to all operating theatres.

The MkIIC was also capable of carrying external fuel tanks or bombs on the underwing hardpoints. A typical Hurricane MkIIC operating in the Middle East was 'tropicalized' and armed with four 20mm Hispano cannons, and external fuel tanks, if modified for the role of fighter, or two 250lb bombs instead of the fuel tanks, if carrying out a bombing role.

Note: The table (right) includes only RAF operational squadrons that operated the MkIIC for more than three months during the periods shown. It does not include squadrons of the SAAF, REAF or IAF, which also operated the MkIIC in North Africa and the Far East. The table does not include detachments of periods of less than three months, nor does it show training or reconnaissance squadrons which may occasionally have operated the MkIIC. Sources vary and there were often cases when a squadron operated different marks of Hurricane at the same time.

The MkIID – Tank Buster

The need for heavier armament to destroy armoured vehicles was recognized as early as 1941, and led to Hawker working on an anti-tank version of the Hurricane – the

A MkIV, armed with rocket projectiles.

RAF operational squadrons equipped with the Hurricane MkIIB, 1941-44		
UK (1941-43)	**NORTH AFRICA (1941-44)**	**FAR EAST (1941-44)**
1/3/17/32/43/56/79/	30/33/73/74/	17/28/30/
121/128/133/174/175/	126/127/134/	135/136/146/
242/245/247/253/257/312/	238/241/249/274/335	258/261/273/
401/402/486/504/601/607/615		605/607

MkIID. The prototype MkIID (Z2326) first flew on 18 September 1941, although it did not enter operational service until April 1942, when it arrived with 6 Squadron at Shandur in Egypt. A total of 300 MkIIDs were built, and operated with five squadrons (5, 6, 20 and 184 Squadrons and 7 Squadron SAAF).

Armed with two 40mm Vickers 'S' cannons, one under each wing, and two 0.303in machine-guns (used for ranging), the MkIID was essentially designed for service with the 8th Army in North Africa, where it was given the affectionate names of the 'Tank Buster' or the 'Tin Opener'. Its main role was to help eliminate the heavy German tanks operating in the North African desert, hence its extremely heavy armament! Otherwise, the MkIID was essentially the same as any other Hurricane although, because of the environment in which it was designed to operate, it was fitted with the tropicalized air filter.

The Mark IV

One development of the MkII was the Hurricane MkIIE, which appeared early in 1943, constructed from the same assembly jigs at the same production lines. The main differences were in the wing design and in the addition of extra armour protection. With the addition of more external stores, there had been a problem in the maintenance of armament and electrical services mounted in the wing. Therefore, during 1941, Hawker developed a wing (known as the 'universal wing') that could carry the necessary external stores without any change to the wiring of the aircraft. Also, because of its likely role as a ground-attack aircraft, this version had additional armour fitted to the forward fuselage and around the radiator; this added 350lb (160kg) in weight.

Built at Kingston, KZ193 was modified as the MkIIE prototype and first flew on 23 March 1943. It was powered by a Merlin 27 engine – a two-speed, single-stage supercharged engine, which was later built in Glasgow. After 270 MkIIEs had been built, it was decided to give this variant

the designation 'Hurricane MkIV'; the designation 'MkIII' had been reserved for Hurricanes powered by American Packard-built Merlins. It appears that not all production MkIVs were powered by the Merlin 27, as there seem to be many cases of aircraft powered by Merlin 24 and 32 engines.

The first designated Hurricane MkIV was KX405, which was powered by a Merlin 32 engine, and fitted with a four-bladed Rotol propeller. However, the production MkIVs retained the three-bladed propeller for the Merlin 24 or 27 engines. A total of 524 MkIVs were built, most of which went overseas to the Middle East and the Far East, although some did remain in the UK, serving with 137 Squadron at Manston, 164 Squadron at Fairlop and 184 Squadron at Detling until March 1944, when the type was phased out of service.

The Hurricane MkIV was armed either with two 40mm cannons, or fitted to carry 500-lb bombs or rocket projectiles (RPs).

Only three MkVs were built with the prototype (NL255), shown here, in January 1944. Powered by an uprated Merlin, driving a four-bladed propeller, the MkV was prone to overheating and the project was cancelled.

RAF operational squadrons equipped with the Hurricane MkIIC, 1941-44		
UK (1941-43)	**NORTH AFRICA (1941-44)**	**FAR EAST (1942-45)**
1/3/43/96/151/	32/33/73/80/87/94/123/134/	5/11/17/28/30/34/42/60/67/79/
247/253/257/309/615	208/213/225/229/237/238/253/	113/135/136/146/176/
	274/336/451	258/261/607

Summary of Hurricane MkII/IV/V variants		
VARIANT	**ARMAMENT**	**NUMBER BUILT (APPROX)**
IIA	8 x 0.303in Browning machine-guns	Not known (100?)
IIB	12 x 0.303in Browning machine-guns	3,100
IIC	4 x 20mm Oerlikon cannons	4,700
IID	2 x 40mm Vickers 'S' cannons	300
IV	2 x 40mm cannons or rocket projectiles	524
V	2 x 40mm cannons	3 (prototypes only)

One of two MkIVs modified to MkV standard was KZ193, fitted with a four-bladed prop.

A rocket-armed MkIV weighed about 1,000lb (455kg) more than a standard Hurricane. The rocket installation could be fitted underneath the wings of the Hurricane MkIID as well as of the Hurricane MkIV, and was of a quite basic design. Generally, four 60-lb rockets were mounted under each wing on long rails, with a protective plate located under the leading edge to protect the wing from the cordite blast. Squadrons involved in rocket attacks, such as 184 Squadron, were equipped with MkIV RP and MkIID cannon Hurricanes. The choice of which aircraft to use would depend on the nature of the task; the MkIV RPs were used against shipping in the Channel, and the MkIIDs were used against trains or other vehicles over occupied Europe.

Although it was a more rugged aircraft, it appears that the MkIV was not particu-larly popular with the pilots who flew it. The speed of the MkIV was not dissimilar to that of an earlier MkI, and the excess weight made this aircraft less manoeu-vrable than the MkII. Indeed, the external stores and additional armour eventually brought the weight of the MkIV to more than 9,000lb (4090kg).

The Mk V

Only one prototype MkV (NL255) was built, and a further two Hurricane MkIVs (KZ193 and KX405) were modified to MkV standard, with the intention of developing a specific variant for service in the Far East. The MkV was powered by an up-rated Merlin 32 engine (giving 1,700 hp), driving a four-bladed Rotol propeller, fitted with a tropicalized air filter and armed with two 40mm cannons. The first flight was made on 3 April 1943, but ground and air tests at Boscombe Down showed that the up-rated engine gave the MkV little advantage over the standard MkIV, and was prone to overheating, so the project was cancelled.

CANADIAN-BUILT HURRICANES

The MkX

The designations MkVI to MkIX were reserved for likely British projects, so the first Canadian-built Hurricanes were designated as MkXs. Before the outbreak of war, the Royal Canadian Air Force (RCAF) had nineteen Hurricane MkIs. With the ever-increasing order for Hurricanes saturating the production lines in the UK, Hawker began to sub-contract work. L1848 was sent to the Canadian Car and Foundry Company of Montreal, together with plans for production aircraft to be built in

One of many MkXIs built by the Canadian Car and Foundry Corporation, this example (BW950) served with the RCAF during 1942.

Several Canadian-built MkXIs and MkXIIs were fitted with skis and a tail-skid and served with the RCAF until 1943. Typical of many Canadian Hurricanes, this example is shown without the propeller spinner.

Canada and then shipped to the UK.

The first aircraft built in Canada was P5170, which made its first flight from St Hubert airport on 10 January 1940. More than 150 Canadian-built Hurricanes were completed, powered by Rolls-Royce Merlin engines, before they began to use the American Packard-built Merlin 28s; the aircraft were then designated MkX. The Merlin 28 engine was a two-speed, single-stage supercharged engine, producing 1,390 hp, and was developed during early 1941 for use by the RAF; it was also fitted to the Lancaster MkIII and Canadian-built Lancaster MkXs.

A total of 434 Hurricane MkXs were built and shipped to the UK. The majority of these were armed with eight 0.303in Browning machine-guns, although some were fitted with either twelve machine-guns or four cannons for operations in other theatres. There were subtle differences in the airframe from the standard British-built MkI; for example, the exhaust glare shields were angled up on the Canadian-built aircraft, not horizontally mounted, as on the standard MkI.

The MkXI

The Hurricane MkXI was essentially the same as the MkX, but fitted specifically for service with the RCAF. A further variant, the MkXIB was powered by a Packard-built Merlin 29. This engine produced 1,390 hp and was developed from the Merlin 28 during 1941 for the Canadian-built Hurricanes and the Curtiss Kittyhawk II. (An unusual point worth noting was that most Hurricanes were flown in Canada without propeller spinners.)

The MkXII and Other Variants

Also developed entirely for use by the RCAF, the MkXII was essentially the same as the MkIIB. As with the MkXI, the MkXII was powered by the Packard-built Merlin 29 engine, and was developed to deter any possible attacks by German U-boats against Canadian shipping, although this seems never to have happened. A total of 474 MkXIIs were built, and equipped ten squadrons of the RCAF. In addition, a number of Sea Hurricane MkXIIAs were built, bringing the total number of Hurricanes built by the Canadian Car and Foundry Company to 1,451.

Above: **The length of ammunition belts is clearly visible, as armourers re-load the Browning machine-guns of this Hurricane from 245 Squadron during the summer of 1941.**

Right: **The number of armourers is somewhat exaggerated for this press photo of a Hurricane of 249 Squadron during re-arming at North Weald in April 1941; its pilot, Fg Off Pat Wells, looks on.**

One experimental aircraft used for trials was a MkX (AG310), which was fitted with a fixed-ski arrangement for service in Canada. Several MkXIs and MkXIIs were converted with skis and a tail-skid, and served with the RCAF until 1943.

Armament

Browning 0.303in Machine-Gun

Designed by John Browning in America, the 0.303in Browning machine-gun became the standard weapon for the RAF from the mid-1930s, and was fitted to all early Hurricanes. The gun was 44in (110cm) long and weighed 22lb (10kg). It was recoil operated, with a cyclic rate of 1,150 rounds per minute, a muzzle velocity of 2,660 feet per second (800m/s), and a maximum range of about 3,000 feet (900m). It was mass-produced in Britain, mainly manufactured by BSA, and generally proved most reliable, with only the occasional problem being caused by extreme cold or blockages arising from poorly assembled ammunition belts. This latter problem was reduced by the armourers running the ammunition belt through a belt-positioning machine to make sure that each round was aligned properly. The ammunition used varied but was most commonly ball rounds, or tracer,

Supported by trestles, a Hurricane of 87 Squadron has its guns aligned by the armourers.

incendiary or armour-piercing.

When installed in the Hurricane wing, the gun barrels lay inside blast tubes, with the ammunition being fed to the guns through feed chutes. Protective patches were placed over the leading edge of the wing to stop dirt entering the end of the barrel.

Hispano-Suiza 20mm Cannon – MkIIC

As early as the mid-1930s, the need for a heavy-calibre weapon was realized. The advantage of explosive shells meant that fewer hits were needed to destroy an enemy aircraft, as well as giving the fighter more capability against ground targets; this would be particularly useful against armoured vehicles. As there were no British projects at the time, nor were there likely to be any, the decision was made to purchase the Hispano-Suiza Moteur Cannon. This 20mm (0.78in) cannon was the product of the Swiss Oerlikon company and adapted for fitting into fighters by Hispano-Suiza in Paris. The decision was made to build these cannons under contract and a production factory was built at Grantham; the first cannons were fired during 1938. As war broke out, the number of cannons required increased, and three other factories were built to meet the demand – a second one at Grantham, one in Newcastle, and one in Poole.

The principle of the early 20mm cannon was relatively simple, with the aircraft's pneumatic system being used to provide the pressure for re-cocking the cannon. A more powerful compressor than that normally fitted to the Hurricane for gun-firing was required. A round was fed into the chamber

and fired. Gas pressure was then fed on the piston to unlock the breech and force the breech block rearwards, extracting and ejecting the empty case from the chamber.

The cannon was essentially designed to be fitted into the Hispano engine and fired through the aircraft's propeller, so it had to be adapted for wing-mounting, as in the Spitfire and Hurricane. The cannon was initially fitted in small numbers to the Spitfire MkIB during 1940, but problems with the feed of ammunition meant that its full introduction into service was delayed until the following year.

Another problem in fitting the 20mm cannon into the wing was that the cannon was too long. The long barrel was designed

to give increased muzzle velocity, but initially it stuck out of the leading edge of the wing by about two feet. This problem led to a modified version of the cannon, the MkII, with a barrel 12in (30cm) shorter, which became the standard production variant as fitted to the Hurricane MkIIC. This production cannon had a cyclic rate of 650 rounds per minute, a muzzle velocity of 2,900 feet per second (870m/s), and weighed 109lb (50kg); four cannons were fitted to the Hurricane MkIIC, two in each wing. Although the firepower of the MkIIC was awesome, the weight of four cannons plus ammunition was a severe limitation. Therefore, it was not unusual for pilots to have two of their cannons removed to reduce the overall weight, helping to improve the overall performance and turn rate of the aircraft.

Later modifications to the Hispano 20mm cannon included an increase in the cyclic rate of the cannon to 750 rounds per minute and further reductions in weight (to 84lb/38kg) by a change in the design of the cocking device. The result of these changes was a lighter and faster cannon, known as the MkV, which entered service during the latter part of the war.

Vickers 'S' 40mm Cannon – MkIID and MkIV

The 40mm cannon came about as a result of trials carried out before the war to determine what size explosive shell was required to destroy an aircraft with just one hit; the answer was 40mm (1.56in),

The Browning machine-guns and supporting trestles are clearly visible as armourers carry out checks on the same Hurricane of 87 Squadron.

Armed with four 20mm cannons, the MkIIC was the most common of Hurricane MkIIs with 4,700 built.

and work began to produce a cannon based on this finding, capable of being mounted in a fighter. The result of this work was the Vickers' Class 'S' cannon, the prototype of which was first fired in 1939.

Known more commonly as the Vickers 'S' gun, the cannon was too big to be internally mounted in the wing of a fighter. Hardpoints had to be fitted under the wings of the Hurricane, on to which the podded cannon could be mounted. The first 40mm cannon was fitted to a Hurricane at Boscombe Down and assessed during September 1941. Trials showed that the recoil produced when firing both cannons caused the Hurricane to slow and dip nose down. This problem never went away, and Hurricane pilots had to learn to pitch slightly nose up just before firing.

Each cannon weighed 300lb (135kg), had a cyclic rate of 125 rounds per minute with a muzzle velocity of 1,800 feet per second (540m/s). The problem of weight was an enormous one, not helped by the weight of the ammunition – each armour-piercing shell was 6in (15cm) in length and weighed 2lb (1.14kg). The number of rounds carried was usually about fifteen per cannon. The shell was solid, with a tungsten nose which was capable of penetrating 2in (50mm) of armour.

The charge was designed so that it would break up on entering the armoured vehicle or tank to cause as much damage as possible.

One Hurricane (Z2326) was fitted with Rolls-Royce BF (belt-fed) 40mm cannons, and went through various air tests during late 1941. These cannons were bigger than the Vickers 'S' gun and carried fewer rounds (ten to twelve). Following a major failure of the Rolls-Royce BF cannon, any ideas of producing it for the MkIID were shelved, and it was decided that the Vickers 'S' gun would be the MkIID's standard armament. The first squadron to be equipped with the Hurricane MkIID was 6 Squadron, based at Shandur in Egypt, which took delivery of its first aircraft during the spring of 1942.

Despite the weight of the 40mm cannons, the MkIID still weighed less than a fully armed MkIIC when fitted with external fuel tanks. Although the cannon was mounted in a fairing beneath the wing, there was no excessive drag; the top speed of the MkIID was still about 320mph (510kph), and it had a service ceiling of 32,000 feet (9600m). The majority of MkIIDs served in North Africa and the Far East.

Gunsights

Fitting guns to a fighter is one thing, but obtaining the correct firing solution and hitting a moving target is something else. The fine art of air-to-air gunnery poses a number of problems. First, the pilot has to assess the range of his opponent, and his closing speed. Second, if his opponent is evading, he has to determine how much 'lead' is required to make sure that the bullets hit his opponent and do not pass behind. Finally, when firing at range, he has to consider the gravity drop, due to the weight of the bullet and the fact that it is slowing down and dropping before it reaches the target. All these problems are reduced as the fighter gets closer to his target, but in most dogfight situations this is easier said than done.

Ever since guns have been fitted to aircraft, simple sights have been developed to help solve these problems. When the Hurricane first entered service, the standard gunsight was the Barr and Stroud GM2, known as the Reflector Sight MkII. The concept of the reflector sight was quite simple, using a procedure known as stadiametric ranging. A large illuminated circular graticule was projected through a lens on to a circular glass reflector screen

3in (7.5cm) in diameter. The graticule was bisected by a cross, the horizontal bar being broken by a gap which was varied by the pilot to represent an opponent's wingspan (32 feet/8m for a Bf 109, for example), and the range at which he wished to open fire, with an illuminated dot making aiming easier.

In 1941 the circular reflector glass was replaced by a larger, square glass. A sight for use by night fighters was also adopted, incorporating a green diffuser cell to enable tracer to be seen more clearly at night. Various modifications to the MkII were made, particularly for use in the air-to-ground role; for example, for aiming rocket projectiles, taking into consideration the increase in gravity drop. Indeed, many pilots made their own changes to suit themselves. These modifications led to the MkIII gunsight fitted to Hurricane MkIIDs and MkIVs for use with the 40mm cannons and RPs; one main difference was the removal of the reflector screen, allowing the graticule to be projected straight on to the windscreen.

The problem of determining how much lead was required to hit a crossing target remained until the development of the gyroscopic gunsight (GGS). The theory of the GGS was based on the idea that an attempt to follow a crossing target was opposed by a gyroscope and the amount of resistance was dependent on the target's

The MkIV could carry either two 40mm cannons or rocket projectiles. Shown here is LB774 at Langley in June 1943, fitted with two 40mm Vickers 'S' guns.

crossing speed. The GGS MkI was developed and tested before the GGS MkIID fighter version, manufactured by Ferranti, was introduced into service late in 1943. The sight was more complicated than the MkI but worked on the same basic principle. A mirror was fixed to the end of the gyro and reflected an illuminated graticule, consisting of a ring of six small diamonds, on to a reflector plate. The pilot

would identify the aircraft he was attacking and manually set the wingspan of the target aircraft. The diameter of the ring of diamonds was initially set to maximum and adjusted by a twist grip on the throttle. As the pilot closed on his target, he had to track the target in the centre of the ring, keeping the target's wingspan as close to the ring as possible, until the ring was at a minimum diameter. This corresponded

This early MkIID (Z2326) was delivered to Boscombe Down and fitted with Rolls-Royce BF (belt-fed) 40mm cannons. After a failure with one of the cannons, the decision was made to keep two 40mm Vickers 'S' guns as the MkIID's standard armament.

Armourers loading a 250-lb GP bomb to the underside of a MkIIB.

The first Hurricane to be fitted with rocket projectiles was this MkIID (BP173), which went through trials late in 1942.

to the optimum range at which the guns were harmonized when the pilot opened fire, typically about 200 yards (180m).

General-Purpose Bombs

The concept of fighters being used to drop bombs was not new; indeed, aircraft had been used in the new role of fighter-bomber during the First World War. During the latter stages of the Battle of Britain, intruding Bf 109s had dropped bombs against lightly protected targets, with some success. The speed and ruggedness of the Hurricane made it ideal for the carriage of external stores, and it was not long before the potential of the aircraft as a fighter-bomber was realized.

During the early stages of the war, the RAF's standard bomb was the 250-lb general-purpose (GP) bomb. These bombs were either short-finned or long-finned, and fusing was either instantaneous or delayed. The Hurricane was first used as a fighter-bomber with the introduction of the MkIIB, fitted with a faired bomb rack under each wing, and with two 250-lb bombs, and used to carry out low-level attacks against shipping in the Channel and over France. During 1942, the Hurricane first carried two 500-lb bombs and was used to attack more hardened targets. The extra weight and drag of these bombs reduced the aircraft's airspeed significantly, and the fact that the Hurricane had to drop from low altitude (to reduce bombing

The eight rocket projectiles fitted to BP173 are clearly visible.

Above: **The control column spade grip, showing the firing push button.**

Below: **A Sea Hurricane MkIA.**

errors) meant that Hurricane pilots were susceptible to ground fire.

Rocket Projectiles

Late in 1942, rocket projectiles (RPs) were fitted for the first time to a single-seat fighter – Hurricane MkIID BP173 – at Boscombe Down, with later trials being carried out at the A&AEE at Farnborough. The first Hurricane unit to be equipped with RPs was 164 Squadron at Middle Wallop. The squadron had just been equipped with Hurricane MkIIDs in March 1943 when it was sent to No 1 Specialised Low Attack Instructors School at Milfield to convert to the Hurricane MkIV, before returning to Middle Wallop during the following month. In June, the squadron moved to Warmwell to continue working up for its first operations.

The first rocket attack by Hurricanes was made against the gates of the Handsweert Canal in Holland on 2 September 1943. The mission was flown by sixteen aircraft from the three rocket-equipped Hurricane squadrons at the time: eight from 164 Squadron led by Sqn Ldr Des McKeown, four from 137 Squadron, and four from 184 Squadron. Despite

several direct hits against the gates, problems with the fusing of the warheads caused minimal damage. However, the accuracy of the attack was encouraging, and the problem with the fusing would soon be solved.

When carrying a full load of rockets, the Hurricane proved quite draggy and, as it was not possible to fit external fuel tanks, its operational range was reduced. In this case, pilots had to take care with throttle handling in order to get the maximum range from the aircraft. This often led to very slow transit speeds to the target area in order to conserve fuel. Whether firing rockets or the 40mm cannon, the best range to open fire was at about 600 yards (550m). The aircraft were also usually armed with two 0.303in Browning machine-guns, although these were of little use, as the rockets were harmonized to the gunsight.

Weapon Switches

The machine-guns or cannons were normally fired by the push button on the control column spade grip. Pressing the button activated a small compressor, taking air from the engine, which

SEA HURRICANE I.A
MERLIN III
APRIL 1943

An early Sea Hurricane MkIA on the catapult of a CAM-ship.

provided pressurized air to the gun-firing actuators. In the case of the Hurricane MkIID and MkIV aircraft, the 40mm cannons were fired electro-pneumatically by a push button in the throttle lever; this could only happen by first operating the cannon master switch on the left side of the cockpit. In the case of a misfire there was a cannon-cocking lever, also on the left side of the cockpit.

RPs were fired in the same manner as the 40mm cannons, using the push button on the throttle lever. An RP selector switch, located below the left side of the windscreen, was used to select the rockets to be fired, either in pairs or as a salvo.

If either 250-lb or 500-lb bombs were carried, there was a bomb-fusing and selector panel situated aft of the right side of the cockpit. On the panel there were two selector switches and two nose- and tail-fusing switches. Releasing the bombs was done by depressing the same push button on the throttle lever. It was recommended that any remaining rockets or bombs were either fired or jettisoned prior to landing.

There was also a camera that operated when the guns, cannons or RPs were fired, or when the push button on the control column was depressed. Finally, there were recognition flares that were selected and fired by a lever on the left side of the cockpit.

The Sea Hurricane

When the Second World War began, the Royal Navy had six aircraft carriers. Within the first year this number had reduced to four, with the loss of HMS *Courageous* and HMS *Glorious*. The need for good air protection of the fleet had long been recognized, and during the early days this role had been carried out by aircraft such as the Gloster Sea Gladiator, the Blackburn Skua and the Fairey Fulmar. The idea of sending the Hurricane to sea as a carrier-based fighter came about during the Norway campaign in 1940, not to provide the Royal Navy with air protection, but to give adequate fighter cover to ground forces. In the days before the addition of external fuel tanks, the Hurricane MkI would not have been able to reach Norway from the

UK. The plan was to fit floats to a MkI, but the campaign came to a swift end in June before a Hurricane could be modified. The seeds of an idea had been sown, although attention returned, for the time being, to the Battle of Britain struggle, during which a number of volunteer Fleet Air Arm pilots played a valuable role.

Although Hurricanes were soon to fly off HMS *Argus* during the reinforcement of Malta (see Chapter 5), it would be some time before the Hurricane was properly developed for operations at sea. By the end of 1940, the air threat to the Merchant Navy had become more severe, as the Luftwaffe increased the number of attacks against convoys. It was decided that thirty-five Hurricane MkIs would be converted to MkIA 'Sea Hurricane' standard, for operation from merchant ships. They would be catapulted into the air when necessary, to engage any threat. The modification to the merchant ships consisted mainly of a rocket catapult fitted to the forecastle of the ship, and two 75-foot (23-m) rails, slightly angled away from the ship's structure. The idea was that the ship sailed full speed into wind, and the solid-fuel rockets accelerated the

Hurricane to a safe flying speed (about 80-85mph/125-135kph). As for any plans to recover the Hurricane – there were none! The only hope was that, if the Hurricane was in range of land, it could recover safely; otherwise, the sea was the only option, the preferred option being to bale out close to the ship rather than to ditch. As far as the Navy was concerned, Hurricanes were expendable – if each one prevented one ship being sunk, it had done its job.

The ships converted to operate the Sea Hurricane were of two types – Fighter Catapult Ships (of which there were only a handful), and thirty-five Catapult Aircraft Merchantman (CAM) ships. The CAM ships were crewed by the Merchant Navy, with the Hurricanes being flown and maintained by the RAF, the pilots being volunteers from Fighter Command. Early in 1941, a Merchant Ship Fighter Unit (MSFU) was set up at Speke near Liverpool, under the command of Wg Cdr Edward Moulton-Barrett. The number of Hurricanes for conversion was soon increased to 250, all of which were either

modified at the Hawker or Gloster production lines, or at Hanworth by General Aircraft Limited.

The first Sea Hurricane squadron was 880 Squadron at Arbroath, which took delivery of its first aircraft in January 1941. The first successful launch and interception by a Sea Hurricane occurred on 2 August 1941, when Lieutenant Bob Everett, operating from the Fighter Catapult Ship HMS *Maplin*, shot down a Focke Wulf Condor while protecting a convoy from Sierra Leone. This success brought Everett the award of a DSO. The fact that convoys now had limited protection from the air against attacking aircraft became a useful deterrent. Bad weather during the winter made the launch of aircraft impossible, so the majority of Sea Hurricanes were returned to maintenance units to be modified to near MkII standard.

Following the MkIA, the exact distinction between the various types of Sea Hurricane is complicated. Once the decision to modify the Hurricane for operation from aircraft carriers had been

made, an A-frame arrester hook was fitted to P5187 in March 1941. This Hurricane was a Canadian-built MkX already modified to MkIA standard, and became the prototype for the Sea Hurricane MkIB. By the end of the year, more than 100 MkIBs had been modified with arrester hooks and were serving with the Fleet Air Arm in the carriers HMS *Argus*, HMS *Eagle*, HMS *Formidable* and HMS *Victorious*, with 801, 806 and 885 Squadrons. The complication continues, as the majority of these MkIBs were later fitted with four 20mm cannons and became Sea Hurricane MkICs, which entered service early in 1942. When the older Merlins were replaced by XX-series engines, seventy of these MkICs became Sea Hurricane MkIICs.

Finally, about fifty Canadian-built MkXIIs were converted to become Sea Hurricane MkXIIAs, although it is doubtful whether the Canadian Navy used any. The majority are known either to have operated with the RCAF, or to have been delivered to the Royal Navy, where they were re-designated as Sea Hurricane MkIIs.

Fleet Air Arm Sea Hurricane MkIBs (fitted with the A-frame arrester hook) on the deck of one of the Royal Navy's carriers.

The Sea Hurricane MkIC was fitted with the A-frame arrester hook (as with the MkIB), and armed with four 20mm cannons; it entered service in 1942.

One of the best-known actions involving Sea Hurricanes took place in the Mediterranean during Operation Pedestal (the re-supply of Malta), in August 1942. Four Royal Navy carriers were involved, with thirty-nine Sea Hurricanes of 801, 880 and 885 Squadrons embarked in HMS *Eagle*, HMS *Indomitable* and HMS *Victorious* respectively. Tragically, HMS *Eagle* was sunk on 11 August, with the loss of all but four of her Sea Hurricanes, which were airborne at the time. During the action on the following day, HMS *Indomitable* was hit, and her damage made it impossible for her to operate any aircraft. HMS *Victorious* was the only remaining carrier, with a somewhat over-crowded deck. The convoy had been heavily hit, but enough supplies reached Malta to help the island through the siege.

The number of aircraft lost had been high, mainly due to the sinking of HMS *Eagle*. There had, however, been a number of successes for the Sea Hurricane pilots, most notably Lieutenant 'Dickie' Cork of 880 Squadron. Born in London, Cork had joined the Fleet Air Arm before the war. During the Battle of Britain he served with 242 Squadron, during which time he

destroyed five enemy aircraft. For this the RAF awarded him the DFC, later changed by the RN authorities to a Distinguished Service Cross. Cork then became one of the first Sea Hurricane pilots to serve with 880 Squadron, during which time he was embarked in HMS *Furious* and HMS *Indomitable*. During Operation Pedestal, he took command of 880 Squadron following the death of its commanding officer, and personally destroyed four enemy aircraft – two German and two Italian – during four sorties on 12 August. This won him a DSO, and brought his personal total to nine. Sadly, Cork did not survive the war, as he was killed in the Far East in April 1944.

Sea Hurricanes were also very much involved during the Allied landings in North Africa in November 1942, as part of Operation *Torch*. More than forty Sea Hurricanes were embarked in the escort carriers HMS *Avenger*, HMS *Biter* and HMS *Dasher*. Although the overall operation was a success, it was marred by the sinking of HMS *Avenger* on 15 November, with the loss of all her Sea Hurricanes and most of the crew. Operation *Torch* marked the beginning of

the end for the Sea Hurricane, as more capable American-built carrier-borne fighters became available. Sea Hurricanes did, however, remain in the Mediterranean theatre until mid-1943.

Photo-Reconnaissance Hurricanes

A small number of Hurricane MkIs were modified for photo-reconnaissance duties in the Mediterranean, the Middle East and the Far East. Airframes were generally modified in theatre, with the Hurricane being fitted with up to three 8- or 14-in F.24 cameras in the lower part of the rear fuselage, for either vertical or oblique photography. The first aircraft modified were for use by No 2 Photographic Reconnaissance Unit (PRU) at Heliopolis in Egypt during 1941. Equipped with various types of aircraft, No 2 PRU later became 680 Squadron in February 1943, when it formed at Matariya. There, it was responsible for photo-reconnaissance of enemy movements in North Africa and the Mediterranean.

CHAPTER FIVE

Malta

The Fortress Island

The island of Malta, situated in the central Mediterranean to the south of Sicily, is small, measuring no more than 8 miles (13km) from one side to the other. However, lying between the European mainland and North Africa, it was the site of a vital fortress for the British. Malta had to be held at all costs, so that the British could continue to threaten the German re-supply line to North Africa.

The Malta Fighter Flight

Although peacetime plans provided Malta with four fighter squadrons for its defence, this number of aircraft could not be spared, as Britain faced its own struggle during the summer of 1940. Malta's only air defence was provided by a handful of Gloster Sea Gladiator MkIs of the Fleet Air Arm, which had been boxed up and placed at the Navy yard at Kalafrana ready for transfer to the aircraft carrier HMS *Glorious*. The loss of the carrier in April meant that these air-

craft were no longer required, so the Air Officer Commanding Malta, Air Cdre 'Sammy' Maynard, had 'acquired' them.

Of the eight boxed Gladiators, four were assembled to airworthy standard, using the remaining four aircraft as spares. There was then the problem of pilots to fly the Gladiators, as there were none officially based on the island. A handful of pilots, both Fleet Air Arm and RAF serving in staff appointments, volunteered, and the Malta Fighter Flight (sometimes referred to as the Hal Far Fighter Flight) was thus formed, on 6 June 1940. Three of these aircraft later became known affectionately as 'Faith', 'Hope' and 'Charity', and took their own place in history.

The Campaign against Malta

The Italian Campaign

Italy entered the war on 10 June 1940, and immediately set about attacking Malta,

carrying out the first air attack on the following day. This was the start of a two-month air campaign against the island, an attempt to destroy the British air and naval installations, and to break the morale of the Maltese people. One of the Gladiators was soon lost, but the remaining three put up a most determined resistance against overwhelming odds for several weeks, as the Italians launched more and more air attacks.

Reinforcements

The determined resistance of the Gladiators demonstrated Malta's immense will to survive but, if the island was to have any long-term chance, reinforcements were urgently required. Two Hurricanes destined for the Middle East arrived in Malta on 21 June, and were quickly commandeered by 'Sammy' Maynard. Five more Hurricane MkIs on their way to North Africa arrived in Malta during the following week; three were 'detained', and never left the island!

So confident were the Italians about the relative ease of the task that their Savoia-Marchetti SM.79 bombers were sent to Malta without fighter escort. Throughout July, the five Hurricanes and the three Gladiators continued to resist significant Italian air attacks, but more Hurricanes were required if Malta was to survive. The fall of France made the usual staging to Malta impossible, and the only way for Hurricanes to reach the island was now by aircraft carrier of the Royal Navy; the idea was that, once the ship was in range (about 350 miles/560km), the Hurricanes could fly off the carrier to land on Malta. This reinforcement plan took place on 2 August, when twelve more Hurricane MkIs of No 418 Flight were flown off the aircraft carrier HMS *Argus*, landing at Luqa airfield. These two units, the Malta Fighter Flight and No 418 Flight, were immediately merged to form 261 Squadron, under the command of Sqn Ldr Denys Balden.

Hurricane (P3731) 'J' of 261 Squadron at Ta Kali in 1941.

Success in Defence

A Hurricane MkII (Z2961) of 185 Squadron being 'turned round' between sorties.

Success in Defence

It soon became obvious that Malta was not going to be an easy target. The Italians tried more attacks, this time with fighter escort; when these failed, attacks were carried out by night. In response, 261 Squadron also flew night air defence, demonstrating its ability to match any moves carried out by the Italians. The Germans had also flown a number of dive-bombing attacks against Malta, but Ju 87 losses, and priorities elsewhere, resulted in the temporary withdrawal of German air assets, leaving the Italians to maintain the campaign. Everything the Italians tried was countered by the squadron, with the high-level combat patrols being carried out by the Hurricanes and the low-level patrols being carried out by the Gladiators. This proved a successful tactic and, eventually, the number of air attacks against the island temporarily decreased until later in the year.

Further Reinforcements

An attempt to reinforce Malta further was carried out in November, when twelve more Hurricanes were flown from the carrier. This time, however, tragedy struck. Because of the threat from enemy shipping, the Hurricanes took off from further away from Malta than they had done previously. A stronger headwind than anticipated meant that only four Hurricanes landed safely on the island; the other eight ended up in the Mediterranean, having run out of fuel.

During the short rest period towards the end of 1940, more aircraft of different types were flown into Malta. It gave the island a chance to strike back at the enemy; Wellingtons, which formed 148 Squadron, carried out bombing attacks against bases in southern Italy and Libya.

For the time being, Malta was relatively quiet and 1940 ended with Malta actually hitting back. The island had struggled to survive with the minimum of assets, yet it refused to be beaten. The determination of the Maltese people and the few air crew based on the island, which had helped resist the early air attacks during the summer of 1940, had set the scene in the Mediterranean. The island of Malta was to become a thorn in Hitler's side.

First Half of 1941

The Fortress of Malta

As the Germans began a new offensive against Malta during the early days of 1941, the important objective for the British and the Maltese was defence. The island became a fortress. Most aircraft not capable of being used in air combat were sent to the safety of British bases in Egypt, leaving those left behind to 'dig in' and prepare for more. The natural geography of Malta made it an ideal site to defend; it was basically an island of solid yet easily

workable rock. The airfields were strengthened and aircraft pens were constructed.

There were only three main airfields on Malta. Luqa was the biggest of the three, and was located between Hal Far in the south and Ta Kali; there was also an emergency operating strip at Safi. On such a small island, airfields were not difficult to identify. It was vital for the airfields to remain open, so, as in all operational theatres, it made sense to disperse aircraft. Not only were the Hurricanes dispersed, but they were also kept in aircraft pens, built by the ground crew using anything that might help protect the aircraft from damage caused by bombs exploding near by. Eventually, the airfields of Luqa and Hal Far, and the Safi operating airstrip were connected by a maze of taxiways. The Hurricanes were so vital to the defence of Malta that they simply could not afford to be lost, particularly on the ground.

The Hurricane pilots faced particular problems on Malta. When operating from bases back home during the Battle of Britain, a pilot had had the option of landing elsewhere if his airfield was under attack or out of action. Also, the air battle had been fought over a large area and pilots had been able to use the vast amount of airspace to gain height and any tactical advantage. On Malta, the situation was very different. Air attacks against the island affected all three operating airfields,

This MkI (Z2827) of the Malta Night Fighting Unit is captured on film after a wheels-up landing in July 1941.

and the pilots had little time to gain any advantage against attacking aircraft. Normally, the Hurricanes would be scrambled off and the pilots would head out to the south, over the Mediterranean, gaining as much height as possible, before turning back northwards to meet the attackers.

Germany Joins the Campaign

The Germans re-joined the air battle over Malta early in 1941, adding significant weight to the air attacks against the island. The Gladiators were withdrawn from the battle during January 1941, leaving the Hurricanes of 261 Squadron to provide the

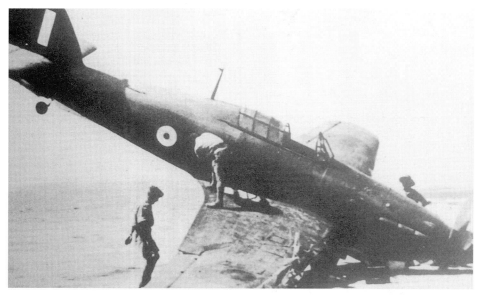

Not all landings were perfect! A crashed Hurricane at Ta Kali.

main air defence of the island. Operating mainly from Ta Kali, with a detachment at Luqa to disperse assets on the ground, the Hurricane pilots each flew up to five sorties a day as the number of air raids increased once again.

The Hurricane squadron scored notable successes and, during one four-day period, between 16-19 January, claimed forty enemy aircraft destroyed. Similar numbers were claimed during the following three months, as the temperature of the air war increased. However, the squadron did not escape loss; five Hurricanes were lost on 22 March, and seven more during April.

Despite the squadron suffering losses, reinforcements still managed to get through, often under the cover of darkness, and success continued into the spring of 1941. With the air combat based around an island, and mostly over the sea, it was impossible to confirm many of the claims of the number of enemy aircraft destroyed. However, the proof of the squadron's success is evident in the fact that Malta survived.

Squadron and Unit Changes

With more, slightly improved Hurricanes arriving on Malta, a second Hurricane unit formed at Hal Far in May. On 12 May, 185 Squadron was officially formed, under the command of Sqn Ldr Peter 'Boy' Mould, DFC. It was initially made up of personnel from 261 Squadron; this squadron ended its association with Malta when it disbanded at Ta Kali on 21 May, later re-forming in July at Habbaniya in Iraq. Its association with the island was never forgotten, and the crest of 261 Squadron proudly includes the Maltese Cross, as does the crest of 185 Squadron.

Although 261 Squadron disbanded at Ta Kali on 21 May, it was replaced the same day by 249 Squadron. Under the command of Sqn Ldr 'Butch' Barton, DFC, 249 Squadron was undoubtedly one of the most experienced Hurricane units. Born in Canada, Robert Barton joined the RAF before the war. In May 1940, he was posted to 249 Squadron, and served as a flight commander with the squadron throughout the Battle of Britain. In December 1940, he was given command of 249 Squadron at North Weald, by which time he had eight confirmed kills and had been awarded the DFC, in October. Many of his pilots were also veterans of the Battle of Britain and had operated almost continuously for the past year without rest.

The squadron had embarked in HMS *Furious* at Liverpool on 12 May and had sailed to Gibraltar, where it transferred to HMS *Ark Royal* for the last stage to Malta. Without subjecting Ark Royal to unnecessary risk in the Mediterranean, the plan was to fly the Hurricanes off the carrier once within range of Malta. On 21 May the carrier was considered to be close enough to the island and the squadron's twenty-four Hurricanes, fitted with long-range fuel tanks, took off for Ta Kali, led by a Fleet Air Arm Fulmar. The Fulmar suffered an engine problem, and was forced to return to the carrier. The Hurricanes

The RAF's association with the island of Malta has never been forgotten: a detachment of Tornado F3s in the Falkland Islands was numbered as No 1435 Flight (formerly the MNFU), and the BBMF Hurricane (PZ865) has recently been displayed in the markings of 261 Squadron, based on Malta during 1940-41.

also had to return, to wait for a second Fulmar to get airborne and lead the way. One of the Hurricanes (Z4830) was flown by Fg Off Pat Wells, himself a veteran of the Battle of Britain, and his log book shows a flight of five and a half hours! Because the Hurricanes were so short of fuel, the pilots landed on the island where they could; some made Ta Kali, while others landed at Luqa and at Hal Far.

Having been with 249 Squadron since June 1940, Pat Wells was an experienced Hurricane pilot. He had already achieved a confirmed kill of a Heinkel He 59, as well as sharing a Messerschmitt Bf 110, but he had not had an easy time during the Battle of Britain. He had already twice baled out of Hurricanes, after being shot down and wounded, and Malta did not prove much luckier. Five days after the squadron arrived at Ta Kali, the airfield was attacked by Bf 109s. Wells was in his Hurricane, when it was hit in the gravity tank and caught fire. Wells had been hit by a

cannon shell in his right ankle, but he managed to vacate the burning Hurricane. He was transferred to Imtarfa Hospital, and it would be another two months before he was fit to resume operational flying.

Turning Defence into Attack

The first Spitfire reinforcements arrived in Malta during April and May 1941, and the island maintained its resistance until the Germans withdrew, temporarily, from the air battle in May 1941 to prepare itself for the invasion of Russia. This relatively quiet period gave Malta a much-needed rest and allowed more aircraft to be flown in. Many of the strike aircraft returned from Egypt, with more being flown from the UK, and it was now the turn of the British to strike back. Targets were enemy shipping on the re-supply line to North Africa, and bases in Sicily. There was also

a change in the command structure, with AVM Hugh Pughe Lloyd being appointed the Air Officer Commanding Malta, in June.

On 6 June, Flt Lt Pat Hancock claimed the destruction of a Heinkel He 111, giving 185 Squadron its first success. By the following month, the squadron was operating by day and night as it continued the defence of Malta. It not only achieved success against aircraft, but also had a certain amount of success against German E-boats that were carrying out attacks against Malta's Grand Harbour. The squadron also began to take on a more offensive role, carrying out fighter sweeps over Sicily.

As Malta was a staging post for the Middle East, it was not uncommon for personnel en route to other squadrons to be 'delayed' there, helping in the island's struggle. Personnel from 46 and 238 Squadrons are known to have served with the resident Hurricane squadrons during June and July. Squadron records show this to be the case, but it is unlikely that either squadron had any of its own aircraft on Malta during this period. In June 1941, a

Although this is not a very clear photo, the loaded bomb racks can be seen on this MkIIB of 185 Squadron at Hal Far during 1942. The ground crew about to see off the aircraft are Royal Navy, showing that everyone helped in Malta.

flight of 46 Squadron pilots en route to the Middle East stopped off in Malta, and ended up forming 126 Squadron at Ta Kali. Using whatever Hurricane MkIIs were available, the squadron was operational within days. It remained at Ta Kali and scored notable success in the island's defence. It eventually converted to Spitfire MkVs in March 1942, and moved to Luqa. The badge of 126 Squadron contains the Maltese Cross, signifying its formation on the island.

When there were no air attacks against Malta, the Hurricane pilots took their chance to get back at the Italians. By the beginning of August, 249 Squadron at Ta Kali had received a number of Hurricane MkIIs (mainly IICs), and had begun to carry out offensive sweeps over Sicily and reconnaissance sorties between Pozzallo and Scicli. The squadron's pilots had to learn how to adapt to the different roles and the different characteristics of the various marks of Hurricane. Bomb racks capable of carrying four 40-lb bombs under each wing were fitted to the MkIIs, giving the Hurricane a limited capability in the air-to-ground role.

Pat Wells had recovered from his wounds suffered during the air attack on Ta Kali on 26 May, and had been promoted to the rank of Flt Lt. His log book for the month of July shows three different Hurricane variants – MkI, MkIIA and MkIIC. For the month of August it shows a variety of operational sorties, ranging from defensive patrols over Malta to offensive sweeps over Sicily, and reconnaissance sorties. These reconnaissance sorties were generally carried out at about 10,000 feet (3000m), and lasted just under an hour. If the pilots saw any enemy activity, they attacked it; on 29 August, Flt Lts Pat Wells and John Beazley attacked an Italian schooner. Flying MkIIAs, and armed only with machine-guns, Wells and Beazley could not sink the schooner, but the sight of the two Hurricanes attacking was enough to make the Italian crew jump overboard!

The Hurricanes defending Malta were, generally, more than a match for the enemy bombers. The MkIIs gave the pilots improved performance at higher altitudes, although any escorting Bf 109s always caused problems. Although the pilots of

249 Squadron had originally believed that they were destined for the Far East, they had been told that they were needed more on the island. They were also told that they would stay for no more than one year; for some, it would be the end of the war before they returned to the UK!

The Malta Night Fighting Unit

Because of the increasing number of night attacks against Malta, it was decided to form a special Hurricane unit. The Malta Night Fighting Unit (MNFU) was formed at Ta Kali on 30 July 1941, under the command of Sqn Ldr 'Polly' Powell-Shedden. Another veteran of the Battle of Britain, George Powell-Shedden was twenty-five years old. He had joined the RAF in 1935, had served overseas with 47 and 33 Squadrons before the war, and was posted to Coltishall in July 1940, where he flew Hurricanes with 242 Squadron throughout the Battle of Britain. During the battle, he was credited with at least three kills before being shot down on 15 September 1940. Recovered from his injuries, Powell-Shedden returned to flying the Hurricane and was posted as a flight commander with 258 Squadron, before taking command of 615 Squadron at Valley in April 1941; three months later he was posted to Malta specifically to form the MNFU.

For his two flight commanders of the MNFU, Powell-Shedden chose Flt Lt 'Cass' Cassidy and Flt Lt Donald Stones. Ernest Cassidy was twenty-four, and had joined the RAF before the war. He had first flown Blenheims with 25 Squadron, before converting to the Hurricane, and had joined 249 Squadron at North Weald in October 1940. Cassidy had been one of the squadron's pilots to fly off HMS *Ark Royal* in May, and had already achieved success in Malta when he shot down an Italian Savoia-Marchetti SM79 torpedo-bomber on 9 July. He would soon achieve his second kill within the first week of the MNFU being formed – a Fiat BR20 on the night of 5-6 August.

Known as 'Dimsie', Donald Stones already knew Powell-Shedden, having flown out to Malta with him on 21 July. Stones was yet another veteran, having flown Hurricanes with 79 Squadron during the Battle of France and the Battle of Britain. When he arrived in Malta, he was just twenty, but had already been credited with ten kills, and had already earned the award of the DFC.

The pilots selected for the MNFU were taken from both squadrons at Ta Kali and their Hurricanes had to be 'borrowed', as none were specifically made available. The unit operated a mix of MkI and MkIIs, depending on what was available at the time. Night tactics had to be discussed and tried; night-fighting in an aircraft that was essentially designed for daytime fighting was to prove a new challenge for the pilots. Close liaison with the anti-aircraft batteries was necessary, as the searchlights were vital in aiding the Hurricane pilots.

One young man to enjoy early success as a night-fighter pilot was Plt Off David Barnwell. Unlike many of his colleagues, Barnwell had no previous combat experience. He had arrived in Malta straight from training, and had spent only a few weeks with 185 Squadron before joining the MNFU. Nevertheless, by the time he became a night-fighter pilot he had already achieved his first kill – an Italian Macchi MC200 fighter on 11 July – followed on the 25th by the shared destruction of a Fiat BR20. On the night of 5-6 August, Barnwell destroyed two more Fiat BR20s, bringing his personal score to three. Barnwell was described as a natural night-fighter pilot and he was

rewarded for his efforts with a DFC in September. Sadly, Barnwell, at just nineteen, was killed defending the island of Malta. On 14 October, he was in combat with Macchi MC202s which were strafing Luqa airfield. Having shot one down, he was never seen again. This was undoubtedly a sad loss for the MNFU, but it was also a tragic blow for the Barnwell family – David's two brothers had already been killed in action with the RAF.

Within weeks, the MNFU had six Hurricanes, very distinctive in their all-black

Aged just 22 years old, Sqn Ldr Bryan Wicks was a veteran of the battles of France and Britain, before he was sent to Malta to command 126 Squadron at Luqa; within weeks he was killed. He is commemorated on the Malta Memorial.

paint scheme. The MkIs were gradually replaced by MkIIs as more aircraft became available for Malta. Life for the pilots was very tiring. Typically, five or six Hurricanes were available on readiness each night. The pilots were scrambled at night in just the same way as they were by day. Many long hours were spent by the telephone in the readiness hut, awaiting orders to scramble; the pilots would pass the time 'cat-napping', or reading by a dim red light. This was the only lighting in the hut, designed to help preserve night vision, as it can take several minutes for the eye to adjust fully to darkness. Having spent the night on operations, the pilots were able to rest the next day (although this was not always an easy task on the

island of Malta). Late in the afternoon, they would report for duty again. There would then be night-flying air tests to do on the Hurricanes, before assembling in the readiness hut to wait for whatever lay ahead that night.

Malta is a very small island and it was subjected to many attacks, making rest for the night-fighter pilots almost impossible. There was little chance for them to establish any kind of social life, and no opportunity to get off the island even when on stand down. As a result, like many who served on Malta, the pilots of the MNFU became very close to the local people and many established a life-long bond with the Maltese and their island.

One of the more unusual tasks that the MNFU was asked to perform was submarine escort. These vital assets in the Mediterranean war often went into Malta for replenishment or repairs. Having to surface, they would arrive under darkness at night and the Hurricanes would escort them in.

The MNFU was re-named 1435 (Night Fighter) Flight on 2 December, and command was handed over to Sqn Ldr Innes Westmacott. Innes Bentall Westmacott was already an experienced fighter pilot by the time he took over command of 1435 Flight. He joined the RAF in 1937 and had served in the Middle East prior to the war. Having converted to the Hurricane in the spring of 1940, Westmacott was posted to 56 Squadron at North Weald. Within the first month of joining the squadron he had destroyed two Messerschmitt Bf 110s and shared in the destruction of a Dornier Do 17. Westmacott's involvement in the Battle of Britain came to an end on 31 August when he was shot down; he was badly burnt, and it was several weeks before he could return to the squadron.

Westmacott arrived on Malta in April 1941 and joined 261 Squadron. He destroyed a Bf 109 at the end of the month and claimed a probable kill on a Heinkel He 111 early in May. When 185 Squadron formed in Malta later in the month, Westmacott was appointed flight commander of 'B' Flight. He was shot down the next day and baled out. Having been wounded in the action, Westmacott was appointed to ground duties on Malta before his continuous protests resulted in a return to flying. When 1435 Flight was formed from the MNFU, Westmacott was given his chance and appointed as the new commanding officer.

Into 1942

New Hope

The news that the United States had entered the war following the attack on Pearl Harbour on 7 December brought much relief and hope to those besieged on Malta. The island had struggled through 1941, often cut off from the rest of the world, but now things looked brighter. Malta entered the new year with hope and expectation. The Flight enjoyed its best night of action on 27-28 January 1942, when its Hurricanes shot down four enemy aircraft; there was one each for Fg Off Denis Winton, Plt Off Jackie Grant, Plt Off F. R. Palmer, and Sgt J. E. Wood. Sadly, the Flight lost Plt Off A. S. Mackie earlier in the evening, shot down by a Bf 109 while carrying out a night-flying air test over Ta Kali.

The beginning of 1942 also saw the arrival of Bristol Beaufighters, which had been specifically equipped with AI (air interception) radar. The Germans increased the effort by day and the arrival of the Beaufighters as night-fighters meant that the Hurricane pilots could be released to support the day fighting. The long-awaited fighter reinforcements arrived in Malta during the spring and early summer, which meant that 1435 Flight was expanded to full squadron strength. The last of the Hurricanes were replaced by Spitfires during the Spring and 1435 Squadron was officially formed at Luqa on 2 August. Incidentally, 1435 Flight has never been forgotten. Despite several squadrons having been disbanded since the war, 1435 Flight remains to this day and now operates Tornado F3s from Mount Pleasant in the Falkland Islands. The association with the island of Malta is still evident as the unit wears the Maltese cross

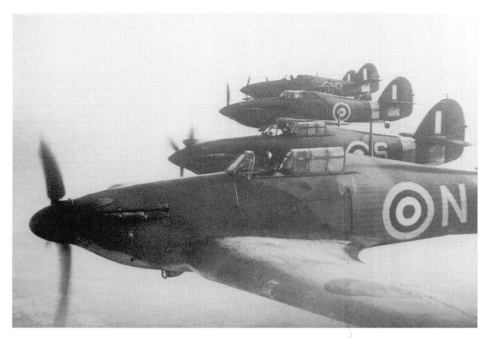

Operating from the Royal Navy carriers *Eagle*, *Indomitable* and *Victorious*, Sea Hurricanes of the Fleet Air Arm played a vital role during Operation Pedestal in August 1942. Although supplies reached Malta, the convoy proved costly, with the loss of two carriers, with only *Victorious* surviving.

on its crest and aircraft; three of the Tornado F3's tail letters are 'F', 'H' and 'C' and they are affectionately known as 'Faith', 'Hope' and 'Charity'!

Continued Defence

The situation by day was again becoming desperate, as the struggle for Malta's survival continued into 1942. The air wing had reduced to no more than a dozen serviceable Hurricanes at any one time, complemented by a handful of Spitfires. The Royal Malta Artillery and the Army's Royal Artillery also played an important role in the defence of the island. An ever-increasing anti-aircraft barrage was put up day after day. Not only did the batteries deter the Italian and German attackers,

but many enemy aircraft also fell to Malta's guns.

The airfields on Malta continued to be attacked throughout the first months of 1942, particularly Ta Kali, as it was the main fighter airfield. George Powell-Shedden was promoted to wing commander and given command of Ta Kali air base throughout this difficult period – on 20 March, for example, three separate raids were made against Malta by a total of almost 500 enemy aircraft, with nearly 100 tons of bombs falling on Ta Kali alone.

605 and 69 Squadrons

In January a small unit had formed in Malta with Hurricane MkIIBs at Hal Far, and had been given the name of 605

Hurricane units based on Malta, August 1940 - April 1942			
UNIT	**LOCATION**	**DATE**	**VARIANT**
46 Squadron	Luqa/Hal Far	Jun-Jul 1941	MkI/IIC
69 Squadron	Luqa	Jan 1941 - Feb 1942	MkI/IIA
126 Squadron	Ta Kali	Jun 1941 - Mar 1942	MkI/IIB
185 Squadron	Ta Kali/Hal Far	Apr 1941 - Mar 1942	MkI/IIA/IIB
229 Squadron	Hal Far	Mar-Apr 1942	MkIIC
238 Squadron	Ta Kali	Jun 1941	MkI
249 Squadron	Ta Kali	May 1941 - Mar 1942	MkI/IIA/IIB/IIC
261 Squadron	Luqa/Hal Far/Ta Kali	Aug 1940 - May 1941	MkI
605 Squadron	Hal Far/Ta Kali	Jan-Feb 1942	MkIIB
MNFU/1435 Flight	Ta Kali	Jul 1941 - Apr 1942	MkI/IIB

Squadron. This caused some confusion, as a 605 Squadron had already been operating Hurricanes in the Far East. Caught up in the heavy fighting as the Japanese advanced, it appears that the 'original' squadron had been prematurely written off. The Far East 605 Squadron did not officially disband until the end of February, so for a period of two months the RAF had two 605 Squadrons!

The Malta-based 605 Squadron operated from Hal Far throughout January and February 1942, also operating a small detachment at Luqa. It moved to Ta Kali at the end of February and then appears to have disbanded. The problem of the two 605 Squadrons was finally resolved when the 'official' 605 Squadron re-formed in the UK in June 1942, under the command of Wg Cdr Peter Townsend, DSO DFC. After this date there were no further references to the Malta-based 605 Squadron.

Another unit to have operated Hurricanes in Malta was 69 Squadron, based at Luqa. The squadron was essentially equipped with Martin Maryland MkIs for reconnaissance duties, but it also operated a number of different types of aircraft, including a few Hurricanes until February 1942. These Hurricane MkIs had the machine-guns removed and cameras installed in their place. This considerably reduced the overall weight of the aircraft, and enabled these reconnaissance variants to reach altitudes in excess of 35,000 feet (10,500m).

The End of the Hurricane Units

The Hurricane pilots had had to learn to adapt in order to get the best out of their aircraft. As in other theatres, it was not uncommon for those who flew the MkIIC to remove the outer two 20mm cannons. Although this reduced the firepower by half, the aircraft was much lighter, and had better manoeuvrability. The pilots were also assisted by visual controllers who used VHF radio from certain vantage points around the island to help direct the Hurricanes towards the attacking aircraft.

By April 1942, all of the Hurricane units on Malta had either disbanded or had been re-equipped with Spitfire MkVs. In addition, 229 Squadron had just arrived from Egypt, only to disband at Hal Far at the end of April; it would later reform at Ta Kali with Spitfire MkVs in August.

The Hurricane days on Malta had come to an end. Aircraft still passed through Malta en route to and from North Africa and the Middle East, but there would be no more Hurricane squadrons. The part played by the Hurricanes, their pilots and ground crews in the defence of Malta was enormously important. From the early days of the Gloster Gladiators 'Faith', 'Hope' and 'Charity', to the arrival of the Spitfire MkVs, the Hurricanes had bridged the gap and ensured the survival of the island. In recognition of the outstanding heroism of those responsible for Malta's defence, King George VI awarded the George Cross to the island on 15 April 1942. Nevertheless, the struggle was far from over and the people of Malta had to withstand hardship until 1943, when the island became an ideal supporting base for the Allied landings during Operation *Torch*.

Wg Cdr George 'Polly' Powell-Shedden commanded the MNFU during 1941 and then Ta Kali, during the difficult period of 1942.

Wg Cdr (later Gp Capt) George Powell-Shedden, DSO DFC

George Ffolliott Powell was born in Cowes on the Isle of Wight on 1 April 1916. The second part of his surname (often spelt 'Sheddan' or 'Sheddon') was inherited from his grandfather, Sir George Shedden. George Powell-Shedden (affectionately nicknamed 'Polly'), initially joined the Army's Royal Military Academy at Woolwich but transferred to the RAF in 1935. Following pilot training he was posted to 47 Squadron at Khartoum, where he flew Fairey Gordons in support of the ground forces in the Sudan. At the outbreak of war in Europe, Powell-Shedden was posted to Gloster Gladiators as a flight commander with 33 Squadron at Mersa Matruh in Egypt. He soon returned to the UK, where he converted to the Hurricane and joined 242 Squadron at Coltishall in July 1940.

During the Battle of Britain, Powell-Shedden destroyed a Bf 109 on 7 September, and two days later a Do 17. On 15 September he destroyed another Do 17, before being shot down by Bf 109s. He spent the next two months recovering from his injuries before being posted as a flight commander to 258 Squadron at Leconfield. In April 1941, Powell-Shedden was promoted to squadron leader and given command of 615 Squadron at Valley on Anglesey; their duties included convoy and shipping patrols over the Irish Sea.

Three months later, in July 1941, George Powell-Shedden's association with the island of Malta began. He was posted to Malta to form the new Malta Night Fighting Unit (MNFU) with a handful of Hurricanes at Ta Kali at the end of the month. As a night-fighter pilot, Powell-Shedden added to his personal score, destroying an Italian Fiat BR20 during the night of 11-12 August, and a Cant Z1007 on 8 September. In December, the MNFU was re-numbered as 1435 Flight and Powell-Shedden was awarded the DFC, promoted to wing commander and given command of Ta Kali.

The struggle for Malta frequently brought out the best in people. Unlike most other theatres of war, the island was often cut off from the supply line and improvisation was important. There were very few fighters based on the island and continuous air attacks made life most difficult. Powell-Shedden led from the front, commanding the highest respect from those who worked with him and for him.

Having commanded Ta Kali during the difficult period of early 1942, Powell-Shedden left Malta in July and was posted to the Middle East before later returning to the UK and being appointed to staff duties at the Air Ministry. In January 1944, he joined 96 Squadron at West Malling, where he flew the de Haviland Mosquito MkXIII, before he was given command of 29 Squadron at Drem in March, also equipped with Mosquito MkIIIs. Promoted to group captain in December 1944, Powell-Shedden was given command of Castle Camps and then awarded the DSO in April 1945. After the war, he remained in the RAF and carried out staff appointments at the Air Ministry and Fighter Command before commanding Jever in Germany during the early 1950s. He retired from the RAF in 1961 and became a farmer and stockbroker before retiring in London. His contribution to Malta's defence and his association with the island will long be remembered.

CHAPTER SIX

Benedict Force

Murmansk, Russia

The Eastern Front

Hitler invaded Russia on 22 June 1941 as part of Operation *Barbarossa*. In an attempt to divert Luftwaffe resources away from the Eastern Front, Fighter Command increased the number of fighter sweep and escort missions across the Channel. Despite these efforts, the situation on the Eastern Front continued to deteriorate, leaving Stalin with little option but to appeal to Britain for support.

Two Squadrons to Russia

Towards the end of July 1941, Winston Churchill agreed to send two squadrons of Hurricanes to the Murmansk area in northern Russia for two reasons: first, to help protect the area of Murmansk so that much-needed supplies could still reach the Red Army through the vital ice-free port; and, second, to train Russian pilots and ground crews in the flying and maintenance of the Hurricane. Some of Fighter Command's most experienced pilots were taken from their units to form these two squadrons. Many of them had gained valuable experience during the Battle of Britain, and they were sorely missed by Fighter Command for several months.

The response to Churchill's pledge was immediate. The two units formed for this special task were 81 and 134 Squadrons, both re-formed at Leconfield at the end of July. The man chosen to lead the wing throughout the campaign in northern Russia was Wg Cdr Henry Ramsbottom-Isherwood. Born in New Zealand in 1905, Henry Neville Gynes Ramsbottom-Isherwood had served as an officer in the New Zealand territorial army before being commissioned into the RAF in 1930. He had served in India and the Middle East before becoming a test pilot during the build-up to war, and had been awarded the AFC in 1940.

81 Squadron

Following the outbreak of war, 81 Squadron had re-formed in France as a

Wg Cdr Ramsbottom Isherwood, Officer Commanding No 151 Wing, pictured briefing with Russian officers.

communications unit. However, after the fall of France during the summer of 1940, it had returned to the UK and had disbanded. The squadron re-formed at Leconfield on 29 July 1941, and was initially made up of pilots from 'A' Flight of 504 Squadron. This unit had distinguished itself during the previous summer and many of its pilots were already combat veterans. Chosen to lead this new unit was Sqn Ldr Tony Rook. Born in Nottingham in 1918, Anthony Hartwell Rook was commissioned into the Auxiliary Air Force in 1937, and was one of two Rook cousins who had both served with 504 Squadron with distinction during the battles of France and Britain. Both had already, coincidentally, achieved kills during the same combat on the same day, 27 September 1940, when the squadron had scored notable success. Tony Rook led 81 Squadron in Russia, while his cousin

A veteran of the battles of France and Britain, Sqn Ldr Tony Rook commanded 81 Squadron throughout the campaign in Russia.

Micky Rook was posted as a flight commander to 134 Squadron; both Rooks would, therefore, continue to serve together on the Eastern Front.

Another '504 veteran' joining 81 Squadron was Plt Off 'Artie' Holmes, who had achieved fame on 15 September 1940 when he shot down the Dornier Do 17 which was believed to have bombed Buckingham Palace. Two other '504 vets' were Fg Off Alan McGregor and Flt Sgt 'Wag' Haw, a promising youngster who, at twenty-one, was beginning to prove himself as an excellent fighter pilot.

134 Squadron

In similar circumstances, 134 Squadron re-formed at Leconfield on 31 July, essentially consisting of pilots from 17 Squadron. This squadron had also served with distinction during the Battle of Britain; its new commanding officer was

The converted flat-deck carrier HMS *Argus*, from which the Hurricanes took off for the airfield at Vayenga, near Murmansk, on 7 September 1941.

Sqn Ldr Tony Miller. Born in Calcutta in 1912, Anthony Garforth Miller had been commissioned into the Auxiliary Air Force before the war, and had assumed command of 17 Squadron at Tangmere during August 1940. He was a natural choice to be the first commanding officer of the new squadron. His two flight commanders could not have been more contrasting in appearance: at six feet four inches, Micky Rook was at one time apparently the tallest pilot in the RAF (and probably the tallest person to fly the Hurricane); the other, Jack Ross, was less than five feet tall, and probably the smallest pilot to have flown the Hurricane!

The only other Battle of Britain veteran from 17 Squadron to join 134 Squadron was Neil Cameron. He had served as a sergeant pilot with 1 and 17 Squadrons during the battle, and was commissioned on joining 134 Squadron. After the war he went on to a most distinguished career in the RAF, becoming Marshal of the RAF Sir Neil Cameron, KT GCB CBE DSO DFC in July 1977.

The arrival of the RAF at Vayenga created much local interest.

A Russian guard meets the RAF pilots.

151 Wing Travels to Russia

The two squadrons were the spearhead of 151 Wing, which officially formed at Leconfield on 12 August 1941. While its pilots were spending a few days on leave, thirty-nine Hurricane MkIIBs were sent from Hawaden to Liverpool, where twenty-four were prepared for flying and put on to HMS Argus; these would be the first Hurricanes to land on Russian soil. The remaining fifteen were packed in crates and placed as cargo on other ships. On returning from leave on 16 August, the pilots flew in Handley Page Harrows from Leconfield to Abbotsinch on the outskirts of Glasgow. The final destination for both squadrons was still secret and most had no idea where they were going, except that it was overseas. They were transported by truck to Gourock, where the main party boarded various ships.

The convoy that sailed for Russia on 21 August consisted of some thirty ships, including the flat-decked HMS Argus, which accommodated most of the squadron's pilots, the cruiser *Sheffield*, and the destroyers *Active* and *Electra*, with most of the wing's ground crew and support personnel embarked in S.S. *Llanstephen Castle*. The RAF detachment bound for Russia totalled 550 men, and it was well out to sea before they were told of their final destination.

Argus was an old Italian merchant ship that had been captured during the First World War and later converted as a flat-decked carrier. The superstructure had been removed, which meant that a flight deck of some 350 feet (100m) was available. For the pilots on board, the voyage proved rather dull, with very basic living conditions. The twenty-four Hurricanes carried below deck were only partly assembled. Although the majority of the pilots had flown MkIs, they had no experience on the MkII. The improved Merlin XX series engine would give them better performance and the twelve 0.303in machine-guns would improve the fire-power. Nevertheless, the fact remained that they would have to take off on a short flight deck, which was something that none of them had ever done before!

Arrival

After three weeks aboard Argus, the moment had come. The twenty-four Hurricanes had been assembled and were now ready for departure. Each was carrying a reduction in armament of only six guns, in order to reduce the all-up weight. The procedure used for take-off was for Argus to steam into wind at her maximum speed of seventeen knots. It was the morning of 7 September and a typical early autumn day in northern Russia: overcast, grey and cold. The pilots gathered on the flight deck to await their turn for departure. First off was 134 Squadron, led by Tony Miller,

followed by 81 Squadron. Sgt 'Wag' Haw was seventeenth off and his log book shows the flight to Vayenga airfield lasting one hour and ten minutes.

On arrival in Russia, the wing was placed under the command of the Head of the Soviet Navy and Naval Air Service, Admiral Kuznetsov. That same day, a conference was held at Archangel between the RAF staff in Russia and Adm Kuznetsov, and it was decided not to make 151 Wing operational until all the guns and ammunition had arrived at Vayenga. At that time, each Hurricane was fitted with just six guns and 130 rounds of ammunition, and a signal had to be sent to hasten delivery of vital armament and spares. Although these supplies were delivered within forty-eight hours, it was found that the guns had gun blast tubes and sears from Hurricane MkIs, which would not fit, and did not have fire and safe mechanisms attached. Following much improvisation in local workshops, two aircraft from each flight of each squadron were stripped of their guns, enabling each flight to have four aircraft of eight guns.

The Campaign Begins

Vayenga - The Base

The airfield at Vayenga (otherwise spelt 'Vaenga' or 'Vianga') was located just over 20 miles (35km) to the north-east of Murmansk, facing the Arctic Ocean, 170

HQ No 151 Wing.

miles (275km) north of the Arctic Circle. It was to be home to the two squadrons throughout the campaign. It was a large base with no real runway, just a large area of hardened sand surrounded by hills and woods. It had none of the facilities normal to an RAF base – no radar to provide early warning, and only limited communications. This meant that the pilots could only meet the threat once they were already airborne, using their eyes and the smoke puffs of the local gunners to locate the enemy aircraft. One other point of concern to the Hurricane pilots was the question of aircraft recognition amongst the Russian ack-ack gunners.

Despite these complications, the pilots had to concentrate on the task ahead. They were there for two reasons: first, to help defend the port of Murmansk, and second, to help convert Russian pilots to their new Hurricanes once they had been unpacked and assembled. The first snow was due and the pilots were unsure just how long they would be expected to carry out their task before the long, severe Russian winter set in.

The arrival of the RAF created tremendous local interest at Vayenga, and they had to host important visits from senior

Russian officers and officials. No flying was carried out on the first three days, for a number of reasons: the British ships had sailed on to Archangel to off-load the main party of the convoy more safely, out of reach of enemy air activity, and there was much site maintenance to be done before the wing would be ready for opera-

Hurricanes of 81 Squadron at Vayenga, September 1941.

tions; second, the weather was already deteriorating; and, third, the Russian food had already posed a problem, and it would be several days before some individuals would adjust to the change in diet!

Z5227 at Vayenga, wearing the code letters 'FE' (81 Squadron), and the number '53'; numbers as well as letters were used to make recognition easier for the Russians. When the aircraft were eventually handed over to the Russians, the RAF roundels were replaced by the red star; the code letters were removed but the numbers remained.

Assembling the Aircraft

Fifteen Hurricanes were taken to Archangel, where an 'erection party' responsible for assembling the aircraft made them ready for use at Keg-Ostrov airfield. This engineering detachment of two officers, one warrant officer, three flight sergeants, two sergeants and thirty airmen was led by the wing engineering officer, Flt Lt Gittins. Conditions at Keg-Ostrov were poor, and many of the specialist tools required for assembling the Hurricanes were missing.

Basically, the procedure was as follows: unpack each Hurricane from its packing case (about one hour); jack it up and attach the basic fuselage components; lower it on to the undercarriage and push it into the hangar; fit the wings and tail units. The aircraft were then fuelled and armed before ground-testing. The process was slow and, despite the party working in three groups, the facilities were not available. Aircraft components had been packed in a hurry in the UK, and there were obvious difficulties in unloading and unpacking the components in terrible weather conditions. However, improvisation and hard work by the erection party meant that the first three Hurricanes were completed and air-tested on the sixth day,

and all fifteen Hurricanes were assembled and tested within the first nine days. It was a magnificent achievement! The squadrons were ready for action only six weeks after Churchill had promised Stalin his support.

Operations Commence

The first sorties took place from Vayenga on 11 September, when the squadrons

Before the weather turned, the pilots of 81 Squadron used a Ford estate wagon to get around.

each flew eight aircraft on local familiarization sorties; the front line was not far away, about 15 miles (25km) in places, and it was essential that the pilots knew their way around before engaging the enemy for the first time. It was deemed necessary to

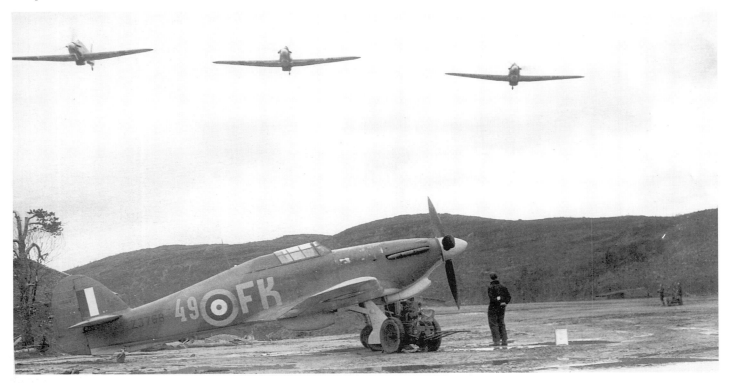

Three Hurricanes fly over Z3768 of 81 Squadron towards the end of September, as the weather began to deteriorate. Note the code letters 'FK', which were used as well as 'FE'.

Hurricanes of 134 Squadron. The squadron used the code letters 'GV' and 'GO' while operating in Russia, as seen on the two nearest aircraft.

make certain adjustments to the Merlin engines to compensate for the low-octane fuel and the cold operating temperatures. The 95-octane fuel in particular led to the Merlin engine cutting out on pilots during the first day; this happened to Jack Ross in Z3763, and Neil Cameron in Z3978. That same night the first snow fell.

During the following morning, various supplies began to arrive at Vayenga. Six more Hurricanes were flown in from Archangel, having stopped to refuel at Afrikanda. Three more Hurricanes were stranded at Afrikanda, after failing to start following refuelling. This meant that a starter battery and accumulators had to be sent to Afrikanda from Vayenga, so that the aircraft could be recovered the following day.

First Success

The first combat patrol was flown that same day, 12 September, by three Hurricanes of 134 Squadron. Although enemy bombers were sighted, no combat took place. This was followed by a patrol by 81 Squadron and two escort missions by 134 Squadron for Russian bombers. Although these first missions did not lead to any activity, Hurricanes were soon in combat for the first time. Later that same day, at 3.05 p.m., the four Hurricanes of 81 Squadron were scrambled to meet enemy aircraft sighted to the west of Murmansk. Leading the patrol was 'Wag' Haw (Red Leader), with Plt Off Jimmy Walker (Red 2), Sgt 'Ibby' Waud (Blue Leader), and Sgt 'Nudger' Smith (Blue 2) completing the section. They soon sighted five Messerschmitt Bf 109s escorting a Henschel 126 in the distance. Pressing home a determined offensive, Haw delivered a close-quarter attack against one Bf 109, which burst into flames before rolling inverted and crashing to the ground. In less than thirty minutes, the Henschel 126 and two of the other Bf 109s were also shot down, one by Walker and the other by Waud, who also claimed the HS 126. Success was theirs, although, sadly, 'Nudger' Smith was killed during the encounter.

Wag Haw's report for that first encounter shows that the combat took place at 3.25 p.m. to the west of Murmansk. He continued:

> Whilst leading a patrol of Hurricanes over the enemy lines I intercepted five Bf 109s escorting a HS126. My height was 3,500ft. The enemy aircraft were approaching from ahead and slightly to the left, and as I turned towards them, they turned slowly to the right. I attacked the leader and as he turned I gave him a ten second burst from the full beam position. The enemy aircraft rolled on to its back and as it went down it burst into flames. I did not see it crash owing to taking evasive action, but Red 2 confirms that it crossed him in a 70-degree dive at 500ft, smoke and flames still pouring from it.

News of this first success travelled fast to the highest of authorities. The RAF's Chief of the Air Staff, ACM Sir Charles Portal, sent the following signal to Adm Kuznetsov, to commemorate the first operations carried out by 151 Wing in Russia:

> British squadrons are now operating from Soviet territory against the common enemy. On this first and memorable occasion of our two Air Forces fighting side-by-side on Russian soil I send you the warmest congratulations of all ranks of the RAF on the skilful and heroic resistance maintained by the Soviet Air Forces

When the weather deteriorated, the ground crews soon learnt to improvise, by using any available help!

Pilots having fun and games in the snow beneath a makeshift aircraft shelter.

The pilots soon learnt to make the best use of skis for getting about the airfield.

against the German invaders. Permit me to express the confident hope that this may prove the beginning of even wider and closer collaboration between our two Air Forces.

Adm Kuznetsov's reply included the following:

I am sincerely happy at the fact that the lucky chance of beginning operations against the common enemy side-by-side with the RAF on an important part of the Front has fallen to the Air Force of the Soviet Navy. I take this opportunity of expressing to you, Air Chief Marshal of the British Royal Air Force, my sincere regards and respect.

The Hurricanes had been in Russia for just four days and enjoyed their first success, but the loss of 'Nudger' Smith was

sadly felt by all, serving to remind the pilots of the seriousness of the task ahead. He was buried two days later on a piece of high ground overlooking Murmansk Sound.

During the next two days, the weather was very bad, although both squadrons were involved in local patrols. The last six Hurricanes to be erected at Keg Ostrov flew into Vayenga on 16 September, with the remainder of the erection party arriving during the following day. By this time, 81 Squadron was flying sixteen fully armed Hurricanes, each with all twelve guns. However, there were still the occasional problems caused by grease blocking the gun mechanisms due to the extremely cold conditions.

Further Success

On 17 September, there was further success, when 81 Squadron was scrambled to intercept a number of enemy aircraft to the west. The weather conditions were ideal, and the enemy was soon sighted. The engagement took place at 6.55 p.m. over the enemy lines to the west of Murmansk and, during the forty-five minutes the sortie lasted, the squadron shot down four aircraft, including another Bf 109 for 'Wag' Haw. His combat report reads:

I was leader of Yellow Section. Two Bf 109s dived over and passed in front of us. I attacked the second enemy aircraft as he turned and dived westwards. I made an astern attack at about 200 yards range, firing a three-second burst with no visible effect. The enemy aircraft then turned to the right across me and I delivered a quarter attack from about 150 yards, firing another burst of three seconds. During this attack smoke began to pour from the enemy aircraft, a large piece flew off him and he rolled onto his back and went into a vertical dive. An enemy pilot who baled out was identified by the Russian Observer Corps as being the pilot of the machine which I attacked. The piece of the enemy aircraft which flew off was probably the hood being jettisoned.

Apart from being scrambled to intercept enemy aircraft, Hurricanes from both squadrons were involved in carrying out escort duties for Russian bombers attacking targets across the front line. Some of these were relatively short-range missions, while others were longer. One of the longer missions took place on 24 September, when Hurricanes provided an escort for Russian Pe-2 dive-bombers. The route

went over the area of Petsamo (to the west of Murmansk), across Finland and into Norway, before returning to Vayenga, and took one and a half hours.

Training

By the end of September, the pilots of 151 Wing had begun their secondary task – training Russian pilots to fly the

Skis were not the only way of getting about! Note the protective covers fitted to the aircraft of 134 Squadron in the background.

By the beginning of October, the temperature had dropped significantly and snow had arrived, making conditions for the ground crews particularly difficult.

Hurricane. The Russians believed very strongly in leading from the front. The first Russian pilot to fly the Hurricane was Admiral Kuznetsov on 25 September. As the Head of the Soviet Naval Air Service, he was given his own Hurricane (Z5252), with his own number and a red star painted on it. The next day, the second Russian pilot to fly the Hurricane was Lt Col Boris Safonov, a 26-year-old ace fighter pilot of the 72nd Regiment of the Soviet Naval Air Service, and the third was Kapitan Kuharienko. Both of these famous pilots would later feature in the success of the Hurricane in Russia.

It worked out that most of the training flying was carried out by 134 Squadron, in particular by Jack Ross, who formed an excellent partnership with his Soviet counterpart, Kapitan Kuharienko. Another of the Russian instructors involved in this early training programme was Kapitan Yacobenko, who later went on to command the first Soviet Hurricane squadron. The RAF pilots found their

Russian colleagues keen to learn about the Hurricane. They all adapted quickly and showed remarkable determination and plenty of guts. It was not uncommon for a Russian pilot to carry out his first flight in the Hurricane in marginal weather conditions, but they seemed to have no fear.

As well as the flying training, the RAF ground crews had started training their Russian counterparts in servicing and maintenance techniques. Snow had continued to fall, much more heavily now, and the RAF and the Russians were in a race against time before the worst of the weather set in. Vayenga was covered in snow and ice, and routine maintenance was proving increasingly difficult.

The End of the Campaign

27 September

On 27 September, Wag Haw destroyed another Bf 109, bringing his personal score to three in two weeks. The combat took place at midday about 45 miles (75km) to the north-west of Murmansk. Haw's report reads:

I was White leader in a formation of four Hurricanes when I sighted four Bf 109s approaching us from the west. The leader of their second section tried to do a beam attack on me but I turned towards him and after three complete turns I was on his tail. I gave him several short bursts and while doing this we lost height down to 3,000ft. As I fired the last burst but one, the enemy aircraft came out of its turn, climbed steeply, and then stalled and went into a spin, white and black smoke pouring from it. I did not see what happened to it, as there was an enemy aircraft on my tail. I got rid of this and returned to base.

This third kill for Wag Haw was confirmed.

During the two weeks of combat, the Hurricane wing had destroyed ten enemy aircraft for the loss of just one. It had managed to operate from Vayenga with relatively little interruption, apart from the occasional attack by German bombers, none of which scored any notable success. There was, however, a tragic accident on 27 September, when two ground crew were holding down a Hurricane (BD825) during engine run-up. The aircraft got airborne, but it stalled just after take-off, and the pilot, unaware of the crew's position, crash-landed, with severe injury

Although relatively short, the campaign and conditions in Russia were hard work, shown in the expressions on the faces of these pilots after another sortie.

to himself and tragically killing both men on the ground.

The weather took a turn for the worse during the final few days of September, and conditions at Vayenga deteriorated badly.

Final Claims

Due to a certain amount of being in the right place at the right time, all the early combat success had belonged to 81

Squadron – the squadron's pilots had destroyed twelve enemy aircraft – but it was soon the turn of 134 Squadron to get some reward for their efforts. On 6 October, Tony Miller led 134 Squadron to success, when it shot down two Junkers Ju 88s, and claimed a further three probables.

These aircraft destroyed, and a further kill by 81 Squadron, proved to be the final claims, bringing the wing's total to fifteen enemy aircraft destroyed for the loss of one Hurricane. These remarkable figures may even have been an under-estimate. Many more aircraft were claimed as probables, but the nature of the surrounding countryside, with so many deep lakes, meant that wreckage could not be found, and these probables could not be confirmed.

The Weather Worsens

By the end of the first week of October, the RAF's task was nearing its end – there was no further operational flying, and the training of the Russian pilots with the newly assembled Hurricanes was almost finished. The training did not go without incident, however – two Hurricanes crashed on landing during the first week of October, without injury to the pilots. Similar accidents had happened at the Hurricane training units in the UK and, considering the weather and operating conditions, the Russians were considered to be remarkably quick learners.

On 9 October, a blizzard hit Vayenga

A Hurricane of 134 Squadron shortly before No 151 Wing returned to the UK.

By the middle of October the heavy snow had arrived and pilots often relaxed by learning to ski.

and, during the next two days, there were further heavy snow showers. At this time, only the Russians were flying Hurricanes, as this extreme change in weather brought to an end the RAF's campaign in northern Russia. By 12 October, most of the wing's Hurricanes, and the newly assembled aircraft, had been handed over to the Russians, and the RAF detachment prepared to leave Russia. The next week was spent in more training with the Russian pilots and ground crew, with some operational sorties being flown by the wing. By the end of the week, more than twenty Russian pilots were operational on the Hurricane.

Departure of the RAF

The First Russian Hurricane Squadron

The first Russian unit to equip with the Hurricane was 1 Russian Hurricane Squadron, which formed at Vayenga on 18 October under the command of Kapitan Yakobenko. The following day, the first Russian Hurricane Wing of three squadrons was formed at Vayenga under the command of Lt Col Safonov, with Kapitan Kuharienko as his second in command. Safonov went on to become one of

Russia's most famous fighter pilots; he loved the Hurricane and had become a very good friend of the RAF fighter pilots at Vayenga. In his 224 operational sorties, he shot down thirty enemy aircraft, before being killed in action on 30 May 1942, while protecting one of the many Allied convoys into Murmansk. He was twice made a Hero of the Soviet Union, as well

as being decorated with the Russian Order of Lenin and the Order of the Red Banner.

A Job Well Done

With the formation of the first Russian wing, the task of 151 Wing was complete. There was no possibility of keeping the RAF in Russia, because of the immense logistical problems involved in supporting a detachment so far from the UK. There was now the question of what to do with

The arctic conditions meant new problems for the ground crews with storing ammunition and ground equipment.

Two veterans of Murmansk, 'Wag' Haw (left) and 'Ibby' Waud in 1944.

Flt Sgt (later Sqn Ldr) 'Wag' Haw, DFC DFM Order of Lenin – 81 Squadron

Born on 8 May 1920, Charlton Haw was educated at Tang Hall School in York, before working as an apprentice lithographer. He joined the RAF Volunteer Reserve in 1938 and carried out his elementary flying training at Brough. Aged just nineteen, he was called for active service on 1 September 1939 and, following initial training at Bexhill, was posted to No 5 Flying Training School at Sealand. On completion of training on the Miles Master, he was posted directly to 504 Squadron, on 19 June 1940. He flew Hurricane MkIs with the squadron throughout the Battle of Britain, during which he achieved his first 'kill', shooting down a Messerschmitt Bf 110 over Bristol on 27 September.

Haw remained with 504 Squadron until the formation of 151 Wing, and he was posted to the newly re-formed 81 Squadron at Leconfield on 28 July 1941. He flew Hurricane MkIIBs with the squadron from Vayenga, near Murmansk, and was the top-scoring RAF fighter pilot in Russia during this short campaign. Having left the Hurricanes behind in Russia, the squadron returned to the UK and converted to the Spitfire MkV. In March 1942, Haw was commissioned, and continued to serve with 81 Squadron until the end of July. He then served as a flight commander with 122 Squadron at Hornchurch, again flying the Spitfire. In February 1943, he was given command of 611 Squadron at Biggin Hill and then 129 Squadron at Hornchurch from November 1943 until July 1944, during which time the squadron converted to the Mustang MkIII. Haw was awarded the DFC on 17 October 1944, after which he was rested from operations.

After the war 'Wag' Haw commanded 65 Squadron from 1946 to 1948, then lost his flying category on medical grounds, which resulted in him leaving the RAF in 1951 to become the landlord of a pub in Sussex. He then acquired a boarding kennel, and developed a pet-food business, which he ran for the rest of his working life. Still very much remembered by the Russians, he visited Moscow in 1985 as a guest to join celebrations for the 40th anniversary of the end of the war. He lived near Farnham in Surrey until his death in December 1993. In May 1995, 'Wag' Haw's unique group of medals went to auction at Christie's, where it was snapped up by the author of this book!

151 Wing; if it could not stay in Russia, where should it go? It was first suggested that it should be sent to the Middle East where it would be most welcome; after much discussion, however, it was decided not to go ahead with this plan, because of the major problem of transporting the wing such a great distance. In the end, it was decided that 151 Wing would return to the UK and then disband.

It was four weeks before the RAF detachment was ready to leave Russia, and the main challenge became how to keep 550 airmen occupied, now that their task was complete. Temperatures were as low as -30 degrees centigrade, and, in fact, this marked the beginning of one of the coldest winters in the Murmansk area; later, temperatures would drop as low as –47 degrees centigrade. A limited amount of physical exercise was possible, but most of the pilots and ground crew preferred to go to the Russian squadrons to assist in further training when necessary.

The wing embarked in various Royal Navy ships from 20 November, and began the long journey home. The largest group joined the cruiser HMS *Kenya* at Murmansk, setting sail on 28 November, and arriving at Rosyth in Scotland on 7 December. With the disbandment of 151 Wing, its members were sent off for some well-earned leave. They were surprised to be hailed as national heroes on their return, unaware that news of their exploits had preceded them.

The expedition of 151 Wing had undoubtedly been a success. The Russians

One of many Hurricanes delivered to Russia, this MkIIB (BM959) of the Soviet Air Force is shown after crash-landing in Finland during 1942.

were now fully operational with the Hurricane, and the wing had helped ensure that the Germans had made no further gains on the Eastern Front, leaving the vital port of Murmansk free. The RAF's Hurricane pilots had led from the front, achieving confirmed kills of a ratio of fifteen to one, plus many more probables, possibles and damaged, the final sum of which will never be known. As well as these obvious achievements, the wing had made many friends and helped boost relations between Britain and Russia during a critical time of the war. Russia had been desperate for help when Stalin made his first appeal to Churchill but, coincidentally, the day that the wing returned home was the day that the United States entered the war. The beginning of the severe Arctic winter meant that Russia was safe for the time being and by the following year things would be much more promising. As soon as 151 Wing had left Murmansk, the Russians immediately began the request for more Hurricanes. By the end of the war, a total of 2,952 Hurricanes had been sent to Russia as part of 14,000 aircraft sent to

'Wag' Haw, pictured with former Russian comrades after the war.

Hurricanes sent to Russia from 1941	
MARK	NUMBER
MkIIA	210
MkIIB	1,557
MkIIC	1,009
MkIID	146
MkIV	30

the Eastern Front by Britain and the United States; this represents more than 20 per cent of the total number of Hurricanes built.

The Russians made certain modifications to the standard marks of Hurricane; they fitted 0.5in machine-guns, and developed tandem variants, including one with a dorsal gun position. There was also at least one Sea Hurricane MkIa (V6881), which was 'adopted' by the Russians. It had originally been launched by catapult from the SS *Empire Horn* during a convoy patrol and, following action with an enemy aircraft, was unable to return to the

ship, landing instead at Keg Ostrov airfield.

The Russians were enormously appreciative of the efforts of 151 Wing, and awarded the Order of Lenin to four of the pilots who took part in the expedition. This show of gratitude was unique, the only time that the Order of Lenin was awarded to any Allied forces during the Second World War. The four awards were made to Wg Cdr Ramsbottom-Isherwood (for leading the overall RAF detachment), to Sqn Ldrs Tony Rook (OC 81 Squadron) and Tony Miller (OC 134 Squadron), and to the top-scoring pilot, Flight Sgt 'Wag' Haw of 81 Squadron. This award of a Soviet Order to Haw, a non-commissioned officer, was unique; the citation given with it is most interesting, handwritten by the Commander of the Soviet Northern Fleet, and dated 29 November:

To Pilot of the Royal 'Military' Air Fleet of Great Britain,
SERGEANT HAW C.F.

I congratulate you with the high Government award of the Union of Socialist Republics, the 'Order of Lenin'. Your manliness, heroism and excellent mastery in battles of the air have always assured victory over the enemy. I wish you new victories in battles against the common enemy of all progressive nations, i.e. – German fascism.

Signed Vice-Admiral A. Golovko

The unique group of medals awarded to 'Wag' Haw, left to right, DFC, DFM, 1939-45 Star with clasp 'Battle of Britain', Air Crew Europe Star with clasp ' Atlantic', Defence Medal, War Medal, Air Efficiency Award, Order of Lenin.

CHAPTER SEVEN

The Desert War

A tropicalized MkI pictured at Cairo, Egypt, in late 1940. When the Italians entered the war in June 1940, the RAF presence in the region was very small and reinforcements were hard to come by. Hurricanes sent to the desert were modified with a tropicalized air filter, to protect against dust and sand.

The air war in North Africa covered a vast area stretching from the western Mediterranean to central Africa. Much of the fighting took place over the desert of North Africa, an area unfamiliar to the Hurricane and its crews. The conditions in which the pilots and ground crews found themselves made operational flying difficult. Many of the operating airstrips were simply prepared areas of sand, and when it was windy, such routine tasks as aircraft maintenance proved almost impossible. Initially, Hurricanes of the RAF were involved against Italian forces, although more capable and experienced German forces started arriving in the theatre during 1941. Although the main

war was fought in the skies over the Western Desert, there were many smaller and more local conflicts, including those in the Middle East and East Africa.

The Situation

Squadrons Present

The original RAF overseas command structure appointed control of the region to Middle East Command, which controlled a huge area, including Egypt, Palestine, the Sudan, Trans-Jordan, East Africa, Iraq, and the Balkans. During the early months of the Second World War,

the strength of British forces in the Middle East and North Africa was never enough to meet any considerable threat. Fewer than thirty RAF squadrons covered the entire area, just five of which were equipped with fighters, in the shape of old Gloster Gladiator biplanes. When Italy entered the war on 10 June 1940, the very existence of the British in this theatre immediately came under threat. Although the Italian threat was not very great, it was enough to cause the British high command to be concerned about the protection of the sea routes through the Mediterranean and the Suez Canal.

Through the Italian-held Libyan ports, such as Tobruk, Italy began to build up large forces in Cyrenaica, with the intention of attacking eastwards through Egypt and on to the Suez Canal. The RAF presence in the Middle East at that time was

A MkI of 33 Squadron being re-armed at Fuka during 1940. The squadron had been in theatre since the outbreak of war, and fought with distinction during the First Libyan Campaign.

very small – just nine squadrons of aircraft, none of which were equipped with modern fighters. In fact, there was just one Hurricane, an old aircraft that had been sent out to Khartoum before the war for trials in the tropical environment. This one aircraft suddenly became a major focus of attention, flying all over the Middle East in order to fool Italian reconnaissance aircraft into believing that there were a number of Hurricanes in theatre!

Gladiators of 80 Squadron had been in Egypt since May 1938, having arrived at Ismailia to help provide air defence of the area. The squadron had been based at Amriya since the outbreak of the war in Europe and, following the declaration of war with Italy, it acquired a handful of Hurricane MkIs. With these, it formed a special flight to operate alongside its Gladiators, and went into action for the first time on 19 June. One of the Hurricanes (P2639) was flown that day by 24-year-old Fg Off Peter Wykeham-Barnes. While patrolling with Gladiators of 33 Squadron based at Qasaba he shot down two Italian Fiat CR42s, the squadron's first success of the war.

One other pilot who flew Hurricanes with this special flight was Fg Off John Lapsley. Born in India, Lapsley was one of the squadron's most experienced pilots having served with 32 Squadron and then 80 Squadron before the war. Lapsley's first success with the Hurricane was on 17 August, when he destroyed three Italian

Savoia SM.79s in one sortie. Having already gained early experience with the Hurricane, John Lapsley and Peter Wykeham-Barnes were posted from 80 Squadron to help form 274 Squadron, the first Hurricane unit in theatre. Also based at Amriya, 274 Squadron was formed on 19 August, under the command of Sqn Ldr Patrick Dunn, DFC. The new squadron was initially equipped with the few Hurricanes that moved across from 80 Squadron, supplemented by Gladiators. It soon became operational, and claimed its first victories of the war on 10 September, when John Lapsley shot down two Italian SM.79s over Maaten Bagush. These kills made Lapsley the first Hurricane ace in North Africa.

The early encounters did not go unrecognized, and Wykeham-Barnes and Lapsley received the first fighter-pilot DFCs for the North African theatre.

Reinforcements

Reinforcing the Middle East and North Africa with Hurricanes was a major problem. The most critical point at that time was that Britain was struggling for its own survival, and fighters such as Spitfires and Hurricanes could not be readily spared. When the decision was made to send a small number of reinforcements, it simply had to be the Hurricane rather than the Spitfire, for two reasons: first, there were more Hurricanes in operational service and, second, the more sturdy design of the Hurricane's undercarriage meant that it was better suited to operating from ill-prepared airstrips.

For the Hurricane, the early route was via France and Malta before flying on to the Middle East. This route posed several problems. First, flying across France during 1940 was not safe and, second, any fighter landing in Malta was likely to be kept there! Another route was via Gibraltar and North Africa, although this was generally preferred by the larger aircraft reinforcing the Middle East. It soon became apparent that the preferred (and safer) route was by sea to Takoradi in the Gold Coast (on the west coast of Africa), where the aircraft were reassembled and made ready for the long flight across Africa into theatre; this route took much longer.

The first Hurricanes to arrive in Africa via this longer route were those of 73 Squadron, which had embarked on HMS Furious and sailed from Liverpool in

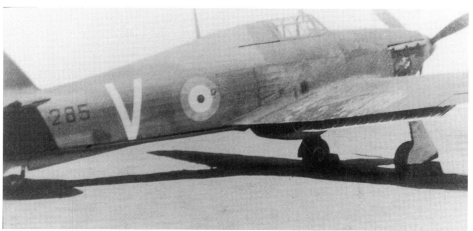

A MkI of No 1 Sqn SAAF pictured at Port Sudan in 1940.

The nose markings of a MkI of No 3 Sqn SAAF.

November 1940. After just over two weeks at sea, the Hurricanes flew off the ship and landed at Takoradi. Many more supplies for the Hurricanes operating in the Western Desert came via this route and arrived in theatre through Takoradi, from where they were moved forward to the various operating bases in North Africa. These supplies ranged from small aircraft components to replacement aircraft, which were then flown across Africa for delivery to squadrons operating from small airstrips in the desert.

The build-up of land forces in the Western Desert had continued through the summer of 1940. There had been little or no air activity with the Italian Regia Aeronautica during October and November. Instead, the time had been spent preparing for the forthcoming advance into the desert by the British ground forces, which would require air support from the Hurricane squadrons. In preparation, 274 Squadron moved from Amriya to Sidi Haneish South on 7 December. The second Hurricane unit in theatre was 33 Squadron, which had been in Egypt since before the war. Its Gladiators had been replaced by Hurricanes in September 1940, when it moved to a satellite airfield at Fuka to carry out patrols and ground-attack sorties against Italian troops and positions. The arrival of 73 Squadron at Heliopolis during the first few days of December 1940 brought the number of Hurricane squadrons in theatre to three. The first few days had been hard work for

both the pilots and ground crews of 73 Squadron, who had only just completed the long journey from the UK.

The Campaigns

The First Libyan Campaign, December 1940 – January 1941

Gen Sir Archibald Wavell launched the First Libyan Campaign on 9 December 1940. For many of the Hurricane pilots, this was their first taste of action. During the opening encounters on the 9th, Fg Off Tom Patterson, a Canadian pilot serving with 274 Squadron, gained his first success, when he shot down an Italian CR42 in the area of Barrani-Sofafi. Another squadron pilot also gained his first success on the opening day; Plt Off Stan Godden shot down an Italian SM.79, the first of his seven kills achieved in theatre.

One of 274 Squadron's pilots also in action on the first day was Fg Off 'Imshi' Mason. Initially posted to 80 Squadron, Ernest Mason had been detached to form the nucleus of 274 Squadron at Amriya. On the opening day of the campaign, he was in action over Sidi Barani during the morning when he shared in the destruction of two Italian SM.79s. By the end of the first week of the campaign, he had personally destroyed three Italian aircraft and, by the end of the second week, his total had risen to five. Mason's wingman during the campaign was Lt Bob Talbot, a

South African pilot who was attached to the squadron from 1 (SAAF) Squadron; Talbot gained his first success on 19 December, when he destroyed an Italian CR42 in the area of Sollum-Gambut.

Sadly, none of these four pilots of 274 Squadron, who all enjoyed early success during the First Libyan Campaign, survived the war in North Africa. Three were dead within six months. Tom Patterson was killed on 25 April 1941, when he collided with a Messerschmitt Bf 110; Stan Godden was shot down and killed on 1 May, during an engagement with Bf 109s; and Bob Talbot was killed on 3 June, during operations against a German occupied airfield. All three had become early Hurricane aces in North Africa – Talbot with nine kills, Godden and Patterson each with seven kills – but none received any formal recognition for their achievements. 'Imshi' Mason went on to achieve fifteen kills flying Hurricanes in North Africa, for which he was awarded the DFC, before he was killed in action on 15 February 1942, while leading an attack on Martuba airfield.

Not to be outdone by the other squadron pilots on the opening day of the campaign, both Peter Wykeham-Barnes and John Lapsley were also successful. Lapsley destroyed an Italian CR42, and Wykeham-Barnes destroyed a CR42, and shared in the destruction of two SM.79s. The careers of these two men were remarkably similar. Both had been the first to fly the Hurricane in North Africa, having served with the special flight of 80 Squadron and 274 Squadron, and they had also received the first fighter-pilot DFCs in North Africa. Both men went on to achieve success during the First Libyan Campaign, Lapsley finishing the campaign with a total of eleven kills, and Wykeham-Barnes with a total of ten. Both remained in the post-war RAF and achieved the rank of Air Marshal, being knighted for their services. Wykeham-Barnes eventually retired from the RAF as AM Sir Peter Wykeham, KCB DSO* OBE DFC* AFC, and Lapsley retired as AM Sir John Lapsley, KBE DFC AFC.

Operating from Fuka airstrip during the early part of the campaign, the Hurricane pilots of 33 Squadron achieved similar success to those of 274 Squadron. One of the most successful pilots in North Africa was Fg Off 'Woody' Woodward of 33 Squadron. Born in Canada, Vernon Crompton Woodward joined the RAF in August 1938 and was posted to 33

Squadron in Egypt just before the war. Like many of the pilots to serve in North Africa during the early months of the war, Woodward gained his combat experience with the Gladiator, and he achieved four kills during June and July 1940. He converted to the Hurricane in September and was in action on the first day of the Libyan Campaign, destroying two CR42s over the frontier of Libya. By the end of the campaign he had destroyed three more, bringing his overall total to nine. 'Woody' Woodward went on to serve in Greece before returning to Egypt at the end of May 1941. By then, his score had risen to eighteen (fourteen while flying Hurricanes), for which he was awarded the DFC, to which a bar was later added in 1943.

One of the most amazing feats of the war was achieved during the First Libyan Campaign, and involved one of 33 Squadron's pilots. Fg Off Charles Dyson was an experienced pilot, having served with the squadron since before the war. He had been involved in attacks against Arab dissidents during 1938 and had been awarded the DFC. On 11 December 1940, he encountered a formation of six Italian CR42s; he shot down all six, before having to force-land his Hurricane. He made his way back to base on foot, arriving several days later, where he related his exploits. Although it seemed difficult to believe at the time, an Army signal reported the destruction of seven aircraft as, apparently, one of the CR42s had collided with an SM79 after Dyson had shot it down. Charles Dyson is therefore recorded as having destroyed seven aircraft in one sortie, and was awarded an immediate bar to his DFC.

The campaign also saw two other pilots from 33 Squadron achieve notable success. The Rhodesian Fg Off Peter St Quintin ended the campaign with seven kills and the Canadian Fg Off John Mackie achieved six; sadly, Mackie would soon be killed while serving with the squadron in Greece.

The third Hurricane squadron taking part in the campaign also achieved significant success. Initially operating

from Heliopolis, 73 Squadron soon found itself back in action once again. For some of the pilots there seemed to have been little rest since the battles of France and Britain. Now, in the skies over North Africa, their previous combat experience would stand them in good stead. The young Canadian Flt Lt James Duncan 'Smudger' Smith was one of these pilots. Having seen action with the squadron during the Battle of France and the Battle of Britain, Smith had already been credited with two kills by the time he arrived in Egypt. He scored his first kill in North Africa during the campaign, when he destroyed an Italian SM.79 over Bardia on 14 December. During the next four days, he destroyed two more SM.79s, bringing his overall total to five. Sadly, 'Smudger' Smith did not survive the war; he was killed over Tobruk in April 1941.

In similar circumstances, Fg Off Alfred Marshall found himself in action with 73 Squadron during the campaign. He had also seen action during the Battle of France, and had already achieved his first kill of the war. On 16 December, Marshall destroyed two Italian SM.79s over Bardia. By the end of the campaign, Marshall had a total of seven kills, and he went on to be credited with sixteen kills, before being killed in November 1944.

Another of 73 Squadron's pilots involved

during the campaign was Fg Off Jas Storrar. He had seen action over France and during the Battle of Britain with 145 Squadron and was already a Hurricane ace, with eight kills and several more shared or probables. He had been awarded the DFC in August 1940, and was posted to 73 Squadron for the deployment to Egypt. By the turn of the year, the squadron had moved to Sidi Haneish and Storrar achieved his first success a few days later when he destroyed an Italian CR42 on 6 January. A few weeks later, he destroyed a number of aircraft on the ground during an attack against Benina airfield. Storrar was eventually credited with twelve kills, ten of which were while flying Hurricanes.

Hurricane MkI of 274 Squadron at Amriya, Egypt, in November 1940, shortly before the squadron deployed to Sidi Haneish South for the First Libyan Campaign.

The remarkable early success of the Hurricane pilots meant that there was little further air activity with the Italian Regia Aeronautica during the latter part of the First Libyan Campaign. The Hurricanes were used increasingly to support the land war, carrying out attacks against Italian ground forces. In an amazingly swift advance, the port of Tobruk fell to the British in January 1941, and by the following month British forces had taken all of Cyrenaica.

East Africa, January – April 1941

The Italian entry into the war in June 1940 created a serious problem in East

A MkI (P2627) of 274 Squadron on patrol over the desert in December 1940.

Hurricane squadrons and locations in the First Libyan Campaign, 9 December 1940 to 27 January 1941		
SQUADRON	**LOCATION**	**DATE**
33 Squadron	Fuka	9 Dec 1940 - 15 Jan 1941
33 Squadron	Amriya	15-27 Jan 1941
73 Squadron	Heliopolis	9-30 Dec 1940
73 Squadron	Sidi Haneish	30 Dec 1940 - 27 Jan 1941
274 Squadron	Sidi Haneish South	9 Dec 1940 - 27 Jan 1941

Africa, with the normal re-supply shipping route through the Red Sea being threatened. Quickly gaining the upper hand, the Italians had advanced swiftly into the region and captured Berbera in August 1940.

The number of British aircraft opposing Italian forces in Abyssinia, Eritrea and Somaliland was relatively small, and most were of the older generation. Nevertheless, British and South African forces had continued to build in the area throughout the winter months of 1940-41. Supported by air cover, the South African forces advanced into Eritrea during January 1941, followed soon after by an advance into Somaliland and Ethiopia. The major British effort came from the squadrons based at Sheikh Othman in Aden, and from there a number of bombing missions were flown against Italian forces in Abyssinia and Somaliland. The build-up of British and South African forces in the Sudan and Kenya meant that a swift campaign was possible.

Providing part of the air cover during the campaign in East Africa were some of the first Hurricane MkIs provided to the South African Air Force (SAAF); the first of these were delivered to 1 (SAAF) Squadron at Port Sudan during the last few weeks of 1940. Capt Ken Driver was one young South African pilot involved in the first Hurricane operations. Born in Pretoria in April 1918, Driver had only just been posted to 1 (SAAF) Squadron when he found himself carrying out patrols over the Red Sea in the area of Port Sudan. He achieved his first kill on 16 December, when he destroyed an Italian SM.79 over Port Sudan. During operations over Eritrea, Driver personally accounted for twelve Italian aircraft (half of which were destroyed on the ground), an achievement that brought him the award of the DFC.

He went on to serve with 1 (SAAF) Squadron in the Mediterranean theatre before being shot down on 14 June; he spent the next four years as a prisoner of war.

Hurricanes of the SAAF also provided air cover during the advance through Somaliland and into Ethiopia. Hurricane MkIs had also been delivered to 3 (SAAF) Squadron, when it became involved in the action during the early weeks of 1941. One of the squadron's flight commanders was Capt Servaas Theron, a 22-year-old from Cape Province. The following two months of the advance saw Theron personally destroy five Italian aircraft in the air, as well as accounting for eight more on the ground, bringing him the award of the DFC in March. He went on to serve in the Mediterranean and European theatres during the Second World War and later in Korea, eventually leaving the SAAF as a brigadier, having received the DSO and bar, and the AFC.

The other flight commander of 3 (SAAF) Squadron found fame as well while flying the Hurricane during the advance. Capt 'Jack' Frost was also twenty-two when he came across three Italian Ca 133 bombers attacking an army camp. He shot down all three, in full view of the soldiers on the ground, an act that brought him the immediate award of the DFC. Frost flew Hurricanes with the squadron throughout the rest of the advance, during which he destroyed seven Italian aircraft in the air and at least twenty-four more on the ground. Frost became South Africa's top-scoring pilot of the war. He went on to fly Tomahawks with 5 (SAAF) Squadron in the Middle East, and was eventually credited with at least fourteen kills in the air. Sadly, 'Jack' Frost failed to return from operations in June 1942; his remarkable efforts were later rewarded by a bar to his DFC, in August 1943.

Mogadishu was taken in February, and British troops entered Addis Ababa on 6 April. The Italian presence in East Africa was over, with the Hurricanes of the SAAF playing an important part in the victory. A total of five SAAF squadrons were equipped with various marks of Hurricane during the war, and all served in the Middle East and North Africa.

Iraq and Syria, June–July 1941

British interest in Iraq went back several years before the start of the Second World War. The large British base at Habbaniya, about 50 miles (80km) to the west of Baghdad, had been constructed during the inter-war years. As the war in the Middle East progressed into 1941, the airfield at Habbanjya played an important part in supporting British involvement in the region, and in helping to preserve British oil interests in the Middle East.

Syria had been seen to support German movements in the region during 1941, and Britain felt that German forces operating from Syria would prove a threat to the oil fields and the Suez Canal. Realizing that there was no alternative other than to occupy the country, British and French forces advanced into Syria on 8 June. Included in the air support were Hurricanes from 80 Squadron, operating out of bases in Cyprus and Palestine, and from 208 Squadron, based at Heliopolis.

The Hurricane pilots of 80 Squadron, only recently involved in the evacuation from Greece and the subsequent air war over Crete, found themselves in action once again. The Vichy French fighters put up resistance, particularly over the supporting ships of the Royal Navy, and several air combats took place. One squadron pilot who had previously distinguished himself in the skies over Greece was Fg Off 'Cherry' Vale of 80 Squadron.

In the two days between 11-12 June, Vale destroyed a Potez 63 and two Dewoitine 520s over the fleet off the Syrian coast. These three kills brought his total number of aircraft destroyed to thirty, twenty of these while flying Hurricanes with 80 Squadron. Vale became the fifth top-scoring Hurricane pilot of the war.

At the end of June, a detachment of four Hurricane MkIs and a handful of Gladiators formed 127 Squadron at Habbaniya under the command of Sqn Ldr Bodman. The Hurricane force operating against Syria was further increased when 213 Squadron joined the campaign on 2 July. Operating from Palestine, the squadron carried out ground-attack sorties until the Vichy French were defeated and a formal ceasefire was announced on the 12th.

North Africa

The Important Ports

Following the successful British advance in the First Libyan Campaign during the period from December 1940 to January 1941, British forces were established in the port of Tobruk. The Mediterranean ports in North Africa, including Benghazi and Tobruk, were hugely important, as they represented the vital supply lines to the desert. Whoever controlled them would control the desert war, and they would change hands many times before the war in the desert was over.

The Hurricanes of 73 Squadron immediately moved to Gazala West, from where they could carry out defensive patrols over the shipping that was re-supplying the

British forces in North Africa through Tobruk. In addition, a detachment of Hurricanes from 6 Squadron arrived in Tobruk from its base at Qasaba. Until February 1941, 6 Squadron had been equipped with Lysanders, to provide tactical reconnaissance for the army during the offensive in the Western Desert. The Lysander had proved capable as a reconnaissance aircraft, but was incapable of defending itself against any fighter opposition. It was only when the squadron took delivery of its first Hurricanes that it was deemed more capable of carrying out this role.

The Pendulum Swings

All had gone well for the British in North Africa up to this point. The furthest British advance had reached El Agheila, but General Wavell was unable to support his forces. British forces were fighting for survival at home, in the Atlantic, on Malta and in the Balkans, with every commander badly needing reinforcements; at that time, it seemed to those in the desert that North Africa was at the end of the supply line. However, the problem for the British was only just beginning. Having seen the Italians fail, Germany decided to concentrate on the war in the Mediterranean and North Africa; it was important for them to secure the southern flank of Europe if their eventual assault on Russia was to be successful. In the Balkans, Germany had invaded Greece and Yugoslavia, as well as putting forces into Romania and then Bulgaria in March. In addition, German forces had arrived in Sicily, from where more pressure could be put on Malta, and large numbers of German forces had entered North Africa through Tripoli.

A MkI of 73 Squadron pictured in the desert early in 1941 after the First Libyan Campaign.

The desert war in North Africa stepped up a gear with the arrival of General Erwin Rommel and his Afrika Korps and, within a short period of time, the British land forces were in retreat towards Egypt. The Hurricanes of 6 Squadron departed from Tobruk, leaving the Hurricanes of 73 Squadron as the RAF's only fighters in Cyrenaica. The few Hurricane pilots of 73 Squadron once again performed great heroics during April 1941. Fg Off George Goodman already had seven kills and a DFC for his service with 1 Squadron during the battles of France and Britain. He added a further three kills to his total, as well as sharing in the destruction of two more during April 1941. Sadly, he was killed just a few weeks later, during an attack against Gazala airfield.

Another pilot who fought with distinction was the Frenchman Lt James Denis, who had been sent to North Africa by the French Armée de l'Air on a special mission, but found himself attached to 73 Squadron. In just nine days during April, he destroyed seven enemy aircraft over Tobruk, for which the British rewarded him with a DFC, before he returned to his own air force.

By the end of April 1941, the situation had become desperate and the five surviving Hurricanes of 73 Squadron withdrew to Sidi Haneish.

Re-organization

Following a relatively stable period, British forces were able to build up in Egypt once more. The campaign in the Western Desert saw the creation of the Desert Air Force (DAF), from which the lessons learned would later help victory in northern Europe. The DAF consisted of aircraft from every Allied nation involved with the air war in the Western Desert; the Hurricane had been the first modern fighter to appear in this theatre during the summer of 1940, and had become present in larger numbers by March 1941. The newly formed DAF carried out a number of attacks against German positions in the desert, as well as attacks against the German-held Mediterranean ports, including Benghazi and Tripoli. Hurricanes were also used in the night-fighter role, to counter any German incursions over the area.

As part of the changing organizational structure in Africa, Air Headquarters for West Africa was set up at Fourah Bay, Free-

A MkI (Z4036) of 451 (RAAF) Squadron, one of three Australian squadrons to operate in the Western Desert during 1941.

town, in October 1941. To help protect the re-supply route through Takoradi on the Gold Coast, a flight of Hurricane MkIs of 95 Squadron, known as the Fighter Flight, had maintained air defence of the area since April 1941. The change to the organizational structure also led to the Fighter Flight forming 128 Squadron,

Hurricane squadrons and locations, August 1941	
SQUADRON	LOCATION
6 Squadron	Wadi Haifa
30 Squadron	Idku
33 Squadron	Amriya
73 Squadron	Sidi Haneish
80 Squadron	Aqir
94 Squadron	Ismailia
127 Squadron	Kasfareet
208 Squadron	Ramleh
229 Squadron	Idku
237 Squadron	Kasfareet
238 Squadron	LG 92
260 Squadron	Haifa
261 Squadron	Shaibah
274 Squadron	Gerawla
450 (RAAF) Squadron	El Bassa
451 (RAAF) Squadron	El Bassa
1 (SAAF) Squadron	Maaten Bagush

under the command of Sqn Ldr Billy Drake. About 10 miles (16km) to the east of Freetown, at Hastings, was a landing strip, which was established in Sierra Leone and used by the Hurricanes for the defence of the harbour of Freetown and the colony. It carried out this role until the end of the war in North Africa.

The Allied Advance, November 1941

Operation Crusader

Hurricanes were used in the air-to-ground role during Operation Crusader, which opened on 18 November 1941, and aimed to crush the Axis powers in the area. British and South African Hurricane squadrons fought side by side as the offensive gathered momentum. One of the Hurricane units to escape from Greece earlier in the year, 33 Squadron had finally evacuated to Egypt with just one Hurricane left. It was temporarily attached to 30 Squadron at Amriya, so that it could re-equip and build up to operational readiness once more, albeit with MkIs, and not with the newer and more capable MkIIs that were arriving in theatre. Now, under the command of Sqn Ldr J.W. Marsden, the squadron had deployed from Giarabub to landing ground (LG) 125 to carry out air-to-ground attacks against Italian positions.

Leading the Hurricanes of 80 Squadron from LG 128 during the advance was Sqn Ldr Mike Stephens, DSO DFC. Born in India, Stephens had joined the RAF in 1938. He served with 3 Squadron in France, where he was credited with eleven victories, and awarded the DFC and bar. On his return to the UK, he was the first commanding officer of 232 Squadron, when it formed at Sumburgh for the defence of northern Scotland. During this time, he shared in the destruction of a Heinkel He 111 over Scapa Flow. He was later sent to North Africa, but was

Fg Off Whitney of No 128 Sqn poses with his MkIIB (BH279) at Hastings, Sierra Leone during 1942.

diverted to Turkey, where he was given the unusual task of training Turkish fighter pilots with a Hurricane unit that had been sent to the west of the country. During this time he was able to add to his score while flying a Turkish Hurricane, when he shot down two Italian S-84 reconnaissance aircraft.

Stephens was then sent to North Africa, where he took over command of 80 Squadron. He brought his personal total to fourteen on 9 December, when he shot down a Messerschmitt Bf 109F over Tobruk, but he had been hit during the same action and had to bale out. He was taken into hospital in Tobruk, where he recovered from his injuries. He was later sent to Malta, awarded the DSO and a second bar to his DFC, and ended the war with fifteen victories.

Another squadron involved in Operation *Crusader* was 213 Squadron. Unlike 33 Squadron, this unit had taken delivery of some MkIIAs and MkIICs to operate alongside its MkIs; the 20mm cannons of the MkIICs gave the Hurricane a much more powerful 'punch' when carrying out air-to-ground operations.

Under the command of Sqn Ldr Lockhart, the squadron had detached from its home base in Cyprus and operated out of Ismailia and Idku during the campaign. The advance was successful and the port of Tobruk was temporarily relieved, with the German and Italian forces being driven back to Benghazi.

The Roles of the Hurricane

Throughout the British campaign during the last weeks of 1941, the long-range capability of the Hurricane MkIIs proved vital in supporting the British Army from bases well away from the front line. This support took many forms, including air support for the troops on the ground, as well as harassing the enemy well behind the German and Italian lines, either by attacking enemy airfields, destroying many aircraft on the ground, or attacking armoured vehicles and other motor transport. The success of many of these sorties maintained the constant pressure on the German and Italian supply lines throughout the region. By mid-December, the advance had reached a point 1,000 miles from Cairo, but the familiar problems of

re-supply brought it to an end, for the time being at least.

Hurricanes also provided air cover above the ports to support the vital supply line from the sea. For months, the enemy carried out constant attacks against merchant ships and Royal Navy escorts providing vital relief supplies to the port of Tobruk; few outside the garrison could have appreciated the part played by the Hurricanes during this time.

The German Advance, Spring 1942

The pendulum swung in North Africa once again, as the British were unable to support their gains in the desert. Reinforcements were desperately needed here, as they were everywhere. The war in the Far East was reaching a critical state, as the British retreated through Burma from the advancing Japanese. And, if the war in the Far East seemed a million miles away, the commanders had only to look closer to home; Malta, for example, was hanging on by its fingertips.

MkIICs of 94 Squadron during 1942. The Hurricane was employed in many roles in the desert, and 94 Squadron was often tasked with tactical reconnaissance. Pilots often preferred to make changes to their aircraft: the lead aircraft in this picture has had two of its cannons removed.

The Germans were able to counter-attack in the desert and Rommel's forces drove the British back towards Egypt once more. The Hurricane squadrons valiantly did as much as possible to resist the advance, but it was too well calculated and too swift. Indeed, without the Hurricane pilots, the British retreat might well have ended in carnage.

Distinguished Pilots

There were several Hurricane pilots who distinguished themselves in the defence against the German advance during this period. One was Sgt James Dodds of 274 Squadron who became the highest-scoring Hurricane pilot of the North African campaign. He was just twenty years old during the spring of 1942 and shot down fourteen aircraft during the six-month period up to June 1942, for which he was later awarded the DFM. From 73 Squadron there was Flt Sgt Ernest Joyce, who destroyed eight enemy aircraft, for which he was also awarded the DFM, and from 213 Squadron there was Flt Lt George Westlake, who destroyed five aircraft and was awarded the DFC. Sadly, Ernest Joyce was later killed while leading 122 Squadron in Europe during June 1944.

The top-scoring American pilot to serve with the RAF during the war also made his mark in North Africa during this period. Flt Lt Lance Wade had travelled to Canada at the start of the war so that he could join the RAF. After training, he was posted to 33 Squadron in North Africa in September 1941. His first success as a fighter pilot was on the opening day of Operation Crusader, when he destroyed two Italian CR42s over the airfield at El Erg. Initially flying Hurricane MkIs, and then MkIIBs and MkIICs, he accounted for a total of ten enemy aircraft in air combat during the period up to July, as well as destroying many others on the ground. Wade was eventually credited with at least twenty-two victories, twelve of which were achieved flying Hurricanes; he was awarded the DFC and two bars, and later promoted to wing commander. Sadly, Lance Wade was killed while flying in an Auster during January 1944. In recognition of the gallant American's achievements with the RAF, the award of a DSO was announced immediately after his death.

The German advance claimed several British lives, including two of the RAF's most popular fighter pilots. The ace New

MkIID 'Tank Busters' of 6 Squadron during 1942. This squadron was the first to be equipped with the MkIID and enjoyed much success during the Battle of El Alamein in October 1942; on the 24th, it destroyed sixteen tanks.

Zealander Derek Ward, DFC and bar, of 73 Squadron, was killed on 17 June; his death was followed a month later by that of George Barclay. At just twenty years old, George Barclay had been awarded the DFC for destroying four enemy aircraft while serving with 249 Squadron during the Battle of Britain. He had later been shot down over France in May 1941, and had evaded capture, eventually returning to the UK via Spain and Gibraltar. He was then shipped out to Egypt and appointed as the Officer Commanding 238 Squadron at LG 92 in July 1942. He quickly added to his score by destroying two German aircraft in two days, but on his second sortie on 17 July he was shot down and killed.

The 'Tank Buster'

One of the few consolations during the spring of 1942 was the arrival of the Hurricane MkIID 'Tank Buster', which was first delivered to 6 Squadron at Shandur, on the Suez Canal, in May. Under Wg Cdr Roger Porteous, DSO, the squadron worked up at Shandur, before moving to various landing grounds in the desert to the west of Alexandria, to carry out the first operations with the MkIID during June. Armed with two 40mm cannons, the MkIID proved an immediate success in the desert, as it countered the deficiency of the British tank being fitted with smaller armament when fighting against its German counterpart. The Hurricane MkIID was soon responsible for the destruction of many tanks and

armoured vehicles; the general tactic was to catch the enemy tanks in the open and dive down to just above the ground to carry out the attack. This new role for the pilots of 6 Squadron was very dangerous, as it involved flying at full throttle at about 250mph (400kph), at less than 50 feet (15m) against columns of vehicles that were armed and well defended. Having opened fire, the pilots noted a marked loss in airspeed. Inevitably, this most demanding of ground-attack roles led to losses for 6 Squadron as it flew at the forefront of desert operations. However, the Hurricane MkIID 'Tank Buster' proved a significant weapon in the desert war.

Hurricane Versatility

Throughout the war in the desert during 1942, the Hurricane performed in many roles – among other things, it was a fighter, and a bomber, it was involved in Army co-operation, and it carried out armed reconnaissance, night-fighting and aerial reconnaissance. The airstrips from which the Hurricane operated varied enormously; some were well prepared, while others were nothing more than a relief landing ground in the middle of nowhere. These airstrips were unnamed and were simply known as LGs (landing grounds), and given a number; for example, LG 123 was situated south of Sidi Hanish in Egypt. These LGs were far from ideal, particularly for the Hurricane MkIs,

The desert war was not all sun and sand – when the rain came, the landing strips turned into a sea of mud. Maison Blanche, Algeria, early in 1943, was the home of 32 and 43 Squadrons after the success of Operation Torch.

which suffered many engine problems as a result of the dusty conditions.

The Hurricane had to be modified to carry out operations in the desert. Filters were fitted to air intakes and radiators to reduce the problems caused by sand, although the fitting of these filters affected the Hurricane's performance by reducing its overall speed by up to 50mph (80kph). Although the MkIICs suffered very few engine problems, the dusty conditions caused occasional problems for

the 20mm cannons. However, the Hurricane was undoubtedly well liked by those who flew it in the desert. Its sturdiness made it capable of operating from almost anywhere, and the ruggedness of the airframe meant that many pilots got back to base in what may well have been a hopeless situation in other types of aircraft.

As well as the dust, small rocks and stones caused all sorts of problems, particularly with chipped propellers, or damaged props unbalancing the aircraft. In

addition, conditions were usually very hot and dry, but it was not uncommon for LGs to become a sea of mud, following heavy rain and thunderstorms late in the day or at certain times of the year. This often led to problems when taking off or landing, with the occasional Hurricane tipping up on its nose in soft sand!

Despite all these difficulties, the ground crews generally kept the Hurricanes flying. Apart from the many operating airfields and LGs, there were also many support units established in the desert to re-supply the squadrons. Repair and salvage units were set up, with small teams of ground crew driving out into the desert to locate downed aircraft, either to recover components from that aircraft or to recover the aircraft itself. The idea was that, after maintenance, the Hurricane could be returned to the front line.

The movement of the land forces in the desert meant that the Hurricane squadrons moved around many times. During the German advance of spring 1942, 238 Squadron was forced to move eleven times during June alone, and 274 Squadron moved ten times between February and July. Overall, however, there had been little change in the number of Hurricane squadrons in North Africa in the year since August 1941. For example, 30 and 261 Squadrons had been sent to reinforce the Far East in February 1942, but 213 and 335 Squadrons had joined the desert war, 213 Squadron having arrived from Cyprus and 335 Squadron having been newly formed. This had come about after the evacuation of personnel from Greece in 1941, with 335 Squadron becoming the first RAF unit to be manned by Greek personnel. Another new squadron was 173 Squadron, which formed as a communications unit at Heliopolis in July 1942; it operated many different types of aircraft during its existence in North Africa, including a Hurricane MkI. Other changes in theatre included 260 and 450 (RAAF) Squadrons exchanging their Hurricanes for Kittyhawks, 237 Squadron moving to Iraq in February, and 229 Squadron moving to Malta in April.

El Alamein and *Torch*

Rommel's advance through the desert was brought to a halt in the same way as the British advance had been previously. The pre-planned British defence line worked

Hurricane squadrons and locations, August 1942		
SQUADRON	LOCATION	MARK
6 Squadron	LG 89	IID
33 Squadron	Idku	IIC
73 Squadron	Shandur	IIC
80 Squadron	LG 92	IIC
94 Squadron	El Gamil	I/IIC
127 Squadron	LG 172	IIB
173 Squadron	Heliopolis	I
208 Squadron	LG 100	I/IIA/IIB/IIC
213 Squadron	Kilo 8	IIA/IIC
237 Squadron	Qaiyara (Iraq)	I
238 Squadron	LG 92	IIB/IIC
274 Squadron	LG 88	IIB/IIC
335 Squadron	Idku	I/IIB
451 (RAAF) Squadron	El Bassa	I
1 (SAAF) Squadron	Maaten Bagush	IIB
7 (SAAF) Squadron	LG 89	I/IIB
40 (SAAF) Squadron	El Firdan	IIB

but, equally, Rommel's supply line could not keep up with his swift advance. Partly, this was because the outstanding work carried out by the RAF's anti-shipping crews, operating out of Malta, stopped Rommel's vital supplies reaching North Africa. There was, once again, a period when neither side achieved any ground. This vital period gave the British a chance to re-group. Gen Bernard Montgomery was appointed in command of the British 8th Army, and he re-built his forces until superiority in numbers was on his side.

The Battle of El Alamein was launched on 19 October, with massive air support being provided by the DAF, which, by then, had some 100 squadrons available. Air superiority for the Allies was immediate, giving the Hurricanes relative freedom over the battle field. The Hurricane MkIID pilots of 6 Squadron, detached to LG 172, enjoyed their most successful day with their new aircraft type on 24 October, when they destroyed sixteen enemy tanks during the day. Operating from the same LG, the Hurricane MkIIDs of 7 (SAAF) Squadron enjoyed similar success as the Allies gained the same ground as quickly as they had lost it during the retreat only a matter of months before. Tobruk was re-gained on 13 November, and a few days later British fighters arrived in Martuba, from where they could safeguard the convoys to Malta, bringing to an end the siege of the island.

One of the most daring episodes during the Allied advance took place between 13-16 November 1942. As part of Operation *Chocolate*, a detachment of 36 Hurricanes MkIICs from 213 and 238 Squadrons, under the command of Wg Cdr Johnny Darween, DSO DFC, landed more than 100 miles (160km) behind the enemy lines and carried out attacks against the Italian and German forces retreating westwards. The detachment spent four days behind the lines, during which time it was reported to have destroyed more than fifteen aircraft and up to 300 vehicles, for the loss of just three Hurricanes.

As the battle of El Alamein was in full swing, Allied landings further along the northern coast of Africa were taking place during November 1942, as part of Operation Torch. Some of the air support for these landings was provided by the RAF operating out of Gibraltar, with more support being provided by the Fleet Air Arm. Included in the Fleet Air Arm's support were thirty Sea Hurricanes, operating from the Royal Navy's aircraft carriers in theatre. Some of the first Allied aircraft to land in Algeria were Hurricane MkIICs of 43 Squadron, which had deployed to Gibraltar from its home base at Kirton-in-Lindsey in preparation for the landings only a matter of days before. After the successful Allied landings, the squadron flew into the captured airfield at Maison Blanche on 8 November, from where it provided air cover for the British 1st Army and its supply ports.

The conclusion of Operation Torch was the eventual link-up of Allied forces with Montgomery's 8th Army, and the final confirmation of a great victory came on 23 January 1943 when the 8th Army entered Tripoli. Some of the last successes in North Africa went to Flt Sgt Don Beard, DFM, of 73 Squadron based at Gambut Main. Flying a Hurricane MkIIC in the night-fighter role, Beard destroyed two Junkers Ju 52s during the night of 9-10 May 1943, bringing his personal total to five. Just three days later, the war in the desert was over, as the final defeat of the Axis powers in North Africa was formally ended on 13 May 1943.

Once North Africa was in the hands of the Allies, the commanders looked to the invasion of Italy as the next vital step towards overall victory in Europe. The forthcoming Allied invasion of Europe across the English Channel would not be ready until June 1944, so it was considered important to open up a second front in the south as soon as possible, in order to help relieve the pressure on the Russians on the Eastern Front.

Fg Off 'Imshi' Mason, 274 Squadron, was the top-scoring Hurricane pilot in the desert war.

Fg Off (later Sqn Ldr) Ernest 'Imshi' Mason, DFC – 274 Squadron

Born in County Durham in July 1913, Ernest Mason joined the RAF in 1938. Although he was originally posted to fly bombers with 45 Squadron, he managed to change so that he could fly Gladiators with 80 Squadron. He was among the first pilots in the North African theatre to convert to the Hurricane in July 1940, and helped to form 274 Squadron.

During the First Libyan Campaign, which opened in December 1940, he was remarkably successful, and during the first two weeks he destroyed five Italian aircraft. By the end of the campaign in January 1941, he had brought his total to thirteen, including three CR42s in one sortie on 26 January, and had been awarded the DFC. He had also acquired the nickname 'Imshi', meaning 'scram' in Arabic, which he was known to shout at local Arabs from time to time.

In July 1941, Mason was promoted to the rank of squadron leader and given command of 261 Squadron on Malta. He led the squadron during the occupation of Iran in August 1941, bringing his total to fifteen on the 26th with the destruction of a Hawker Nisr over Iran; this proved to be the only RAF kill during the occupation. In January 1942, Mason returned to the Western Desert and was given command of 94 Squadron, which was re-equipping with Kittyhawks. While leading an attack against Martuba airfield on 15 February, he was shot down and killed.

CHAPTER EIGHT

The Far East

The Forgotten War

Those who served in the Far East have frequently referred to this campaign as the 'Forgotten War', and it is certainly true to say that the concentration of effort generally remained with the war in Europe. Despite the emergence of Japan as an aggressive power, the Far Eastern front was left almost completely open. When the Japanese attacked the United States Fleet at Pearl Harbor on 7 December 1941, an entire new front was opened, bringing with it the problems of fighting in a part of the world where the logistical difficulties were significant. At the time of the Japanese attack on Pearl Harbour, the RAF's contribution in the Far East was just eight squadrons, with a total of 170 front-line aircraft. This presence mainly consisted of Brewster Buffalos on Singapore Island, and Bristol Blenheims on the Malayan mainland, as well as some Lockheed Hudsons, Vickers Vildebeests and a handful of Consolidated Catalinas. Nevertheless, the situation in the Far East soon changed and air power would, once again, prove decisive in the final outcome of this campaign, with the Hurricane playing a major part.

The Japanese Advance

Problems for the RAF

For the RAF to stand any chance of countering the Japanese in the Far East, much

A classic view of a Hurricane carrying out an attack.

The Chindwin River, Burma, along which Hurricanes carried out many attacks against Japanese re-supply vessels, by day and night.

aircraft were out-performed by the Japanese Zero fighters. Although the improved marks of Spitfire might well have performed better, they were not available for the Far East, and the Hurricane was left to provide the last defence.

The Fall of Singapore, Sumatra and Java

Not only did the Japanese Zero have the advantage in performance over the Hurricane, it was also present in far greater numbers. The Hurricane pilots also lacked any early warning of Japanese raids, as the radar station at Mersing had been dismantled so that it did not fall into Japanese hands. On the 20th the squadron lost three pilots, followed by three more the following day, and a further three on the 22nd, with the additional loss of five Hurricanes. By the end of January 1942, Singapore was defended by just eight Hurricanes, which were all that remained of the squadron.

With the inevitable surrender of Singapore, the remaining Hurricanes of 232 Squadron were sent to Palembang on the island of Sumatra on 1 February, where they joined twenty-eight Hurricane MkI-IBs of 605 Squadron, which had been flown to the island from HMS *Indomitable* the week before. One of the auxiliary squadrons, 605, had sailed for the Far East in December 1941. By the time it arrived in theatre, Singapore was falling, so the squadron was sent instead to

was dependent on the vital supply chain to provide aircraft. The main problem was the vast distance from the UK and the fact that aircraft bound for the Far East had to transit through the Middle East. The air commanders had many difficulties with such limited resources, and it was not uncommon for urgently requested aircraft to be 'borrowed' by other equally desperate air commanders en route.

Given these problems for the RAF, in theory there was little to stop the Japanese forces carrying out a successful invasion of the Far East. They soon landed on the east coast of Malaya as part of the strategy to capture airfields during the thrust against the British Naval base at Singapore. At the time of the Japanese invasion of Singapore, just fifty-one Hurricanes were available, many still in crates, with not enough trained Hurricane pilots to fly them. Those aircraft still in crates were assembled as quickly as possible, and first flew in the defence of Singapore on 10 January 1942. These first Hurricanes had originally been destined for the Middle East, and had to be modified with tropical air filters. Unfortunately, although this modification enabled the Hurricane to operate in this new environment, it reduced the aircraft's overall performance in terms of rate of climb and top speed.

As a further response to the Japanese advance, a number of pilots and ground

crew from 17, 135 and 136 Squadrons, together with sixteen Hurricane MkIIBs, were sent to Singapore to join 232 Squadron, which had arrived in Singapore on 17 January 1942. The squadron's Hurricanes were immediately involved in countering Japanese air attacks and, although they enjoyed some success against the Japanese, their modified

Pilots of 30 Squadron at Ratmalana in 1942. This squadron was part of the reinforcements which arrived in Ceylon from the Middle East during March 1942.

Pilots of 5 Squadron in the makeshift 'ops' area, 1943. Pictured are (standing, left to right) Fg Off Mendizabel, Fg Off Souter, F/S Boyens, Plt Off Lawrence, Fg Off Lee, Sgt Parsons, and (sitting, left to right) Fg Off Snowball, F/S Worts, Fg Off Rashleigh.

Palembang, where it could be used in the defence of Sumatra.

Singapore had been the second major British base to be taken in the Far East, with Hong Kong having fallen a few weeks before. Although the RAF Hurricanes did their best to counter the Japanese advance, it was not long before Sumatra fell, and the Hurricanes of 232 and 605 Squadrons moved to Tjililitan in Western Java, where they joined with 242 Squadron. All three squadrons combined on 25 February to continue the fight until almost all the Hurricanes were destroyed. Java finally fell during early March.

The RAF had suffered badly during the defence of Singapore and Malaya. They had been unprepared to meet such a threat, with the concentration of effort being needed closer to home. What did emerge from the losses was that the Hurricane had already proved itself, having been credited with over 100 kills (for the loss of less than half that number). However, it had arrived in theatre too late, and in too small numbers, to make any difference to the overall outcome of the battle.

The Hurricane would soon arrive in significant numbers in the Far East, and eventually became the workhorse of the air war in that region.

The Retreat from Burma

The British had long recognized the importance of Burma, as any further advances of the Japanese army towards India would have to pass through its plains; it represented a natural barrier which extended from the Himalayas to the Malayan Peninsular. Initially, the only aircraft available for the defence of Burma were a couple of dozen Brewster Buffaloes and Curtiss Tomahawks. Japanese air attacks against Burma had been under way since December, and the major RAF effort was concentrated on supporting the defence line along the river Salween, and on the defence of Rangoon.

Reinforcements soon began to arrive in Burma, providing Hurricanes for both of these tasks. They were also used to carry out attacks against Japanese airfields, and to provide air defence of attacking ground forces. Although there was a certain amount of success, losses were also increasing.

The desperation of the British at that time is indicated by the moves of the

Fg Off Lee with the squadron pet, 'Pip', outside a basha in 1943.

Pilots of 5 Squadron pose by one of the squadron's MkIICs early in 1944.

Hurricanes of 17 Squadron. Under the command of Sqn Ldr 'Bunny' Stone, the squadron had sailed from the UK during November 1941, originally heading for the Middle East. Born in India, Stone was a 'veteran', having joined the RAF in 1936. He had flown Hurricanes since 1938 and had served with 3 Squadron during the Battle of France, during which he was credited with three kills, bringing him the DFC. He flew Hurricanes with 263 Squadron, and was a flight commander with 245 Squadron during the Battle of Britain; at twenty-four years of age, he had been given command of 17 Squadron, in July 1941.

As the situation deteriorated in the Far East, 17 Squadron was diverted without ever going ashore. With the fall of Singapore, the squadron had been sent to Mingaladon on 16 January, with a detachment at Akyab. The airfield of Mingaladon was situated on the northern outskirts of Rangoon, and was right in the forefront of fighting. Although the

squadron had plenty of pilots, it was under-established in its number of Hurricanes. It had no more than ten to twelve aircraft, and a very limited amount of spares and maintenance tools.

The squadron was mainly equipped with Hurricane MkIIAs, but it had managed to 'acquire' the occasional MkIIB fitted with long-range fuel tanks. These fuel tanks offered increased range and endurance – the Hurricane could effectively double its normal radius of action of about 150 miles (240km) – but they could not be jettisoned. In fact, the external fuel tanks proved to be a problem for the pilots during short-notice scrambles, when the aircraft was unable to climb rapidly to height. Nevertheless, the squadron scored some notable successes, with 'Bunny' Stone leading from the front, bringing his total number of kills to six by the end of January, and subsequently being awarded a bar to his DFC.

The Hurricanes offered as much resistance as possible, but the Japanese advance seemed unstoppable, and Rangoon was evacuated on 7 March. It was recognized that the situation was desperate, and the Hurricanes were withdrawn 250 miles (400km) north, to Magwe airfield on the banks of the Irrawaddy in Central Burma.

Although the conditions at Magwe were very basic, the squadron appreciated a pleasant break from the constant hassle of life around Rangoon. They were generally down to not much more than a handful of serviceable Hurricanes on any one day (eight at best), but still managed daily to fly up to thirty sorties. For a few days, the squadron did not come under attack on the ground, but the Japanese advance soon continued further north. The lack of facilities meant that the squadron had to provide its own early-warning system, by keeping one Hurricane in the air

Left: **Pilots relaxing outside one of the squadron's bashas: (left to right) Bill Souter, Keith MacEwan, Rudi Mendizabal, Johnny Lee and Paddy Chancellor.**

Lashio for just a few days, before the Japanese advance once again caught up, leaving the squadron with no alternative but to withdraw to India by any possible means. The defence of Burma was over.

Stabilizing the Burma Front

By April 1942, the surviving air assets in the Far East, including the few remaining Hurricanes, were based in India, where they were able to carry out operations over the Burma Front. For the time being, the Burma Front stabilized and attention turned to other possible Japanese options. Such was the strength of the Japanese Navy, one of the options for the Japanese forces was to carry out an invasion of India from the sea. The island of Ceylon was in a position to prevent this, but only if the air assets could be built up to a sufficiently high level. Airfields were constructed at Ratmalana and China Bay in Ceylon, and reinforcements soon began to arrive. Two of these squadrons were Hurricanes of 30 Squadron (at Ratmalana) and 261 Squadron (at China Bay), which had been brought in from the Middle East on HMS Indomitable. They arrived in Ceylon just in time to help counter the first Japanese air attacks on the island during the next few weeks.

Build-Up of RAF and IAF Squadrons

The monsoon rains arrived towards the end of April, bringing to a halt the Japanese advance in Northern Burma. With the Burma Front stabilized, and the possibility of invading India gone for the time being, Japan consolidated its forces in the area and concentrated on holding its strong position in Burma throughout the remainder of 1942. This period gave the RAF valuable time to re-organize and re-supply. During the retreat to India, the RAF had been at its lowest ebb in the Far East, with the remnants of just five operational squadrons. One of the immediate tasks was to increase the number of squadrons as quickly as possible, and throughout 1942 the RAF's commitment in the Far East increased as a plan to

throughout daylight hours to warn of likely intruders. It was not long before air attacks began again, and the few remaining Hurricanes were moved another 200 miles (320km) north to

Lashio. For the ground crews and the remaining pilots, it was a matter of taking the long journey to safety by any vehicle possible on the long road to Mandalay.

The remnants of 17 Squadron flew from

RAF Hurricane squadrons in the Far East, April 1942		
SQUADRON	LOCATION	MK
17 Squadron	Pankham Fort	IIB
30 Squadron	Ratmalana	IIB
67 Squadron	Alipore	IIB
135 Squadron	Dum Dum	IIB
136 Squadron	Alipore	IIB/IIC
258 Squadron	Colombo Racecourse	IIB
261 Squadron	China Bay	IIB

re-take Burma was formulated. By June, the total number of squadrons had increased to twenty-six, including eleven Hurricane squadrons.

In addition to the build-up of RAF forces in the Far East, the Indian Air Force (IAF) was expanding. The RAF had policed the skies of the North West Frontier during the inter-war years and had provided the only air power in the region until 1933. Although there were limited resources for the Indian Government at that time, it soon recognized the need to develop its own force; 1 Squadron IAF was formed with Westland Wapitis in April 1933. Training was carried out in the UK, but at the outbreak of the Second World War there was still just one IAF squadron. The Japanese attack in the Far East led to the formation of more squadrons, although these were initially equipped with older aircraft. The fall of Burma brought better equipment to the region and the first two IAF squadrons – 1 Squadron IAF at Trichinopoly, and 2 Squadron IAF at Arkonam – began to equip with Hurricanes in September 1942. (Incidentally, the prefix 'Royal' was not officially added to the IAF until March 1945.)

Plans to re-take Burma continued to be formulated during 1942, as the build-up of forces in the region continued. The first part of the plan was to capture the airfields on the island of Akyab as part of the First Arakan campaign, launched on 9 December. Hurricanes continued to arrive in theatre in increasing numbers, replacing less capable aircraft such as the Blenheim, and were included in this campaign, although the lack of air support brought a relatively unsuccessful conclusion.

By June 1943, the RAF had built up a force of some 700 Hurricanes in the Far East, which equipped a total of twenty-three front-line squadrons; these were generally all MkIIs, although some MkIVs had by that time arrived in Ceylon. A true multi-role aircraft, capable of carrying out fighter, reconnaissance or bombing duties, the Hurricane was ideal for jungle operations. In particular, it was in the air-to-ground role that the aircraft proved most useful. Its speed was slow enough to give the pilot maximum manoeuvrability in the target area, but fast enough to get him

out of trouble. The airframe was strong and sturdy enough to withstand ground fire and, on many occasions, pilots were able to take Hurricanes back to base, when other aircraft might not have survived.

5 Squadron, June 1943 – June 1944

Since the outbreak of the Second World War, 5 Squadron had been located in the Far East. When war broke out with Japan, the squadron moved to Calcutta, where it operated Audaxes in the air defence role. Due to the lack of adequate fighters in the region, the squadron re-equipped with Curtiss Mohawks, and moved to Assam in May 1942 to provide air defence and fighter escort for attacks against northern Burma.

At Khargpur

On 1 June 1943, the advanced party of 5 Squadron arrived at Khargpur from Agartala in preparation to receive Hurricanes. The main party of twenty-five vehicles left No 221 Group headquarters in Calcutta the following day, and arrived at Khargpur that evening. By 5 June, its headquarters was fully established and the squadron was

Although the Hurricane MkIID proved that it was capable of penetrating the armour of Japanese tanks, it served primarily in the Western Desert, and only served with 5 and 20 Squadrons during the campaign in the Far East.

Officers of 5 Squadron.

ready to receive its new Hurricane MkIIDs. Conditions were generally good, although the weather was becoming increasingly hot, with storms every evening. The squadron's basha accommodation (constructed of woven reed) had to be made fully rain-proof, and 'luxuries' such as water pumps had to be erected. One main aim was to prevent diseases such as cholera, which was epidemic in some surrounding districts (particularly Calcutta), and all the squadron's personnel were inoculated accordingly.

On 12 June, four officers left Khargpur in one of 31 Squadron's C47 transport aircraft, bound for Allahabad to collect the first of the squadron's new Hurricane MkIIDs. The four officers, Sqn Ldr Hogan, Flt Lt Courtney-Clarke, Fg Off Mendiza-bal and Plt Off Lawrence, delivered the first four Hurricanes to Khargpur during the next couple of days. Various lectures had been given to the squadron pilots and ground crews about the MkIID and its armament. Fitted with two 40mm cannons and two 0.303in Brownings, a squadron of Hurricane MkIIDs represented a potent amount of firepower; its cannon was capable of penetrating the armour of the Japanese Type 95 light tank. The

squadron's pilots still had much to do, including learning new tactics and the

Sqn Ldr G.J.C. Hogan	Fg Off C Courtney-Clarke
Flt Lt Rashleigh	Fg Off N.M. Beyts
Fg Off W.J.N. Lee	Fg Off Mendizabel
Fg Off Ryde	Fg Off B. Snowball
Fg Off W.M. Souter	Fg Off L.D. Thomas
Plt Off W.S.S. Garnett	Plt Off R. Lawrence
Plt Off Seifert	Plt Off A.B. Skidmore
W/O B.A. Ferguson	W/O R. McLauchlan
F/S G.I. Baines	F/S R. Boyens
F/S Morgan	F/S Stafford
F/S E.R. Worts	Sgt B.P. Case
Sgt F.A. Gore	Sgt D. Parsons
Sgt Sweeting	Sgt Watt.

best way to employ the MkIID against the enemy. A short course in army co-operation (known as the Hurricane 'A' course) was run at Simla, where pilots were taught how to support the troops on the ground in the forward fighting areas. Allowances had to be made for the Hurricane's firing parameters (such as speed, dive angle and wind) if the pilot was to be successful in the art of air-to-ground gunnery. Although speed and dive angle could be determined by the pilot, he was not always aware of the wind in the target area. One method used by the squadron to

aid the air-to-ground technique was to fit tracer rounds in the Brownings and use these for sighting, leaving the much more potent 40mm cannon to do the damage.

The Pilots

On 16 June, eight more of the squadron's pilots flew the Hurricanes for the first time to get used both to the aircraft and to the local area. By the end of the month, all the pilots had become familiar with the new type and were ready for operations. The pilots of 5 Squadron in Khargpur in June 1943 are shown left:

Operations and Detachments

The first operations of 5 Squadron took place on the morning of 1 July, when nine cross-country reconnaissance sorties were flown. Similar sorties were flown during the rest of the week, without incident, as the squadron continued to familiarize itself with the Hurricane MkIID and the local area. The first air-to-ground firings of the 40mm cannons took place on the 8th. As the commanding officer, Sqn Ldr Hogan, fired his first burst, a wing panel flew off his aircraft and he had to return to base. At first, witnesses thought it was the wing that had fallen off, but were relieved to see that this was not the case! Having returned to base for rectification, Hogan took off again, and was more successful during this second attempt. One other Hurricane, flown by Fg Off Thomas, also carried out a successful firing, although the aircraft flown by Plt Off Baines suffered a stoppage in the starboard cannon.

During the following days, more firings took place against ground targets and into the sea. There was an increasing number of early problems with the 40mm cannon, such as runaways (when the gun would not stop firing after the pilot released the trigger), and on 14 July the squadron received an engineering order to remove the 40mm cannons temporarily from the MkIIDs. These problems would eventually be sorted out, although it would be a further six months before the squadron could use the gun operationally.

Operations continued without the 40mm cannon. The squadron replaced some of its MkIIDs with MkIICs, and continued to operate both variants together. The early operational sorties flown by the squadron during July 1943 were reconnaissance sorties generally lasting one hour. By the end of July 1943, 5 Squadron had sixteen MkIICs and MkIIDs on strength, as follows:

HW801	HW878	KW745
KW794	KW859	KW865
KW867	KW871	KW873
KW879	KW896	KW898
KX121	KX226	KX228
KX229		

Although the airstrip at Khargpur was perfectly adequate for Hurricane operations, there was the occasional hazard to the pilots. Operating from these basic airstrips in the Far East always caused problems as heavy rainstorms would often make the ground difficult. During July, Plt Off Boyens made a perfectly good landing, only to burst a tyre, which led to the aircraft leaving the runway and tipping nose-over in the soft, unprepared ground.

As in any operational theatre, squadron detachments were not uncommon. These detachments served a number of purposes: the squadron could fly more operational sorties over a larger area, as transit times to and from its main operating base were reduced; the pilots gained more experience in operating from different airstrips, and a greater knowledge of the areas over which they were flying; the squadron aircraft were dispersed, and any attack by opposing forces would have less overall effect. One such detachment was carried out by 5 Squadron in October, when six aircraft (three MkIICs and three MkIIDs) deployed to Ranchi. The detachment was led by Sqn Ldr Hogan and included Fg Off Lee, Fg Off Beyts, Plt Off Lawrence, W/O Worts and Sgt Case; the engineering and support personnel flew to Ranchi by DC3.

On 7 October, Fg Off John Lee led three Hurricanes in a sector reconnaissance as the first operational sorties of the detachment. During the detachment to Ranchi, the squadron took part in several liaison

Above: **Fg Off Johnny Lee, 5 Squadron, was a long-serving member of the squadron and led many attacks against the Japanese during the jungle war. Sadly, he was killed in 1944, after which his DFC was announced.**

Right: **A veteran of the Battle of Britain, Laurence Thorogood served in the Far East as flight commander with 9 Squadron IAF during 1944.**

The MkIIC proved an ideal platform for the war in the jungle and was the workhorse during the campaign in the Far East, serving with no less than twenty-five squadrons between 1942-45. Here, a pilot relaxes with his ground crew during a rest from operations.

visits and exercises with the Army. This would often mean flying simulated attacks against the anti-aircraft sites and various armoured convoys, to benefit the Hurricane pilots in air-to-ground strafe, and also instruct the Army in developing its defensive tactics. Although there was a requirement for two pilots to be on stand-by from dawn to dusk, there was little or no enemy activity before the detachment returned to Khargpur.

Following a brief stay at Amarda Road during December, the squadron moved to Sapam and almost immediately became more involved with more active operations against the Japanese. On the afternoon of 21 December, Flt Lt Sharpe led six MkIICs on an offensive reconnaissance sortie along the Chindwin River from Mawlaik to Paungbyin. The sortie took one hour and twenty minutes, and the Hurricanes attacked various canoes and rafts. This offensive was continued the following day, when Flt Lt Thomas led six Hurricanes along various roads in the areas of Yazagyo, Kalemyo, Kaiewa, Shwegyin, Pyingaing, Chinyaung, Mawtangyi, Indaw and Pantha; this time the sortie lasted two hours and fifteen minutes, during which various targets of opportunity were strafed.

The Hurricane MkII proved to be a versatile aircraft in the Far East campaign.

MkIIDs off the Arakan coast.

| Operating bases of 5 Squadron Hurricanes, June 1943 - September 1944 ||
OPERATING BASE	PERIOD
Khargpur	June - December 1943
Amarda Road	December 1943
Sapam	December 1943 - March 1944
Wangjing	March 1944
Lanka	March - June 1944
Dergaon	June 1944
Vizagapatam	June - September 1944
Yelahanka	September 1944

With the MkIIC capable, generally, of carrying two 250-lb or 500-lb bombs, pilots were often asked to carry out a variety of tasks. Its flexibility was evident two days later, when the next operational sortie, led by Sqn Ldr Hogan, involved six of 5 Squadron's Hurricanes providing fighter escort to Hurricane MkIICs of 42 Squadron. Operating out of Palel, 42 Squadron had been tasked to carry out a bombing attack against Pagoda Hill near Natchaung. Although one of 5 Squadron's Hurricanes had to return to Sapam with engine trouble, the remaining five aircraft successfully provided fighter escort to the target, and then carried out air-to-ground strafing of an ammunition dump.

By the new year, the problems with the 40mm cannons of the MkIID had been resolved, and the cannons were successfully used operationally for the first time on 8 January 1944, when the squadron destroyed twenty-seven Japanese lorries and other supporting vehicles. The squadron's tasks remained varied: during the week of 16-21 January, it carried out offensive river reconnaissance between Mawlaik and Pantha on the 16th, fighter cover for British ground troops at Kyaukchaw on the 18th, air-to-ground strafe of Japanese positions south-east of the Lophei ridge on the 20th, and bombing with specially designed petrol bombs against concentrations of Japanese rafts on the 21st.

The following month saw similar operations, as 5 Squadron continued its offensive against Japanese positions, particularly along the Chindwin River. One example of a successful day was 22 February. In the morning, Flt Lt Johnny Lee and Flt Sgt David Parsons carried out successful offensive reconnaissance sorties against the area of Kalemyo, resulting in the destruction of a loaded Sampan, as well as destruction of Japanese bashas at Myintha and Inbaung. Six more Hurricanes from the squadron carried out successful attacks against fifty-three Lundwins and one motor launch during an offensive reconnaissance sortie along the Chindwin River between Shwegyn, Mingin and Maukkadaw. During the afternoon, the same areas were visited by six more Hurricanes, led by Sqn Ldr Hogan. A total of thirty Lundwins, fourteen Sampans, two large rafts, one large barge and a small shipbuilding yard were strafed.

The pilots were keen to evaluate the success (or not) of the air-to-ground sorties. Whenever possible, a film night took place, when 16mm film from the Hurricane's camera was shown. The pilots were convinced of the importance of using the camera to prove their claims during the post-sortie debrief with the intelligence officer.

A Hurricane serving in the Far East, with typical markings of a single letter (with no squadron code), and small blue and white roundel on the fuselage.

Throughout the spring of 1944, the squadron's commitment at Sapam increased, with more and more incursions into Japanese-held territory. The normal daily routine was to provide at least twelve Hurricanes on readiness at first light; whenever possible this was increased to all available aircraft (up to sixteen). From readiness, the pilots would be tasked in groups of between two and six to carry out various sorties, depending on the requirement. This could be anything from reconnaissance sorties in support of the Army, to attacking convoys of armoured vehicles along tracks, or attacking vessels along the Chindwin River. Sorties were even flown at night when necessary. As many as twenty operational sorties in a day were flown, each generally lasting up to two hours.

In June 1944, the squadron was declared non-operational, and it retired to Ceylon for a well-earned rest from operations before converting to the Republic Thunderbolt in September.

Arakan and Imphal Campaigns

A Swing in the Balance of Power

The build-up of air assets in the Far East had continued throughout 1943, with more and better aircraft arriving in theatre, including more Hurricanes as well as the first Spitfire MkVs. With the continuing expansion of RAF forces, the size of a typical Hurricane squadron was sixteen or seventeen aircraft, with twenty or more pilots. Facilities were generally much improved, including better airfields and operating airstrips. However, it was still a war being fought very far away from home and, despite the improvements, conditions remained almost unbearable at times. In addition, supplies were still short, and news from home seemed to take for ever to arrive.

Nevertheless, the war went on. The combined Allied air forces began a

programme of air attacks against Japanese airfields in an effort to achieve air superiority. Each month, pilots would typically fly thirty operational sorties each, with the squadron achieving anything between 600 and 800 operational sorties. Operations included night attacks on ground targets and vehicles; the Hurricane pilots would get airborne by night, and follow known roads and tracks waiting for Japanese vehicles. Navigation over the jungle by day was bad enough, but by night it was even more difficult. The pilots very quickly become experts in river and waterway navigation, learning to follow these features, visible by day and by moonlight.

South East Asia Command (SEAC) was formed towards the end of the year, bringing together all British Commonwealth and American forces under the command of Adm Lord Louis Mountbatten. The aims of SEAC were primarily to carry out a strategic air offensive against the Japanese, as well as providing direct tactical support for the ground offensive, while maintaining a constant air supply to the troops on the ground. The total force of air power available to Mountbatten was more than 1,000 aircraft and, by now, the balance of air power in the region had swung in favour of the Allies. Yet, there was still much to be done to force the Japanese out of Burma; the nature of the terrain made it almost impossible at times to remove the enemy completely from any one area.

The Siege of Imphal

The Second Arakan campaign, carried out during late 1943 to early 1944, failed almost immediately, due to strong Japanese resistance. However, the Allies slowly established footholds and used air power to defend them. This tactic led to gradual success, although air battles around areas such as Imphal proved to be incredibly tense. This area, covering a large central plain located on the main route from Burma into India, was the scene of much aerial fighting during March 1944, as the Japanese carried out a brilliant countermove and tried to push back towards India. It was essential for the Allies to hold the plains of Imphal but, by the end of the month, some 150,000 men of the British 14th Army were surrounded by the Japanese.

Thirty miles (45km) to the north of Imphal, at Kohima, Allied forces were also surrounded and the siege of Imphal began. The only way to re-supply the ground forces

Hurricane squadrons serving in the Far East, September 1945		
Squadron	Location	Mk
20 Squadron	Amarda Road	IID/IV
28 Squadron	Mingaladon	IIC
1 Squadron RIAF	Kohat	IIB/IIC
2 Squadron RIAF	Willingdon	IIB
3 Squadron RIAF	Risalpur	IIC
4 Squadron RIAF	Yelahanka	IIC
6 Squadron RIAF	Kohat	IIC
7 Squadron RIAF	Lahore	IIC

was by air, and the transport crews flew long hours to keep the supply chain going. The skies were kept relatively clear of Japanese by the RAF's fighters maintaining local air superiority, and carrying out air strikes against Japanese positions. Allied ground forces within the siege areas were also able to make local raids against enemy positions, and by June it had became too difficult for the Japanese to hold the areas of Imphal and Kohima. By the end of June, the Imphal-Kohima Road was in Allied hands, and the tide of the ground war had swung in favour of the Allies. During the siege of Imphal, 5 Squadron had destroyed 705 enemy vehicles or wagons, ninety-eight river crafts, twenty-nine tanks, and four trains.

Allied Victory in the Far East

By the middle of the year, there were thirty-seven squadrons of Hurricanes operating in the Far East, the largest number of squadrons operating the type at any one time; indeed, in terms of numbers, the Hurricane proved to be the most employed aircraft in the Far East. In July, the British troops reached the Chindwin river in northern Burma and, from that time, more and more successes in Burma were achieved. The British began to force the Japanese back through Rangoon, with the RAF in the forefront of the attack. By the end of 1944, most squadrons had re-equipped with the new heavier American-built Republic P-47 Thunderbolt fighter. The remaining Hurricane squadrons were used primarily for air-to-ground duties, using GP bombs and rockets to destroy

A MkIIC (LD803) of No 10 Sqn IAF being turned round between sorties at Kyaukpyu in April 1945.

A MkII (LE947) of No 4 Sqn IAF pictured near Nagpur in February 1946.

ground targets and armoured vehicles, while Spitfires and Thunderbolts carried out fighter escort.

By the spring of 1945, an Allied victory in the Far East was in sight. Mandalay was re-captured during March, and this was followed six weeks later by air and sea landings around Rangoon. Although the air war in the Far East was all but over, the war on the ground would continue, as highly motivated Japanese forces made any progress on the ground painfully slow and costly. The remainder of the war was spent consolidating British positions in Burma and planning for the offensive into Malaya and back into Singapore; plans for this were cancelled following the Japanese surrender in August 1945, after the American atomic bomb attacks on Hiroshima and Nagasaki.

At the end of hostilities in the Far East there were still two RAF squadrons (as well as six Royal Indian Air Force squadrons) operating Hurricanes in front-line duties. This fact is significant – it means that the Hurricane served operationally throughout the Second World War, from day one in Europe right up to the cessation of hostilities in the Far East.

Gp Capt Frank Carey, CBE DFC** AFC DFM

Frank Reginald Carey was born in London on 7 May 1912. He joined the RAF in 1927 as an aircraft apprentice at Halton, before applying for pilot training in 1935. He joined 43 Squadron as a sergeant pilot in 1936 and flew Hawker Furys, before converting to the Hurricane in November 1938. Carey was still serving with the squadron at Tangmere at the outbreak of the Second World War and, within five months, had shared in the destruction of three enemy aircraft, bringing him the award of the DFM in March 1940.

Carey was then posted to 3 Squadron at Kenley and was soon commissioned. He moved across the Channel to take part in the Battle of France, where he distinguished himself beyond all others. During the five days of 10-14 May, he destroyed thirteen enemy aircraft, before being shot down; this remarkable achievement resulted in him being awarded the DFC and bar at the end of the month. He re-joined 43 Squadron as a flight commander, and served with this squadron throughout the Battle of Britain, bringing his personal tally to twenty kills, plus many more un-confirmed or damaged, before crash-landing on 18 August. As a result of his injuries, Carey was rested from operations. When he was fit to fly again, he carried out instructional duties before being posted to form and command 135 Squadron at Baginton in August 1941; once the squadron was declared operational, it was sent to the Far East.

The squadron arrived in Burma in January 1942, and was first based at Zayatkwin, before moving to Mingaladon at the end of the month. Carey was soon in action and his personal score began to increase; he claimed his first Japanese victim within the first few

days of arriving at Mingaladon. He was promoted to the rank of wing commander in February and took over command of 267 Wing, continuing to lead from the front. By the end of February 1942, Carey had brought his personal tally to at least twenty-five kills, all achieved in Hurricane MkIs and MkIIBs. The true significance of Carey's achievement will probably never be known, but the second bar to his DFC was well overdue when it was finally announced in March 1942.

Following the retreat from Burma, Carey was given command of RAF Alipore in India before being given a staff appointment at the Air Headquarters at Bengal. Early in 1943, he formed the Air Fighting Training Unit (AFTU) at Amarda Road, where he was responsible for the training of British, Commonwealth and American pilots destined to continue the air war over Burma. Finally, in November 1944, he was posted away from the Far East as a group captain, assuming command of No 73 Operational Training Unit at Fayid in Egypt. For his outstanding contribution to the war in the Far East, Frank Carey was awarded the AFC and the American Silver Star.

At the end of the war, Carey returned to the UK and carried out various staff appointments. Reverting to the substantive rank of wing commander, he commanded 135 Wing in Germany and flew Tempests until 1949. After further staff appointments, he retired from the RAF in 1960 as a group captain, having been made a Commander of the British Empire. He worked for Rolls-Royce in Australia before returning to the UK, and retirement. The contribution of Frank Carey to the war in the Far East was, without doubt, second to none.

CHAPTER NINE

Europe

Although the Battle of Britain officially ended at the end of October 1940, Britain was far from secure. The heroics of the Few had ensured, for the time being, that Britain was safe from invasion, but the bitter air fighting over southern England did not end.

The Struggle Continues

At the end of the Battle of Britain, the RAF had thirty-four Hurricane squadrons based in the UK, three of which had taken delivery of the new Hurricane MkIIAs by the end of the year. By the beginning of 1941, fourteen squadrons were equipped with MkIIAs or MkIIBs, and the first MkI-ICs were delivered in April. By the summer of 1941, the number of squadrons operating MkIIs had increased to twenty-four; in addition, the first modified MkIIs with tropical air filters had been sent to the Mediterranean theatre.

Raids

The UK-based Hurricane squadrons were mainly involved in various operations across the Channel, such as sweeps and intruder missions. These raids, by day or night, were generally of small numbers and against either selected targets or targets of opportunity; those known as 'Rhubarbs', for example, may have involved just four aircraft. The larger squadron raids were known as 'Rodeos', and the wing raids as 'Rangers'. If the target was shipping in the Channel or in port, the missions were known as 'Roadsteads'. Hurricanes were also used to escort light bombers, such as Blenheims, during raids across the Channel; such a raid was known as a 'Circus' or a 'Ramrod', depending on the bombers' objectives.

Air-to-Air Combat

However, despite the Hurricane fulfilling its new role as a ground-attack aircraft, the bitter air-to-air combat continued throughout the winter of 1940–41. Its

A pilot of 56 Squadron, aided by his ground crew, prepares for a sortie.

ferocity is summed up in this account by Fg Off Pat Wells of 249 Squadron at North Weald. During the afternoon of 28 November 1940, Wells was flying as 'weaver' over Kent. His recollection is as follows:

The position of 'weaver' meant that you flew some 1,000 feet above the squadron and gave warning of an attack or threatening enemy fighters above. Obviously, weaving above the others, you used higher throttle settings and thus more fuel, to add to your worries. It was, in any case, a suicidal position – they all went for you first! As a result, only experienced pilots with good eyes were used. Unfortunately, I fitted both requirements.

It was a bright sunny afternoon and there was a lot of enemy activity over Kent, so we were wide awake, me in particular through previous clashes with Bf 109s. Half way through the patrol at 23,000 feet, I was watching some Bf 109s, some in the sun, but at that time they posed no threat to us and I guessed that the other pilots had seen them anyway so there was no need to alarm anybody. The next thing I

Fg Off Pat Wells, 249 Squadron, taken in 1940 before his encounter with Luftwaffe ace Adolf Galland, on 28 November.

Fg Off Pat Wells (right) pictured after his return to 249 Squadron in 1941. The other two pilots are Plt Off R.H. Munro (left) and Plt Off A.R. Thompson (centre).

knew was an attack from below. I took evasive action and howled on the R/T but nobody heard me nor saw the attack, which was a lethal one. I was able to take some evasive action until my controls were shot away. My Hurricane was well alight but I could see tracer bullets going over the left wing and hear bullets rattling against the armour plate at the back of my seat, so there was no point in baling out into that lot. And so, I sat and fried. He eventually left me diving vertically.

One gets dopey from flames, smoke and lack of oxygen, so my first attempt to get out was a failure – my right foot got caught under the instrument panel. I climbed back in and tried

Although enemies on 28 November 1940, Pat Wells (left) and Adolf Galland became lifelong friends, and are pictured here at a gathering of the Luftwaffe Fighter Pilots Association in September 1995, shortly before Galland died.

again, but this time my left foot got caught. A Hurricane diving vertically and on fire is not easy to exit! As I had earlier seen the suffering of burned pilots in hospitals, I didn't want to be burned so I decided 'to hell with this – I'll go in with the aeroplane'. A lot closer to the ground than I would normally have chosen, I was miraculously thrown out of the cockpit. To prove its reluctance to lose me, and because of its vertical state, the tail of the aircraft hit me and dislocated my left shoulder. However, I still had my right hand to pull the ripcord and this I did. Sheets of skin were hanging from my face and legs and the cold really stung the open nerve ends. I landed in an apple tree, which was prickly without its leaves, adding to my discomfort when falling through it.

I was taken to Leeds Castle Emergency Hospital, near Maidstone in Kent, where I spent a week. All burned pilots were taken to Queen Victoria Hospital at East Grinstead where Archie McIndoe did marvellous work on his so-called 'guinea pigs'. I could smell roast pork for weeks afterwards. I made a good recovery – so good, in fact, that the RAF, being short of pilots, had me back flying within three months.

Pat Wells had been shot down by the famous Luftwaffe pilot Adolf Galland of JG26. In his combat report, Galland stated that he had fired 132 machine-gun rounds and 64 cannon shells during the engagement; under 'fate of enemy pilot' he had written the comment, 'Dead by burning'!

Gallant Poles

As the Spitfire became more available, several Hurricane squadrons, many of them the 'foreign' squadrons, were converted to it. One example was 303 Squadron, the famous Polish unit. Towards the end of the Battle of Britain, the squadron had been retired to Leconfield in Yorkshire for a well-earned rest from operations, and converted soon after to Spitfires. The other Polish units flew the Hurricane for several more months. With 303 Squadron's move north, 302 Squadron moved south to replace it for the final days of the battle; it remained there until May 1941, when it moved to Jurby on the Isle of Man, where its Hurricane MkIs took part in convoy protection. Defensive duties were carried out briefly by 308 and 315 Squadrons, operating Hurricanes at Baginton and Speke until the spring of 1941. Both 316 and 317 Squadrons were equipped with MkIIAs and MkIIBs, with units carrying out convoy patrols, offensive sweeps and bomber escort over France during the summer.

In the same period, 317 Squadron was based at Fairwood Common, led by two of Poland's most famous fighter pilots: commanding the squadron was Sqn Ldr Stanislaw Brzezina, and his senior flight commander was Flt Lt Henryk Szczesny.

One of the many gallant Poles to serve with Fighter Command during the war was Henryk Szczesny, who flew Hurricanes as a flight commander with 317 Squadron at Exeter, and was then given command of the squadron in August 1941.

F/L Henryk Szczesny, 317 Squadron, with his personal Hurricane 'Hesio', and ground crew.

Brzezina, who took command of the squadron. A few weeks later, on 10 July, both pilots destroyed Bf 109s while escorting Blenheims during a daylight raid against Le Havre and Cherbourg. Four days later, Szczesny brought his total to seven by destroying a Ju 88, bringing him a third bar to his Cross of Valour, and a DFC. At the end of the month, the squadron moved to Exeter; Brzezina was given command of 2 Polish Wing (consisting of 302, 316 and 317 Squadrons), and Szczesny took command of 317 Squadron and was awarded the Polish Virtuti Militari.

By the end of the year, all of the Polish squadrons had converted to Spitfires, as had the two Czech squadrons (310 and 312 Squadrons) and the Norwegian 331 Squadron.

Conversion to Spitfires

The first 'Eagle' squadron (formed with volunteers from the US) was 71 Squadron, which had received its first Hurricane MkIs at Kirton-in-Lindsey towards the end of 1940. In May 1941, the second 'Eagle' squadron, 121 Squadron, also formed at Kirton-in-Lindsey, and 133 Squadron formed at Coltishall in August. The three 'Eagle' squadrons flew defensive patrols throughout 1941 before they all converted to the Spitfire before the end of the year.

On 1 March 1941, 1 Squadron RCAF at Driffield, and 2 Squadron RCAF at Digby in Lincolnshire, were re-numbered as 401 and 402 Squadrons respectively, both based at Digby. Initially equipped with Hurricane MkIs, and later MkIIAs and MkIIBs, the squadrons were initially used for air defence but later carried out offensive sweeps over France. In September, 401 Squadron converted to Spitfires, while 402 Squadron moved south and carried out fighter-bomber attacks over France until March 1942, when it also converted to Spitfires.

Night Fighter

The Hurricane served in almost every wartime role imaginable, and it especially proved itself as ideal for an early night

Both men had served in the Polish Air Force during the German invasion of September 1939, and both had fled through France to Britain. They were both posted to 74 Squadron at Hornchurch in August 1940, and flew Spitfires during the Battle of Britain. Known together as 'Breezy' and 'Sneezy', the two men became most popular members of the squadron and excellent fighter pilots.

Szczesny was posted to 317 Squadron in April 1941, and was followed in June by

Czech sergeant pilots of 245 Squadron, (left to right) Sgts Srom, Baumann and Cap.

Hurricanes of 71 Squadron at Kirton-in-Lindsey; this was the first so-called 'Eagle Squadron' and was made up from volunteers from the United States.

A night-fighter Hurricane of 87 Squadron about to get its own flypast at Charmy Down.

Sqn Ldr Ian Gleed DFC commanded 87 Squadron throughout the first winter of night-fighter operations during 1940-41

fighter. Before airborne radars were fitted into fighters, the early techniques involved setting up a combat patrol, using moonlight to aid visual acquisition, in areas where intruders were likely to probe. Other early techniques involved the night-fighter pilot setting up an orbit over enemy airfields, and waiting for aircraft to return before taking them by surprise!

Adapting to Night Flying

The Hurricane was used operationally as a

night fighter as early as 1940. The failure of the Luftwaffe to bomb Britain to defeat by day led to a new campaign of night-bombing attacks against targets in southern England. With no specific training to convert the day-fighter pilot into a night-fighter pilot, this proved to be another new challenge for those flying the Hurricane. They trained by flying at night as much as possible, and carrying out practice interceptions against each other. They were trying to get a feel of what an attack at night looked like, and to get used to assessing ranges in order to shoot down enemy aircraft. The pilot also had to get used to night navigation when flying over

blacked-out countryside.

One of the first squadrons to convert to this new role was 87 Squadron, which had fought with distinction during the battles of France and Britain. During the summer of 1940, the squadron had taken part in night defensive patrols from its base at Exeter. In November, it had moved temporarily to Colerne and, during the following month, it moved to a small airfield at Charmy Down, a new satellite airfield of Colerne, near Bath. Another Hurricane squadron to form as a night-fighter unit was 96 Squadron at Cranage, with the appropriate motto of *Nocturni Obambulamus*, meaning 'we prowl by night'.

Life for the Hurricane pilot as a night fighter was completely different from that with which he was familiar. There were obvious hazards involved in operating out of dimly lit airfields at night. Taxiing the Hurricane often proved difficult even by day, and in the dark there were many cases of ground accidents. Once airborne, the night-fighter pilot had to adapt to very different tactics. Instead of operating as a flight of three within a squadron of aircraft, which he would do by day, he had to learn to hunt alone. A typical night of operations involved spending many hours in a dark hut, with little or no heating, before being scrambled to patrol a line somewhere over the south of England. The

A unit which fought with such distinction during the campaign in Greece was No 80 Sqn.

patrol height for the Hurricane would typically be about 10–12,000 feet (3–3600m), with the weather varying from a clear moonlit night, to thick cloud and far from perfect weather conditions.

The Hurricane was not fitted with any electronic homing devices, so the pilot had to revert to basic stopwatch and compass navigation techniques at night. His task of patrolling was easier on clear nights, when he could follow the patrol line, marked by bright flares on the ground, at 10-mile (16-km) intervals. If the night was not clear, or if the flares were not visible to the pilot, he had to rely totally on timed runs using his stopwatch and compass, turning about at the end of each timed leg on to the reciprocal heading. It should have been possible for the pilot to obtain a navigation fix of his position by using triangulation from voice transmissions, but the Hurricane's TR.9 radio proved to be unreliable, and sensitive to poor atmospheric conditions. At the end of a typical patrol of one and a half hours, the wind would have had quite an effect and it was not uncommon for the pilot to be temporarily unsure of his position.

The Hurricane pilots made certain modifications to their aircraft. The aircraft were painted in a matt black paint scheme, but some more subtle changes were made in an attempt to gain any advantage over the German bombers. The rear-view mirrors were useless at night, so these were removed, in order to reduce drag and increase the overall speed of the aircraft. The bright cockpit lighting was replaced

Above: **Hurricanes and pilots of 249 Squadron at North Weald, April 1941.**

Left: **The scene in 1941 was not very different from that of the year before; pilots of 245 Squadron find time to relax between sorties.**

Above: **Hurricane MkIs of 245 Squadron at Aldergrove, Northern Ireland, May 1941.**

Right: **The artwork on the fuselage of the Hurricane flown by the ace Sqn Ldr John Simpson, DFC and bar, during his time in command of 245 Squadron in 1941.**

by dimly lit red lights, to help preserve the pilot's night vision. In addition, small rectangular shields were fitted horizontally just forward of the cockpit, to reduce the glare from the exhausts.

Any advantage over the enemy bomber helped, but the Hurricane pilot still had to find his target and shoot it down. He had to rely on his eyesight in difficult weather conditions, hoping to pick up the silhouette of a bomber against the background fires in target areas. Sometimes he was lucky enough to get a glimpse of the exhaust flames from the engines of an enemy bomber, or to be supported by searchlights, which could follow a bomber long enough to allow him to pick up the aircraft visually, and then close within range to shoot it down. Shooting the bomber down was another problem within itself. The bright aiming graticule of the Hurricane gunsight was difficult to use at night, so the pilot had to get a feeling for

what looked about right.

The odds were certainly against the Hurricane pilot at night. There were very few interceptions during the winter of 1940-41, but the fact that the Hurricane night fighters were there must have been an unpleasant thought for any attacking German bomber. During the early months of 1941, the night-fighter pilots changed

their tactics. Finding an enemy bomber at night was proving difficult, as the pilot had little or no idea of where to look. He knew the likely targets, but was unsure from which direction the attack would take place. The pilots knew the airfields in France from where the attacks were being launched, so the idea was formulated to take the war back across the Channel. The

MkIICs of 3 Squadron, September 1941.

Combat report from Red and Green Sections of 245 Squadron, September 1941.

plan was simple, although its execution was rather more daring; the Hurricane was to set up an orbit above a German airfield and wait for the bombers to take off or return home.

This tactic often resulted in shooting down a bomber after it had attacked its target, but it did prove more successful. Any kills achieved using the new tactic made the risk of orbiting German airfields at night worthwhile. The pilots were also briefed to attack targets of opportunity in France, rather than return back to base full of ammunition. Pilots learnt to look for any ground targets and the Hurricane soon became useful in night ground-attack. The Hurricane was the first single-seat single-engined fighter of the war to carry out night ground-attacks when aircraft of 87 Squadron carried out various attacks in northern France in spring 1941. And their targets at night were not limited to air or land. Occasionally, Hurricanes returning across the Channel would catch a glimpse of a German E-Boat, or other enemy shipping, and attack it; anything that came

under the category of 'the enemy' was fair game.

A Dedicated Night Fighter

What had begun as a conversion for night-fighter operations had resulted in the Hurricane proving itself as an excellent platform in any role. The effectiveness of the 0.303in machine-guns was questionable, but the versatility of the Hurricane was not. With heavier armament, the Hurricane pilots knew that they would be able to achieve much more; their ambitions were realized, with the introduction into service of the Hurricane MkIIC.

The potential of the MkIIC as a dedicated night fighter was explored further during trials, when an air intercept (AI) radar was fitted into a pod carried under the wing. To balance the extra weight, a 44-gallon fuel tank was fitted under the other wing. This trial seems to have been partially successful, and a number of Hurricanes were fitted with AI MkVI radars and served in the Far East with 176 Squadron during 1943. However, the concentration of effort went into developing the AI radar-equipped Beaufighter as a dedicated night fighter. The AI radar became the crew's eyes at night and a well-trained operator could talk his pilot into an ideal attacking position. The introduction of radar into service changed the entire concept of fighter operations at night, and meant that no bomber would ever be safe, whatever the time of day or night, or the weather conditions.

Greece, 1941

Italy had entered the war on 10 June 1940 and, in an attempt to influence the war in the Balkans, Italian forces invaded Greece from Albania on 28 October. In response to Greek requests, British air and land forces were despatched from Egypt, bringing the British advance in Egypt to a halt – a political point that has been debated ever since. On the other hand, the fact that Hitler committed his forces to the campaign in the Balkans and Greece reduced his capability during the German advance in Russia, so the debate goes on.

Reinforcements

The initial RAF response was to send two squadrons of Blenheims, plus a squadron of Gladiators into theatre, to counter the Italian forces and to defend the area around Athens. The RAF squadrons enjoyed much success over the Italian Regia Aeronautica during the winter, but the RAF contribution had to be increased during early 1941 to meet the increasing threat of the German forces assisting the Italian effort. More RAF units – two squadrons of Blenheims and two squadrons of Hurricanes – were sent into theatre in Greece; 33 Squadron went to Eleusis, near Athens, on 19 February, where it was later joined by Hurricanes of 208 Squadron in the tactical reconnaissance role. The number of Hurricane squadrons was increased towards the end of February, when 80 Squadron, based at Iannina under the command of Sqn Ldr E.G. Jones, DSO DFC, exchanged its Gladiators for Hurricanes.

One of the first pilots to gain early success with the Hurricane was the young Australian Fg Off 'Ape' Cullen of 80 Squadron. Known as 'Ape' because of his size, Richard Nigel Cullen was born in New South Wales in June 1917. Having been brought up in England, he had joined

Commanding 87 Squadron during its night-fighting period of 1941-42 was Sqn Ldr Smallwood, who led a successful detachment to St Mary's in the Scillies, from where the squadron achieved a number of successes at night.

the RAF at the outbreak of war, and was originally sent out to the Middle East as a ferry pilot. He was posted to 80 Squadron in September 1940 and soon found himself in action. By the time the squadron converted to Hurricanes, Cullen had achieved six kills in the Gladiator, his last success in the type being on 23 February. He had to convert to the more powerful and more capable Hurricane with little or no formal instruction, and in a hostile environment, and his courage and skill are evident in the fact that he scored his first kill in the Hurricane, and became a Hurricane 'ace', just five days later. He destroyed an Italian BR20, two SM79s and two CR42s to the south of Valona, all in one day. This was a remarkable feat, and Cullen was rewarded with an immediate DFC. He followed this achievement up just three days later, with four more kills during one sortie on 3 March, when he and his wingman, Plt Off Acworth, intercepted five Cant Z1007 bombers which had just attacked Larissa. Cullen shot down four, with Acworth claiming the fifth. 'Ape' Cullen had proved himself a notable pilot, who adapted quickly to the Hurricane; he had nine confirmed kills in the Hurricane in the

Flt Lt Geoffrey Roscoe, aged 25, killed in February 1942 while serving with 87 Squadron at Charmy.

The Duke and Duchess of Gloucester during a royal visit to 245 Squadron. Many such visits were made to RAF squadrons during the war, serving to boost the morale of pilots and ground crews alike.

Pilots of 87 Squadron at Charmy Down, April 1942.

A pilot of 245 Squadron poses next to his Hurricane at Middle Wallop during the summer of 1942.

Sqn Ldr Smallwood (centre) and pilots of 87 Squadron gather beside one of the squadron's MkIICs at Charmy Down during 1942.

first week. Sadly, Cullen went out on patrol the next day and was attacked by a number of Fiat G50s; he was never seen again.

Two days later, 80 Squadron moved to Eleusis near Athens. The loss of Cullen was felt deeply by everyone on the squadron, but this gallant young pilot had set the pace with the Hurricane in theatre. The squadron, and the Hurricane, would go on to achieve much success in Greece

during the next few weeks.

The Germans now increased the pace. With continued plans for the advance on Russia, Hitler felt that it was necessary to secure the southern flank in the Balkans and, on 1 March, the Germans advanced into Bulgaria. This move was followed by the main advance in the Balkans just a few weeks later. Supported by Italy, Hungary and Bulgaria, the main German offensive against Greece and Yugoslavia began on 6

April 1941. The offensive took place across a front extending 400 miles (650km), and was opposed by less capable Greek and Yugoslav forces, supported by a small number of British forces. The result was a swift advance by the German forces through Yugoslavia and eastern Macedonia.

Aces over Greece

RAF Hurricanes were involved throughout the campaign in Greece. Although vastly outnumbered, the Hurricane pilots were responsible for the defeat of the Italian Regia Aeronautica in the skies over Greece and Crete, and for providing fighter cover for the troops on the ground against overwhelming German opposition. The air fighting during the first three weeks of April was as bitter as any, as the small number of Hurricane pilots fought against huge numbers of enemy aircraft. Several Hurricane pilots distinguished themselves during this period, none more so than the officer commanding 33 Squadron, Sqn Ldr 'Pat' Pattle, who became the RAF's top-scoring fighter pilot of the war before being killed on 20 April. While serving with 80 and 33 Squadrons during the Greek campaign, 'Pat' Pattle achieved more 'kills' in the Hurricane than any other pilot did.

It is probably no coincidence that another of the top-scoring Hurricane aces also achieved fame in the skies over Greece. In common with 'Pat' Pattle, Fg Off William Vale was a former Gladiator pilot serving with 80 Squadron, before converting to the Hurricane during the Greek campaign of early 1941. By this time he had a personal score of ten 'kills'. His first kill while flying the Hurricane came on 3 March, when he destroyed an Italian S81 to the west of Larissa. During the bitter air fighting over Greece and Crete during the German advance in the last two weeks of April (during which time 80 Squadron evacuated to Crete), Vale personally accounted for eleven German aircraft. This brought his personal score to twenty-three, thirteen of which were achieved while flying Hurricanes.

The beginning of May saw Vale and the other squadron pilots flying the handful of surviving Hurricanes in the defence of Crete. In the next two weeks of aerial fighting, Vale added four more to his tally, bringing him a well-deserved DFC and bar, as well as a Greek DFC, for his outstanding gallantry. In July, he was rested from

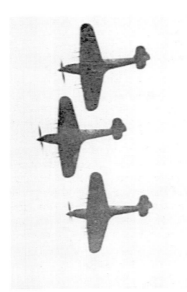

operations, having individually accounted for thirty enemy aircraft, plus many more 'shared' and 'probables'. Vale spent a period in the Middle East before returning to the UK in 1942.

The success of the Hurricane pilots during this period of March-April 1941 demonstrates their aerial dominance 'one-for-one' over the Italians and Germans in theatre. Pattle and Vale, for example, accounted for thirty-six enemy aircraft between them during April alone.

A MkIIC night fighter of 247 Squadron during 1942.

Inevitably, however, there were losses; Fg Off John Mackie of 33 Squadron was one victim, on 15 April. After shooting down a Messerschmitt Bf 109, he was shot down and killed during combat over Larissa airfield. This was a sad loss, as Mackie had been with the squadron since the previous year, and had already accounted for six enemy aircraft during the First Libyan campaign.

There were many valuable contributions from the Hurricane pilots in Greece; Flt Lt 'Woody' Woodward of 33 Squadron had a total of eighteen kills, fourteen in

Hurricanes; Sgt Ted Hewett of 80 Squadron was credited with sixteen kills, thirteen in Hurricanes; W/O Leonard Cottingham of 33 Squadron shot down three Messerschmitt Bf 110s over Piraeus on 20 April; Sgt 'Jumbo' Genders, also of 33 Squadron, destroyed a Messerschmitt Bf 109 and three Junkers Ju 87s on 23 April; and Fg Off Roald Dahl of 80 Squadron became an ace in the same theatre of operations, before becoming one of the best-known children's writers ever.

Surrender

The Germans and Italians had the advantage of much greater numbers, often in a ratio as high as twenty to one; this fact, and the significant advance on the ground, forced the Hurricanes back to just two airfields around Athens in mid-April 1941. On 17 April, Hurricanes of 208 Squadron arrived at Eleusis to carry out tactical reconnaissance sorties, a role they fulfilled for just a few days, before evacuating to Crete. It was left to the remaining Hurricanes of 33 and 80 Squadrons to maintain the air battle. The two squadrons had just fifteen Hurricanes serviceable between them, and these were led by Sqn Ldr 'Pat' Pattle during bitter aerial fighting over the next couple of days. Tragically, Pattle was shot down and killed on 20 April.

2 Squadron RCAF was re-numbered as 402 Squadron in March 1941. Here one of the squadron's MkIIBs (BE417) is loaded with 250-lb bombs prior to a sortie early in 1942.

Italian Regia Aeronautica. It is probable that the experience of most of these pilots in the Gladiator helped them, in fact, during the introduction of the Hurricane in February 1941. Only the presence of the Luftwaffe, with more capable fighters, raised the temperature of the air war over Greece, and the Hurricanes still managed to cause a major delay to the German advance in the region.

Home Front, 1941-42

UK-Based Squadrons

The number of UK-based squadrons equipped with the Hurricane had risen to more than forty during the summer of 1941. For the operational squadrons, the tasks mainly involved sweeps across the Channel, and fighter escort for light bombers during daylight raids. The Japanese attack on Pearl Harbour, and the subsequent advance, had opened up an entire new front, and a number of Hurricanes were crated up and sent out on ships to the Far East. By April 1942, nine Hurricane squadrons had been sent from the UK to the Far East (see Chapter 8). Reinforcements had also been sent to North Africa and the Middle East, with nine Hurricane squadrons being sent during the period from May 1941 to November 1942 (see Chapter 7).

Hurricane squadrons in Greece and Crete, January - May 1941		
SQUADRON	**LOCATION**	**DATE**
33 Squadron	Eleusis	19 Feb
	Larissa	4 Mar
	Eleusis	18 Apr
	Maleme, Crete	27 Apr - 1 Jun
80 Squadron	Iannina	17 Jan
	Eleusis	6 Mar
	Argos	21-25 Apr
208 Squadron	Eleusis	17 Apr
	Argos	22 Apr
	Maleme, Crete	24 Apr - 1 May

The Greek army surrendered on 23 April, and the remaining Hurricanes covered the evacuation of British forces from the region. By the following day, there were just five serviceable Hurricanes left and, in the absence of adequate reinforcements, and with a critical lack of air assets, these aircraft were forced to evacuate to Crete. This handful of Hurricanes from 33 and 80 Squadrons, plus some Fleet Air Arm Fairey Fulmars and Sea Gladiators, continued to provide air defence over Crete from the only two airfields, at Heraklion and Souda Bay. The force was reinforced by one or two Hurricanes a day arriving from Egypt. However, the defence of Crete soon became impossible, and the island fell to an assault by German paratroops during May. Even when the airfields of Crete were denied to them, the Hurricanes carried out long-range sorties across the Mediterranean from airfields in North Africa.

The Hurricane pilots involved in the air war in the skies over Greece have arguably never received enough recognition for

their achievement. They were hopelessly outnumbered and in a most desperate situation; the majority of pilots had to carry out the first part of the campaign in the old Gladiator biplane, but many still achieved remarkable success against the

During 1942, a Hurricane MkI (L1884) was fitted with a second 'jettisonable' upper wing as an experiment in generating more lift during take-off; however, the project was soon cancelled.

Above: **Pilots of 245 Squadron enjoy a moment of fun.**

Left: **Operations board and cartoons of 'A' Flight, 245 Squadron.**

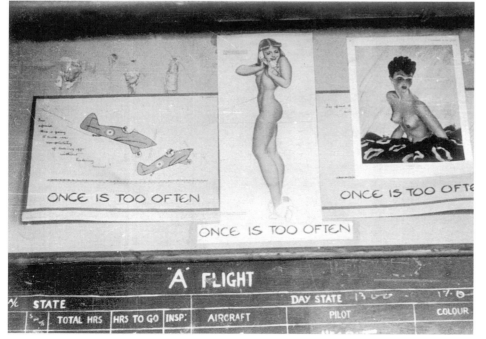

By the end of July 1942, there were only a dozen operational Hurricane squadrons based in the UK. The rest had either deployed to other operational theatres, or had converted to newer types such as the Spitfire or Beaufighter. Those Hurricane squadrons still based in the UK were all equipped with either MkIIBs or MkIICs, and were primarily involved in tasks such as convoy patrols, intruder patrols (many at night), and sweeps across France. In addition to the operational squadrons, there were several other non-operational squadrons equipped with Hurricanes, which were used for many different tasks. For example, 116 Squadron based at Heston used the occasional Hurricane MkI in helping to calibrate radars and anti-aircraft batteries. At Turnhouse, 289

Squadron was equipped with many different types of aircraft, including Hurricanes, with the task of providing detachments around southern Scotland for co-operation and training with various anti-aircraft batteries.

Trials and Development

A number of trials and development programmes were carried out with the Hurricane during the early part of the war, in order to improve the aircraft's capability and performance. Early ideas were based on the desire to increase the Hurricane's range, and varied from it being towed, to it being carried 'piggy-back' by a larger aircraft. These ideas rarely got beyond the drawing board, but one saw the light of day during 1942, when a prototype was built of a MkI (L1884) fitted with a second 'jettisonable' upper wing. This was known as the Hillson-Slip wing, and was an experiment in generating more lift during take-off. The appearance of L1884 was very much that of a 'Hurricane biplane'; although the prototype did fly, the project was cancelled. Other ideas were based on a different engine – including the Rolls-Royce Griffon and the Bristol Hercules – but the fact that Merlins were never in short supply meant that these projects never reached production.

The Dieppe Raid – 19 August 1942

Air Support

Much has been written about the joint British and Canadian raid on Dieppe, which took place on 19 August 1942. The aim of Operation *Jubilee* was to capture and hold the town of Dieppe for a limited period only (a matter of hours), as a form of rehearsal to a larger Allied invasion at some time in the future. It was a raid in which many lessons would be learned, helping to ensure a more successful invasion during the summer of 1944. What is not often appreciated, however, is the scale of the air support. The RAF flew more than 3,000 sorties during the day and more fighter squadrons took part in the day's fighting than were available at any one time during the Battle of Britain.

By August 1942, many Hurricane squadrons had been sent overseas and two-thirds of the seventy RAF squadrons involved in the raid were

UK operational Hurricane squadrons – July 1942		
SQUADRON	**LOCATION**	**MARK**
1 Squadron	Tangmere	IIB/IIC
3 Squadron	Hunsdon	IIC
32 Squadron	Friston	IIB/IIC
43 Squadron	Tangmere	IIB/IIC
87 Squadron	Charmy Down	IIC
174 Squadron	Manston	IIB
175 Squadron	Warmwell	IIB
225 Squadron	Thruxton	IIB/IIC
245 Squadron	Middle Wallop	IIB
247 Squadron	Exeter	IIC
253 Squadron	Friston	IIB/IIC
257 Squadron	High Ercall	IIB/IIC

Above: **A MkIIC (LF638, 5S-P) of No 691 Sqn at Roborough in January 1945. This unit was used for anti-aircraft duties during the latter part of the war.**

Below: **During the latter stages of the war Hurricanes were extensively used by the Operational Training Units.**

A Hurricane MkIV operating with the Balkan Air Force during the summer of 1944. Note the unusual external stores fit of rocket projectiles under the starboard wing and an external fuel tank under the port wing, demonstrating the versatility of the Hurricane. For this mission, it required the extra fuel to reach the target and return, and the rockets to destroy the target.

Hurricane Losses

equipped with Spitfires. The remaining third were made up of Hurricanes, Typhoons, Mustangs, Beaufighters, Blenheims and Bostons. The eight Hurricane squadrons involved were based at five bases in the south: 3 and 245 Squadrons at Shoreham, 32 and 253 Squadrons at Friston, 43 and 87 Squadrons at Tangmere, 174 Squadron at Ford, and 175 Squadron at Warmwell.

The air war during the day was bitter. The Hurricane squadrons were detailed to attack ground targets in the beach area and flew 300 sorties during the day, for the loss of twenty Hurricanes. One of the squadrons to suffer was 3 Squadron, which had moved from its base at Hunsdon to Shoreham to take part in the raid.

This MkIV (LB886) served with 351 (Yugoslav) Squadron during the final stages of the victory in the Balkans, after which it was handed over to the Yugoslav Partisans.

Hurricane MkIVs of 6 Squadron operated as part of the Balkan Air Force from August 1944 until the end of the war, for much of the time from remote airfields in Yugoslavia in support of the partisans. After the war, 6 Squadron moved to Palestine, and then Cyprus, and was the last RAF squadron to operate the Hurricane; the last aircraft left in January 1947 .

With the war over, only a few Hurricanes were kept for peacetime duties. One lucky survivor was Z3687, which was fitted for trials with laminar flow wings, and used by the Test Wing at Farnborough during 1946-48.

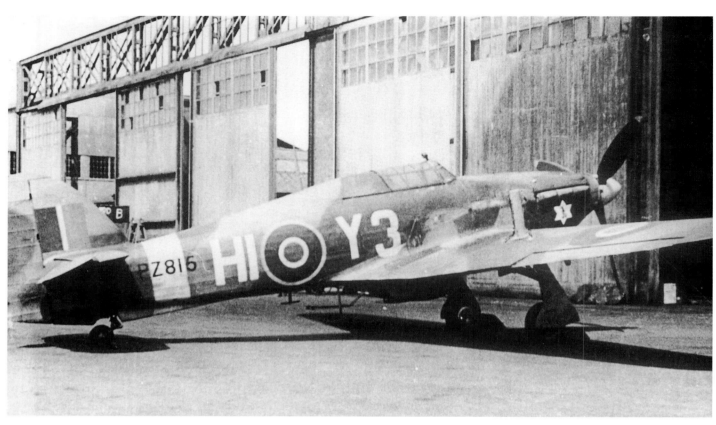

Used for meteorological duties after the war, this MkIIC (PZ815) of No 518 Sqn is pictured at Aldergrove in Northern Ireland early in 1946.

In command was Sqn Ldr Alex Berry, DFC, a New Zealander who had been with the squadron for two years. During his fourth mission of the day, he was shot down by a FW190 and killed while strafing his target. Another squadron commander to lose his life was 25-year-old Frenchman Sqn Ldr Emile Fayolle, DFC of 174 Squadron. The son of an admiral and the grandson of a general, Fayolle had escaped from occupied France and served with 85 Squadron during the Battle of Britain. It was his first mission in command of the squadron and he was last seen heading back across the Channel.

It was a bad day for 174 Squadron, with five Hurricanes lost during the day, and the loss of three pilots, as, indeed, it was for all the Hurricane squadrons. Sqn Ldr Dicky Mould led 245 Squadron at Shoreham. The squadron's first sortie was disastrous, with all but one of the seven Hurricanes either lost or crash-landed, and three pilots killed. Although there were many successful attacks by the Hurricane squadrons during the day, the losses indicate the ferocity of the fighting over the beach area. A total of 100 RAF fight-

ers were lost, with nearly as many Luftwaffe fighters lost or damaged beyond repair; these were losses that neither side, and particularly the Luftwaffe, could afford.

Turbinlite Squadrons

Despite the efforts of the Hurricane pilots, early attempts at providing an

Turbinlite squadrons equipped with the Hurricane, September 1942 - January 1943	
SQUADRON	LOCATION
530	Hunsdon
531	West Malling/Debden
532	Hibaldstow
533	Charmy Down
534	Tangmere
535	High Ercall
536	Predannack/Fairwood Common
537	Middle Wallop
538	Hibaldstow
539	Acklington

efficient night-fighter force were only marginally successful. Any new ideas were welcome, and often put into practice. One such idea, quite simple, was the development of the airborne searchlight, with a Hurricane MkIIC working with an aircraft such as the Douglas Havoc. The Havoc was equipped with an AI radar, a searchlight in the nose, known as the 'turbinlite', and formation lights. The tactic was for the Havoc to locate the enemy aircraft, for the Hurricane to fly under and ahead of the Havoc, and for the Havoc to illuminate the target aircraft using its searchlight, making it easier for the Hurricane to shoot it down. In September 1942, a number of squadrons were formed, which became known as 'Turbinlite Squadrons'. These were numbered from 530 to 539, and each squadron comprised of a flight of Havocs and a flight of Hurricanes.

Although it was a good idea, only one kill was ever confirmed using this method (by Flt Lt Derek Yapp), and this, together with the development of the AI radar in aircraft such as the Beaufighter, resulted in the disbandment of all ten squadrons in January 1943.

Italy, 1943

Invasion of Sicily

With North Africa safely in Allied hands early in 1943, the Allied commanders looked to the invasion of Italy as the next vital step to overall victory in Europe; the German's southern flank in the Mediterranean had always been considered the weakest. The build-up of Allied forces in North Africa in preparation for this new offensive was huge, and included more than 120 RAF squadrons. In summer 1943, Hurricanes were involved in air operations during the preparation for the invasion of Sicily. The islands of Malta, Lampedusa and Pantellaria proved to be key bases from which attacks could be made against Sicily, Sardinia and southern Italy; the Hurricanes were involved in attacking a wide range of targets, and in generally patrolling the skies.

The main assault forces landed on the Sicilian beaches on 10 July 1943. As night fighters, the Hurricane MkIICs of 73 Squadron provided air cover for a glider assault during the early hours. The struggle for Sicily lasted through the month, but the Allies eventually forced the Germans out through the port of Messina. The

UK-based operational Hurricane squadrons and locations – January 1944		
SQUADRON	**LOCATION**	**MARK**
164	Fairlop	IV
184	Detling	IID/IV
438 (RCAF)	Wittering	IV

Allied air forces soon gained air superiority in the region, and this was vital during the main landings in southern Italy, which began on 3 September.

Re-Capturing Mainland Italy

The capture and repair of the major Italian airfields meant that fighters could soon move from their bases in North Africa. In the eastern Mediterranean, Hurricanes were involved throughout the rest of 1943 in the continual harassment of German forces on mainland Greece, Crete and the other Greek islands. Cyprus proved to be an important base from which to launch raids; it could only support a limited number of operations, however, and most units still operated from Egypt.

The plan had been to capture the major Greek islands during the main Allied offensive in the Mediterranean, so that air attacks could be launched against German positions in the Balkans. However, all had

not gone the Allied way in the eastern Mediterranean, and it would be another year before this was possible. Meanwhile, partisan forces in Yugoslavia had continued to cause problems for the Germans during the occupation, and the Allies realized the importance of continued operations in this region. The RAF was involved in numerous special duties operations, as well as carrying out attacks against German positions in support of Yugoslav ground forces.

Initially, the Allied advance northwards through Italy during the latter half of 1943 had been met by a determined defence along the German's Gustav Line. The Allied response to this was to land forces behind the line at Anzio, in January 1944, and then to mount an attack at Monte Cassino in May. The Allied forces

After the war, twenty of the RAF's MkIICs were sold to Persia as trainers in 1947.

advanced to Rome during the following month, before the Germans established a new line of defence (known as the Gothic Line). The Apennine mountains made it difficult for the Allied ground forces to make any advance, although several air attacks were made against opposing forces.

In the end, further Allied landings in southern France during August were necessary, to threaten the German and Italian forces on two fronts. The hard winter of 1944-45 made it impossible for the Allies to take the region, but a spring

formed at Castle Camps, which used its MkIIB for radar calibration.

By May 1944, the Hurricanes of all three squadrons had been replaced by the newer Hawker Typhoons. The following month saw the Allied invasion of the European mainland during Operation *Overlord*. The air power in support of this operation was the greatest ever seen, with more than 3,000 British and American fighters taking part, although it was the Spitfire MkIXs, MkXIVs and the Typhoons which provided the main force. In fact, the only

best known was 5 OTU, at Aston Down in Gloucestershire, which formed early in 1940, and was the unit at which many of the famous Hurricane pilots of the Battle of Britain trained. The last Hurricane OTU was 55 OTU at Annan in Scotland, which closed in 1944.

Although many Hurricanes had been sent overseas since 1941, those that remained had been given to many of the training flights around the UK to carry out many enormously varied tasks. One example was 516 Squadron at Dundonald, formed in 1943 with several different types of aircraft, including Hurricane MkIIBs and MkIICs. There, the Hurricane was given such tasks as laying smoke screens and carrying out simulated attacks against troops on the ground, exercises that were particularly valuable during the build-up to the D-Day landings.

Included in the sales deal with Iran during 1947 were two MkIICs modified as two-seat trainers.

Other non-operational tasks included anti-aircraft co-operation, radar calibration, target towing and gun-laying practice. These flights became squadrons, of which the majority were in the 500 and 600 series, and had formed during late 1943-44 with various types of aircraft, including the Hurricane. It appears, however, that the mark of Hurricane did not particularly matter! One such squadron was 679 Squadron, which formed at Ipswich in December 1943, from 1616 and 1627 Flights, and which carried out anti-aircraft co-operation duties in East Anglia. Initially, it operated MkIICs, and later received MkIVs when they retired from operational service. The squadron remained at Ipswich until the end of the war, when it disbanded.

offensive was launched on 9 April 1945, and a ceasefire brought to the region early in May.

Towards Victory - 1944

Different Uses for the Hurricane

By the beginning of 1944, there were just three UK-based operational squadrons equipped with the Hurricane. Many other units were also equipped with the Hurricane for various tasks. Examples of these were 286 Squadron, based at Weston Zoyland, which used a Hurricane MkIIC for target towing; 288 Squadron, based at Digby, which was equipped with a MkI and MkIIC for anti-aircraft battery co-operation and training; and 527 Squadron,

operational Hurricane squadron in the UK during the D-Day period was 309 Squadron at Drem, which operated MkI-ICs during the period March-October 1944, due to a problem with the squadron's Mustang's engine. Its role during this period was air defence over Scotland, and it remained well north throughout Operation *Overlord*.

The Fate of the Remaining Hurricanes

What happened to the many Hurricanes still in existence? The number of Hurricanes being produced meant that some older MkIs could be released back into the training system, mainly to the Operational Training Units (OTUs). These OTUs were in existence for most of the war, and the Hurricane was an ideal single-seat fighter on which to learn. Probably the

Hurricanes were also used during the war, and after, for meteorological duties over Europe and the North Sea. In fact, Hurricanes had first been used for met duties in the Middle East during 1943. Initially, old MkIs were used but, as MkIIs became available, they were specifically modified – the guns were removed, and met equipment installed. The met flights were formed into squadrons, and it was not unusual for these squadrons to operate several different types of aircraft. One squadron, 521, at Langham, had many

One Hurricane which survived the war and found fame with the Battle of Britain Memorial Flight was LF363.

aircraft on charge, including a Hurricane MkIIC, which it operated until early 1946. Further afield, 520 Squadron in Gibraltar also operated a MkIIC for met duties in the Atlantic. The Hurricane remained in use for met duties in the Far East until 1946. It seems that there was no job for which the Hurricane could not be used!

Victory in the Balkans

The support for Marshal Tito's partisans in the Yugoslav theatre of operations increased in importance as the Allies advanced northwards through Italy. It became possible for the RAF to operate from bases in eastern Italy, across the Adriatic, to attack German positions in Yugoslavia. The Balkan Air Force was formed, and this included Hurricanes, which were involved in carrying out attacks against German positions, and in helping to gain and maintain air superiority over the region during the summer months of 1944. The Axis powers had lost the support of Romania and Bulgaria in the Balkans, which meant that the German forces in Greece were effectively isolated.

By July 1944, 351 and 352 (Yugoslav) Squadrons had been formed at Benina in Libya as Yugoslav-manned fighter-bomber units. One of them, 352 Squadron, was soon re-equipped with Spitfires, but 351 Squadron moved to Canne in Italy to operate with 281 Wing of the Balkan Air Force. Due to the distance across the Adriatic, the squadron operated a detachment of MkIICs and MkIVs from the island of Vis, where it was able to fly missions in support of the Yugoslav partisans.

By September 1944, the Allies were ready to advance back through the Aegean once more. The RAF provided constant air cover for each of the Greek islands to be recaptured. The Russian advance in Eastern Europe led to many of the German forces on mainland Greece withdrawing northwards, to escape back to Germany before being cut off. The Allied forces that landed at Araxos in September were met by less opposition than they had originally feared. British fighters were able, once again, to occupy airfields in southern Greece. Following a short period

of unrest between internal factions in Greece, a ceasefire was declared on 15 January 1945, bringing to an end RAF offensive operations in Greece.

It was some time before the German forces were eventually pushed out of Yugoslavia. The Balkan Air Force had flown thousands of sorties, with the rocket-firing Hurricanes operating from bases in Greece enjoying much success. The campaign in this region ended during the first week of May 1945, when Yugoslav partisan forces linked up with elements of the British 8th Army advancing from Italy. The Hurricanes of the Balkan Air Force flew their last missions, with 351 Squadron disbanding the following month.

Peace Once More

With the war in Europe over, there was a mass disbandment of squadrons – not just the Hurricane units, but across the entire RAF. Within weeks of victory in Europe, all but two of the squadrons that had been operating the Hurricane in the UK were either disbanded or had re-equipped with

Sqn Ldr Henryk Szczesny, VM KW and 3 bars DFC.

Henryk 'Sneezy' Szczesny, pictured with his memorabilia at home in London.
This gallant Pole died peacefully in 1996.

newer types. The only surviving units were 518 Squadron at Aldergrove, and 521 Squadron at Chivenor, which were equipped with several types of aircraft, and carried out meteorological observation duties until 1946.

In the Far East, the story was slightly different. Many of the Hurricane squadrons had re-equipped with aircraft such as the American Thunderbolt, but there were still several squadrons operating the Hurricane up until the victory over

Japan. The Hurricane continued to operate with the Indian Air Force in the Far East until August 1946, when it was replaced by the Spitfire or the Tempest.

The last unit to operate the Hurricane was 6 Squadron, which operated MkIVs in Palestine and the Mediterranean until January 1947. During the last few months of the war, the squadron had been attached to the Balkan Air Force, and had operated from various bases in Yugoslavia in support of the partisan forces. At the end of the

war in Europe, 6 Squadron moved to Palestine to support the Army, which was trying to deal with the internal problems in the area. The squadron operated from Petah Tiqva, Ein Shemer and Ramat David during the rest of 1945 and most of 1946, by which time the first Spitfires were arriving to replace the Hurricanes. In October 1946, the squadron moved to Nicosia in Cyprus, where it operated for the next year, although the last of its Hurricanes were phased out by January 1947.

With the war over, the future of the Hurricane was unclear. It had been designed as a single-seat fighter and, unlike larger aircraft, such as the Lancaster, it was not much required in times of peace. It was also true that the rapid progression in aircraft design and capabilities meant that the Hurricane was approaching the end of its days. A number were retained for further trials and development work at establishments such as Farnborough, but there was little for the Hurricane to do at home. However, the Hurricane continued to serve overseas until the early 1950s.

A number of Hurricanes had been delivered to overseas air forces, including the Indian Air Force, the South African Air Force and the Royal Egyptian Air Force.

Sqn Ldr Henryk 'Sneezy' Szczesny, VM KW and 3 bars DFC - 317 Squadron

Known to his comrades as 'Sneezy', Henryk Szczesny was the perfect example of a gallant Pole who continued the fight against Germany long after his own country had been overrun. Born in the district of Warsaw in 1909, Szczesny joined the Polish Air Force at Deblin in 1931. Operating with an unofficial fighter unit at Deblin during the German invasion of September 1939, he destroyed two He111s while flying the only available PZL P29. When Poland fell, he made his way to England, where he joined the RAF and was posted to 74 Squadron at Hornchurch.

During the Battle of Britain, and in the hectic weeks that followed, Szczesny destroyed four enemy aircraft while flying Spitfires, before being posted to the Hurricane with 257 Squadron. Following a few weeks' rest (during which he was awarded the Polish Cross of Valour [KW] and bar), he was posted to a Polish Hurricane squadron, 317, as a flight commander, when it formed at Acklington. By July, Szczesny had brought his personal total to seven by sharing in the destruction of a Bf 109 and Ju 88 over the Channel. He was awarded two more bars to his Cross of Valour.

During August, Szczesny was promoted to the rank of squadron leader, and given command of the squadron at Exeter. He was then awarded the Polish Virtuti Militari and the DFC. He remained as the commanding officer until March 1942, when he was rested once again from operations. He spent the rest of the year as the Polish Liaison Officer at HQ No 10 Group and HQ No 12 Group, before being posted to Northolt as the squadron leader flying of the Polish Wing. While leading the Northolt Wing during an escort mission against the Renault factory near Paris, on 4 April 1943, he was engaged by FW190s near Rouen. Having shot down one, he was seen to collide with another, being forced to bale out and subsequently being captured by a German patrol. He spent the rest of the war as a POW at Stalag Luft III, before being repatriated at the end of hostilities. Szczesny remained in the RAF as an admin officer and fighter controller until he retired in 1965. He lived in retirement in West London until he died peacefully, at home, in 1996.

Some had also been delivered during the war to countries such as Russia and Yugoslavia, while others had found their way overseas, by one means or another; a typical example was the Irish Air Corps, which had managed to 'acquire' a number of Hurricanes. Of those that were sold overseas, fifty MkIICs were delivered to Portugal, and twenty to Persia, including a couple of two-seat trainers, delivered to Persia in 1947. Those aircraft sold overseas during 1946-47 are believed to be the last serving examples of the Hurricane, and are known to have remained in service until the early 1950s.

Sadly, very few examples of the Hurricane remain and only a handful have remained in airworthy condition. Museums in the UK, Canada and South Africa still exhibit those that have survived, while two of the most famous Hurricanes belong to the Battle of Britain Memorial Flight at RAF Coningsby in Lincolnshire (see Chapter 10). The rest, as they say, is history!

Sqn Ldr 'Pat' Pattle commanded 33 Squadron during the air campaign over Greece, destroying fifty enemy aircraft before his death in April 1941. Pattle achieved thirty-five of his kills while flying Hurricanes, making him both the top-scoring Hurricane pilot and RAF pilot of the war.

Sqn Ldr 'Pat' Pattle DFC and bar – 33 Squadron

Born in South Africa on 3 July 1914, Marmaduke Thomas St John Pattle joined the RAF in 1936. Following pilot training, he was posted to fly Gladiators with 80 Squadron in 1937. At the end of April 1938, Pattle accompanied the squadron to Ismailia in Egypt, to help provide air defence in the local area. When war broke out, Pattle was a flight commander with the squadron which had by then moved to Amriya. In August 1940, the squadron moved to Sidi Haneish South, near the Libyan border, where Pattle experienced air combat for the first time. By the end of his first month in action he had personally destroyed four Italian aircraft in the area of Bir Taieb el Esem.

The squadron then moved to Trikkala in Greece, and on to Larissa to support the Greek forces on the Albanian front, and it was in this theatre of operations that Pattle enjoyed tremendous success. By the end of 1940, he was an established Gladiator ace, with fourteen confirmed kills and many more 'probables' or 'damaged'. The squadron moved to Iannina in January 1941 and, during the following month, the first Hurricane MkIs arrived. Pattle enjoyed immediate success with this new type. His first kill flying the Hurricane was on 20 February, when he destroyed an Italian G-50 near Berat. This was followed on the 28th by four more kills during one day – two Italian BR20s followed by two CR42s over the Tepelene Coast.

During this period of operations, the squadron was mainly involved in carrying out fighter escort for bombers attacking enemy positions. This gave the Hurricane pilots freedom to manoeuvre and several claims were made against Italian aircraft. By the end of February 1941, Pattle had individually achieved twenty-one confirmed kills, and had been awarded the DFC. This remarkable feat was followed by three more kills on 4 March, when he destroyed three Italian G-50s in the area of Himara-Valona, and was immediately awarded a bar to his DFC. He was then promoted to squadron leader, and given command of 33 Squadron at Larissa. It was not long before he added to his score, and on 23 March he led the squadron to considerable success during an attack against Fier airfield; after

destroying an Italian G-50 in the air, he destroyed three more on the ground.

On 6 April, the Germans invaded Greece and the Hurricane pilots found themselves up against better pilots flying more capable aircraft. However, this did not deter Pattle, and he achieved immediate success on the opening day of the campaign by destroying two Messerschmitt Bf 109s over Bulgaria. Two remarkable weeks of air fighting followed for Pattle, with eight more kills during the next six days, five kills on 14 April, six more on the 19th, and four more on the 20th. It seemed to be only a matter of time before his luck ran out, and this happened during his third sortie of the day on 20 April. While leading what remained of 33 and 80 Squadrons from Eleusis, he was shot down and killed over Eleusis Bay.

The actual number of kills achieved by 'Pat' Pattle will never be known, because of the loss of some squadron records covering that period. It is believed that his final total was fifty enemy aircraft destroyed in the air, thirty-five while flying Hurricanes. This total does not include many more which were 'shared' destroyed, or claimed as 'probables', neither does it include the successes he had against aircraft destroyed on the ground. The total of fifty does, however, make him the RAF's top-scoring fighter pilot of the war, as well as the pilot with the most number of kills while flying the Hurricane. Of the thirty-five enemy aircraft he destroyed while flying Hurricanes, nine were while serving with 80 Squadron; the last twenty-six were achieved while commanding 33 Squadron, and all but one during April 1941 in just two weeks of air fighting in the skies over Athens.

Pattle was killed during the final days of the campaign in Greece; soon after, the German advance forced the handful of surviving RAF Hurricanes to evacuate to Crete, and then back to Egypt. Despite the fact that Pattle achieved so much, he received no more recognition of his outstanding success. The air war over Greece has never been recognized as it should have been, and, had he have served in a different theatre of operations, 'Pat' Pattle might well have received the recognition he surely deserved.

The Last of the Many

PZ865

The last of the 14,533 Hurricanes to be built was a MkIIC, PZ865, proudly named 'The Last of the Many'. It was built at the Hawker main assembly plant at Langley during July 1944, and when it rolled off the production line a banner with 'The Last of the Many' was erected above the plant; the same words were inscribed on the port and starboard side of the fuselage of the aircraft.

Flown by Hawker's chief test pilot, Gp Capt George Bulman, PZ865 made its maiden flight from Langley on 27 July 1944. The aircraft was powered by a 1,280 hp Rolls-Royce Merlin 20 engine, and fitted with the standard four 20mm Oerlikon cannons, but PZ865 was not destined for the front line. Indeed, it never served with the RAF at all. Instead, PZ865 was to be preserved as a lasting tribute to

this aeroplane. It was flight-tested and accepted by the Ministry of Aircraft Production, but was allocated back to Hawker for communications trials at Langley. With the war over, PZ865 was bought back by Hawker for private use, and was soon put back into storage by the company.

The aircraft remained in storage until 1950, when it was made airworthy for entry into the 1950 King's Cup air race. A number of modifications were made to the original MkIIC design. The cannons were removed, two extra fuel tanks were installed (giving an extra 25 gallons fuel capacity), and it was painted in a smart royal blue and gold paint scheme; furthermore, PZ865 was given the civil registration of G-AMAU. The aircraft flew for the first time in its new fit on 13 May 1950, and went on to fly in the King's Cup air race on 17 June, entered by Princess

Margaret and flown by Gp Capt Peter Townsend; averaging 283mph (about 455kph), Townsend finished in second place.

Later in the same year, G-AMAU was fitted with an improved Merlin 24 engine. In August, it was flown by Neville Duke, achieving third place in the Kemsley Trophy, and then, the following month, it made the best time in the *Daily Express* Challenge Trophy. The pattern was much the same for the next three years, when the aircraft made several appearances at air shows and air races. In 1956, it was transferred to Dunsfold, where it remained into the early 1960s, by which time it had been returned to its wartime camouflage paint scheme. It had also been fitted with an improved Merlin 502 engine, and flown as part of the Hawker Museum.

This famous Hurricane has starred in

The last Hurricane off the production line in July 1944, PZ865 was bought back by Hawker after the war for private use, and put back into storage by the company until 1950, when it re-appeared for air racing.

some famous films, including *Angels One-Five* and *The Battle of Britain*; it was disguised as H3424 and coded as MI-G during the making of the latter, at Duxford, during 1968.

Battle of Britain Memorial Flight

The Hurricanes

On 29 March 1972, having restored PZ865 to airworthy condition, Hawker Siddeley presented the Hurricane to the Royal Air Force's Battle of Britain Memorial Flight (BBMF) at Coltishall. Initially named the Historic Aircraft Flight, the flight had been in existence since 1957. By 1972, it had four Spitfires and just one Hurricane MkIIC (LF363). The Lancaster was added the following year and, in 1976, the flight moved to RAF Coningsby in Lincolnshire, where it has remained until the present day.

The flight's other Hurricane, LF363, is believed to have been the last Hurricane to enter service, having been delivered to

No 5 Maintenance Unit in January 1944. It was an original member of the flight, but was severely damaged in a crash-landing at RAF Wittering on 11 September 1991. For the next few years, the remains of LF363 were kept as its future was discussed. Eventually, the decision was made to restore the aircraft, although it took the sale of one of the flight's Spitfires to meet the costs. The work, carried out by Historic Aircraft Limited at Audley End, was due for completion late in 1997, ready for the following display season.

The Pilots

During its time as the flight's only airworthy Hurricane, PZ865 has thrilled thousands of enthusiasts. Only a handful of fighter pilots at RAF Coningsby are fortunate enough to get the chance to fly it. These privileged few include the Station Commander and the Officer Commanding Operations Wing, and instructors from 56 Squadron (the Tornado F3 Operational Conversion Unit), who volunteer to fly the flight's fighters in their spare time during the display season.

Once selected to fly for the flight, each

'The Last of the Many' was presented to the RAF's Battle of Britain Memorial Flight in 1972, and has appeared in various colour schemes ever since.

pilot has to complete a work-up on the Chipmunk and Harvard, before being given the chance to fly the Hurricane. The flight's DHC-1 Chipmunk is an ideal trainer, as it has a piston engine and a tail-wheel. The aspiring Hurricane pilot has to fly a minimum of twenty-five hours in the Chipmunk, during which time he learns to master the flying characteristics of a tail-dragger aircraft – somewhat different to those of a Tornado F3 fighter! The pilot then goes to Boscombe Down, where he flies the North American Harvard trainer, to get the feel of a heavier tail-dragger aircraft. The Harvard serves as an excellent lead-in to the Hurricane, as there are several similarities in performance and cockpit characteristics. The pilot gets to fly the Harvard from both the front and back seats, before he returns to Coningsby to begin the ground school prior to flying the Hurricane.

The ground school is carried out by the flight's Fighter Leader, Sqn Ldr Paul Day,

The flight's other Hurricane (LF363) was an original member of the Historic Aircraft Flight when it formed at Biggin Hill in 1957. Following an engine problem, the aircraft crashed at Wittering attempting an emergency landing, and has had to be restored by Historic Aircraft Limited at Audley End.

AFC. The flying career of Paul Day is outstanding. He has flown fighters with the RAF since 1963, having achieved 2,000 flying hours on the Hawker Hunter, 3,000 hours on the McDonnell Douglas F4 Phantom, and 1,000 hours on the Tornado F3. Since 1980, he has flown with the Battle of Britain Memorial Flight, and has more than 1,000 hours on the Spitfire and Hurricane. In 1987, Paul Day was awarded the Air Force Cross for 'services to the RAF in air combat training and services to the Battle of Britain Memorial Flight'.

The Hurricane is the first of the flight's fighters flown by any pilot beginning his time with BBMF. This is mainly because the Hurricane's wider undercarriage track makes the aircraft easier to handle on the ground than the Spitfire. Despite the vast experience of all the flight's pilots, flying the Hurricane for the first time is no easy matter. The pilot has to complete a number of general handling exercises before practising the display routine. This is first carried out at height, well above the hazards of the ground, before gradually

reducing the display height through 500 feet, down to 100 feet. As the flight's Hurricane is a valuable piece of RAF history, the pilot has to have the display routine approved by the Air Officer Commanding No 11/18 Group before he is cleared to fly his first public display.

The Display

Sqn Ldr Clive Rowley is a fighter pilot with the BBMF and regularly displays the flight's fighters during the air show season. In common with the flight's other fighter pilots, Rowley is a Tornado F3 pilot, currently serving as an instructor with 56 Squadron, the Tornado F3 Operational Conversion Unit. Flying the BBMF's historic aircraft is a 'secondary duty', which has to fit in around his primary role and into his own time at weekends. Clive is a very experienced RAF pilot, with over 5,000 hours of flying, all on fighters or training aircraft, including the Hunter, Hawk and Lightning, as well as the Tornado F3. Clive describes exactly what it is like to fly PZ865 during a typical display:

On the Ground

Today I am privileged to fly PZ865 on a typical BBMF display sortie. As I walk out to the aircraft, I am struck by the impressive shape and size; its hunched-back stance and height off the ground make it seem more imposing than other similar-sized aircraft; the four 20mm cannon barrels protruding from the leading edge of the wing give the MkIIC a very purposeful and potent look. The pull-down step on the fuselage, just behind the trailing edge of the port wing, is necessary to enable me to climb up on to the wing; clever, the way it automatically opens up the hand hold in the fuselage side as I pull the step down. The cockpit switches are safe, so I jump down to the ground again to carry out my 'walk round' external checks. This is more of a tradition than a necessity in the BBMF case, as the ground crew have already completed the most thorough of inspections before releasing the aircraft to me. As I walk round, conducting my checks, it is difficult to suppress the feeling of excitement and slight disbelief that I am about to go flying again in this truly classic, and now very rare, 'warbird'.

With the external checks complete, I clamber back up on to the port wing and into the cockpit. Settling into the seat, that wonderful smell of oil and petrol attacks my nostrils – so different from the smell of a jet cockpit. I am assisted in strapping in by the ground crew, who then hands me my 'bonedome', a modern departure from historical authenticity which provides much better head and acoustic protection than the original leather helmets. Despite the relative simplicity of the controls in the Hurricane, compared with modern jet fighters, I am reminded as I scan the cockpit of how complicated it seemed when I first flew the Hurricane; controls, instruments and warning lights seem to be scattered in an almost haphazard manner.

The cockpit of PZ865 is mainly original, although there have been some changes over the years. Most noticeably, the gunsight is missing and a modern multi-channel VHF radio is positioned at the top of the instrument panel, easily in view when I am required to change frequency while maintaining close formation. The left-to-right checks are simple and logical and are completed in a minute or two. I particularly enjoy pumping the flaps down twenty degrees with the manual hydraulic pump handle (you can't do that in a jet!). I leave the flap selector lever in the 'UP' part of the 'H' gate, so that when the engine starts and the hydraulic pump comes on line it will raise the flaps, proving the serviceability of the system. As I look around, I take the opportunity to refresh myself on the picture I will be seeing on landing, in terms of the height of my eyeline from the ground and the nose-up angle of the aircraft.

It is time to start up. As the engine has not been run today, and taking the air temperature into account, I give twelve pumps of fuel from the Kigas priming pump. I confirm that the wheel brakes are on, the throttle is just off the idle stop, the control column is held fully back (to prevent nose-over) and the magneto switches are on. I then press the boost coil button for two seconds with my index finger then, keeping it pressed, also press the start button with my middle finger. Meanwhile, I am holding the stick back with my legs and my right hand is ready to either use the priming pump or to move the throttle. The prop turns very slowly and jerkily for three or four blades and then the engine kicks and the Merlin V12 bursts into life, with puffs of smoke from the exhaust stacks and a cacophony of

noise. What a wonderful sound; I always get a buzz from that on start-up.

The after-start checks are completed in seconds; the engine instruments, particularly the oil pressure, show that all is well. The flaps have travelled up so the flap selector lever is left to neutral and the magnetos are checked. A quick radio call gets me clearance to taxi so I throttle back to idle and signal for the chocks to be removed. Taxiing the Hurricane is easy; the view over the nose is not bad at all, although it can be improved by weaving slightly from side to side. The brakes,

The cockpit of PZ865.

controlled by a lever on the control column spade grip, are easy to use and give differential braking via the rudder pedals for steering. It is important to keep the stick fully back though, especially when braking or opening the throttle, as nose-over could otherwise occur. The Hurricane is not prone to overheating on the ground, because the large radiator is sensibly located under the prop wash on the fuselage's centreline. Indeed, it is necessary to allow enough time for the engine to

Sqn Ldr Clive Rowley, BBMF

warm up for the engine run-up checks, especially as, to preserve engine life, BBMF wait for an oil temperature of 40 degrees rather than the original 15 degrees, before running-up. Once the engine run-up checks are complete, I taxi on to the runway.

With the Hurricane, the final important check on the runway is to move the under-carriage safety catch to 'Select' – this catch prevents the inadvertent 'up' selection of the undercarriage while on the ground, but needs to be in the 'Select' position to permit the gear to be raised after take-off. I then release the brakes and gently open the throttle to +6 boost (much less power than would have been used originally), once again, in the interest of preserving engine life.

Airborne

On take-off, the aircraft tries to swing to the left as power is applied and again when I raise the tail at about 50 knots, but the rudder control is powerful and it is easy to

keep straight by using right rudder. Acceleration is moderate and at 70 knots I ease gently back on the control column to lift off, the aircraft feeling quite heavy on the controls. Once safely airborne, I squeeze the brakes to stop the wheels rotating, and then comes the tricky part – I take my left hand off the throttle and place it on the spade grip of the control column and, flying the aircraft with my left hand, I find the undercarriage lever with my right hand (without looking in), and, pressing the thumb catch, I slam it hard into the 'UP' gate.

The airspeed is increasingly rapidly towards 100 knots as the gear slowly begins to retract and I have to pull the aircraft up into quite a steep climb, or the under-carriage limiting speed of 104 knots will be exceeded, and the gear will fail to lock up, because of the aerodynamic loads on the doors. After what seems like ages, two thumps and the red 'UP' light on the undercarriage position indicator tell me that the gear is locked up. With the under-carriage locked up, I can now lower the nose to a more normal climbing attitude,

permitting the speed to increase to 140 knots, while selecting neutral with the undercarriage lever, and then setting +4 boost with the throttle and 2,400 rpm with the prop pitch control lever. This reduction in rpm slightly reduces the noise, but the noise levels are still unbelievably high, even with the modern 'bonedome' on. As the speed reaches 140 knots, I start a right turn to orbit the airfield to join on the Lancaster which is just beginning its take-off roll. Meanwhile, the Spitfire has turned left after take-off and is now closing to join on the Lanc's left wing. I take care to control the overtake in order to avoid having to throttle all the way back to idle, as this causes the Merlin to pop and bang in a most disconcerting manner.

Close formation flying in the Hurricane is relatively easy. It is an extremely stable platform, not easily thrown out of position by turbulence, and it has immediate power response as I throttle it up or back. Against that, I have to say that it is so stable that it is sometimes difficult to move the aircraft quickly. Also, with the power being trans-mitted through an 11ft propeller, every movement of the throttle requires a movement of the rudder pedals with the feet to keep the nose straight and prevent it from swinging around. However, while this is initially strange to a jet pilot unused to such effects, it quickly becomes natural. I move into close formation, juggling the throttle and constantly moving the stick and rudder pedals to hold position.

We stoop down to the 300ft minimum height in formation and roar across a village fete. My concentration is almost exclusively focused on formatting on the Lancaster, but I catch a glimpse of the venue with people looking up. Next time round I see nothing but sky, Lancaster and Spitfire, because I am on the inside of the formation's turn, looking up. Then we straighten and begin to climb away, both fighters hold position for another minute as we fade from the crowd's view, and then it's time to relax and we slide gently out to a more comfortable position.

The best range speed for the Hurricane at these heights is 140 knots but there is only a small loss of range for speeds up to 160 knots. The prop pitch lever is set to give 1,800 rpm and the throttle to a boost (about 0) to achieve 150 knots cruising speed (equal to 2.5 miles per minute, making timing easier to calculate); even at cruising rpm, the Hurricane cockpit is extremely noisy. There is always a small gap between the windscreen and the canopy (which can be locked open but not shut), which creates considerable wind noise. I have the radio volume turned fully up in the air and still have difficulty hearing what is said. We try to avoid flying the Hurricane through rain, because of the potential for damaging the wooden propeller, but sometimes this is unavoidable and I end up getting wet as the rain comes through the gap in the canopy!

While cruising, I do not relax for a moment, as I am constantly monitoring the engine instruments. Every few minutes I check the fuel tank contents by turning the fuel gauge button to the tank I wish to interrogate and pressing it in. I am also keeping a check on the navigation (using a map and stopwatch). There is no heating or cooling in the Hurricane and the cockpit can either get very hot or very cold, depending on the ambient conditions outside. As I become accustomed to the cockpit environment again I can't help wondering how the wartime pilots coped with these problems on operational sorties. However, my discomfort at low altitudes

and in temperate climes is a small price to pay for the pleasure of flying this wonderful machine.

The Display

We now arrive for the main event – a major air show at a famous airfield. I complete my pre-display checks, including setting 2,650 rpm with the prop pitch lever, and pressing in the cage button on the directional indicator (DI). I will have no heading reference during my display other than what I can see out of the window; the DI would 'topple' as soon as I exceeded 60 degrees of bank if it was not caged. The artificial horizon will also topple and become useless during my routine, and the altimeter will be of limited value in indicating height because of pressure errors. The only instruments I will be referring to during my display are the airspeed indicator (ASI), and the engine performance gauges. The three of us run down the display line on our arrival pass, with the crowd on our left. While remaining focused on the Lancaster, I can see the crowd rush past in the background.

I break the Hurricane up and out of formation, turning right, and position for the first solo display. I fly a long lazy turn up to 1,500ft, building up speed to 180

knots and looking back over my shoulder to get my bearings with the display line and central datum. I roll out to run in at 90 degrees to the display line, head on to the crowd, aiming at the datum and letting the nose drop into a gentle dive. A final confirmation that I have display power set at 2,650 rpm and +6 boost, and I tighten the throttle friction fully and put both hands on the control column spade grip. As I dive down to level off at 100ft on my run-in, the speed builds to 250 knots and the controls are becoming much heavier; I will need both hands to roll and pull into the initial break turn. Again, I wonder how wartime fighter pilots manoeuvred these aircraft at speeds considerably in excess of the 270 knots to which we are now limited.

Approaching the display line, I roll the aircraft left with full stick and a large input of left rudder and pull out into a level 3g break turn (the max 'g' allowed to preserve airframe life). I pull through 120 degrees and then max rate roll to wings level, wait three seconds and pitch up to a 3g pull to approximately 30 degrees nose up. After three seconds in the climb, I roll to 120 degrees of right bank and pull down to 'wingover' back on to the line. I check the airspeed, I still have 140 knots over the top. On the way down from the wingover

Sqn Ldr Clive Rowley strapping in to PZ865 prior to a display.

'PZ' during the 1997 display season, shown in the markings of 261 Squadron, which was based on the island of Malta during 1940-41.

I check the engine instruments and then concentrate on rolling out on the display line and levelling off at 100ft.

As I roar down the line on the so-called 'high speed' pass, the aircraft is bumping in turbulence, and I have to feed on rudder to keep the nose straight as the speed builds. I pull into another 'wingover' and then prepare for the final move, the 'victory roll'. I position by running down the line at 100ft and ensure that I have at least 180 knots before pulling up. Just before display centre I pitch the nose up at 3g, wait until I am passing 500ft, and then roll left with full stick deflection and rudder to co-ordinate. As I pass inverted, I look out the top of the canopy at the ground to see if I've achieved the aim of passing inverted exactly at display centre. Looking back to the front as I complete the roll, I see the Spitfire running in head on to me for his display. We each call 'tally' on the radio and he passes under me at 100ft as I roll

wings level at 800ft – nice takeover!

I fly a climbing turn to crowd rear, looking for the Lancaster also holding there; I will hold at 1,500ft to his 1,000ft. Now it's time to cool off, both the engine and me, as we've both been working hard for the four and a half minutes that the solo display has taken. The engine oil and radiator temperatures have risen slightly and I bring back the rpm to let the engine cool. Once the Spitfire has completed his display, he joins me to hold while the Lancaster displays. Once the Lanc is complete, we all join up to fly a 3-ship formation down the crowd line at 110 knots.

At this particular air show, we are landing so that the crowd will be able to benefit from the presence of our aircraft on the ground as well as in the air. Now I have to concentrate on the circuit and landing. The Hurricane is relatively forgiving of any pilot errors of judgement on landing, more so than the Spitfire, because of its

wide and strong undercarriage. None the less, any tail-wheel aircraft demands respect when landing (especially from us fast-jet pilots), and today is complicated by 10 knots of crosswind. These aircraft were designed to land on grass airfields, more or less into wind, and are not ideally suited to hard runways. I level off downwind at 800ft, throttle back to just above idle to reduce speed, and complete the pre-landing checks. When the speed is below 104 knots, I lower the undercarriage. I select full flap down as I tip into the final turn and correct the big nose-down pitch trim changes with a large movement of back stick and lots of nose-up trim. I fly the final turn at 85 knots, with about 30 degrees of bank, aiming to fly a continuous curved approach to roll wings level at about 200ft; enough straight in to assess the effects of the crosswind.

As the aircraft reaches the correct glide path, steeper than in a jet, I apply a trickle of power to hold the runway aspect and then roll wings level for the final part of the approach. I gradually raise the nose, making sure that I am in trim, and let the speed reduce to 75 knots by about 20-30ft. On this straight part of the approach I am 'crabbing' in sideways, with the nose pointing into the crosswind. One final check of the speed at 70 knots as I go into the landing 'flare', gently raising the nose into the touch-down attitude, slowly closing the throttle. In the Hurricane, closing the throttle causes the nose to drop, and it takes back stick to prevent the aircraft touching down early, with an inevitable bounce. Just before I believe that I am going to touch down, I kick the aircraft straight with rudder, keeping the wings level with aileron. Now I am looking straight ahead, to ensure that I keep the nose straight, but as the nose comes up in the flare it blocks my view, and I have to use my peripheral vision to monitor the runway edges either side of the nose.

With a squeak from the tyres, and the gentlest of skips, we are down. Stick right back now for maximum ground stability, and concentrate on keeping straight with rudder, resisting the aircraft's tendency to swing into the crosswind. No time to relax yet, as the ground roll can be the most exciting part of the sortie in a strong crosswind. Now I'm down to taxiing speed and can relax slightly. I open the cockpit

hood and wave to the crowd, park up and shut down; it's been another successful day – I am one of the lucky few!

A Lasting Memory

PZ865, as with all the BBMF's aircraft, is maintained to an exceptionally high standard by a small number of dedicated engineers. All are full-time members of the RAF and volunteer to serve on the flight. All the lengthy servicing schedules are carried out during the winter months, ensuring that the Hurricane is available throughout the display season. Major servicings are carried out away from Coningsby, under civilian contract. Fortunately, there tend to be few problems in maintaining the Hurricane in terms of spares. Some components are made at the manufacturers from original drawings or, if these are not available, replacement parts are made by copying the original piece. Another source of spares is the general public, who frequently kindly donate parts to the flight.

PZ865 flies a maximum of sixty hours per display season, and will be seen all over the country by thousands of enthusiasts. BBMF sorties often take in several venues, and sorties of more than two hours are not

uncommon. The aircraft is not flown above 10,000 feet (3000m) these days, as the oxygen equipment has been removed. In addition, the aircraft is not flown through cloud, and is only flown visually below any cloud cover. The result of these restrictions is that most transit flying is done at an altitude of 2–4,000 feet (600–1200m), depending on the cloud cover and airspace restrictions.

When not at displays, and outside the display season, PZ865 can be seen at its home base at RAF Coningsby. A visitors' centre has long been established there, annually welcoming some 20,000 members of the public from all over the world and of all ages and all backgrounds. Many are ex-RAF, but many are not, and all share the same fascination for the aircraft on display. During the peak season, the centre is visited by up to 300 people every day, and a number of volunteer tour guides provide tours every half an hour, between 10.00 a.m. and 3.00 p.m., Monday to Friday. As with any historic aircraft, no one knows how many more times the public will be treated to the sight of PZ865 – 'The Last of the Many' – airborne.

The author in the cockpit of PZ865 in the BBMF hangar at RAF Coningsby.

Appendix A

Production

This appendix covers the production of Hawker Hurricanes – where they were built, under which batch, and when they were delivered. The serial block numbers cover the first and last serial number of aircraft built in each batch, but every serial number within the block was not necessarily used. Details of the Hurricane MkIIs do not include whether an aircraft was built as a MkIIB or MkIIC; this is because an aircraft may originally have been built as one MkII variant, and entered service as another. It should also be noted that the batches which include MkIV development are shown. From this appendix, it should be possible to identify where any particular Hurricane was built, and approximately when.

HURRICANE MKI

K5083	Prototype

Built by Hawker Aircraft Ltd at Kingston–upon–Thames, Brooklands and Langley

L1547–L2146	First batch of 600 aircraft, delivered Dec 1937 – Oct 1939 (2 a/c per day)
N2318–N2729	Second batch of 300 aircraft, delivered Sep 1939 – May 1940 (2)
P3265–P8818	Third batch of 500 aircraft, delivered Feb – Jul 1940 (3)
R2680–R2689	
T9519–T9538	
W6667–W6670	
V7200–V7862	Fourth batch of 500 aircraft, delivered Jul 1940 – Feb 1941 (2)
AS987–AS990	

Built by Gloster Aircraft Co at Brockworth

P2535–P3264	First batch of 500 aircraft, delivered Nov 1939 – Apr 1940 (3)
R4074–R4232	Second batch of 100 aircraft, delivered May – Jul 1940 (2)
V6533–V7195	Third batch of 1,250 aircraft, delivered Jul 1940 – Sep 1941 (5)
W9110–W9359	
Z4022–Z4652	
Z4686–Z4939	

HURRICANE MKII

Built by Hawker Aircraft Ltd at Kingston–upon–Thames, Brooklands and Langley

Z2308–Z4018	Fifth batch of 1,000 aircraft, delivered Jan – Jul 1941 (5)
BD696–BD986	Sixth batch of 1,350 aircraft, delivered Jul 1941 – Mar 1942 (6)
BE105–BE716	
BM898–BM996	
BN103–BN987	
BN988–BN992	Seventh batch of 1,900 aircraft, delivered Mar – Nov 1942 (8)
BP109–BP772	
HL544–HL997	
HM110–HM157	
HV275–HV989	
HW115–HW881	
KW745–KW982	Eighth batch of 1,200 aircraft, delivered Nov 1942 – Apr 1943 (8)
KX101–KX967	
KZ111–KZ612	
KZ613–KZ949	Ninth batch of 1,200 aircraft (including MkIVs), delivered Apr – Sep 1943 (8)
LA101–LA144	
LB542–LB999	
LD100–LD999	
LE121–LE999	Tenth batch of 1,350 aircraft (including MkIVs), delivered Sep 1943 – May 1944 (8)
LF101–LF774	
MW335–MW373	
PG425–PG610	
PZ730–PZ865	
NL255	Hurricane MkV prototype

Built by Gloster Aircraft Co at Brockworth

Z4940–Z4989	Third batch of 450 aircraft, delivered Mar – Sep 1941 (3)
Z4990–Z5693	
BG674–BG999	Fourth batch of 450 aircraft, delivered Sep – Dec 1941 (5)
BH115–BH361	

CANADIAN-BUILT HURRICANE MKX/XI/XII

Built by Canadian Car and Foundry Corporation, Montreal and Ontario, Canada

P5170–P5209	First batch of 40 MkI (MkX) aircraft, shipped to UK Mar – Nov 1940
AE958–AE977	Second batch of 350 MkX aircraft, shipped to UK Jun 1940 – Apr 1941
AP945–AP993	
AG101–AG344	
AG665–AG684	
AM270–AM369	Third batch of 100 MkX aircraft, shipped to UK during 1941
BW835–BW884	Fourth batch of 100 MkX aircraft, shipped to UK during 1941
BW885–BW973	Fifth batch of 150 MkXI aircraft, shipped to UK during 1941–42
BX115–BX134	
JS219–JS468	Sixth batch of 250 MkXI/XII aircraft, shipped to UK during 1942
PJ660–PJ872	Seventh batch of 150 MkXII aircraft, shipped to UK during 1942

Appendix B

Squadrons and Locations

This appendix lists each squadron of the RAF and Commonwealth that operated the Hawker Hurricane. It shows the location, base (or bases), and period of operation. Due to the large number of moves the squadrons made, bases are often grouped together, and often cover a period of several months. The mark (or marks) of Hurricane operated during each period is also shown.

1 Squadron

UK	Tangmere	Oct 1938 – Sep 1939	MkI
France	Octeville/Norrent Fontes/Vassincourt	Sep 1939 – Apr 1940	MkI
France	Berry–au–Bac/Vassincourt/Cond≥–Vraux/Anglure	Apr – Jun 1940	MkI
France	Chateaudun/Chateau Bougon/St Nazaire	Jun 1940	MkI
UK	Northolt/Tangmere/Wittering	Jun 1940 – Jan 1941	MkI
UK	Kenley/Croydon/Redhill/Tangmere/Acklington	Jan 1941 – Sep 1942	MkI/IIA/IIB

3 Squadron

UK	Kenley/Biggin Hill/Croydon/Manston	Mar 1938 – May 1940	MkI
France	Merville	May 1940	MkI
UK	Kenley/Wick/Castletown/Turnhouse/Dyce/Skeabrae	May 1940 – Apr 1941	MkI
UK	Martlesham Heath/Debden/Stapleford Tawney	Apr – Jun 1941	MkIIA/IIB/IIC
UK	Hunsdon	Aug 1941 – Apr 1943	MkIIA/IIB/IIC

5 Squadron

| India/Burma | Khargpur/Sapam/Wangjing/Lanka | Jun 1943 – Jun 1944 | MkIIC/IID |
| India/Burma | Dergaon/Vizagapatam | Jun – Sep 1944 | MkIIC/IID |

6 Squadron

Egypt/Libya	Shandur/Gambut/Sidi Haneish/LGs	May – Dec 1942	MkIID
Egypt/Libya	Idku/Bu Amud/Castel Benito/Sorman	Dec 1942 – Apr 1943	MkIIC/IID
Tunisia	Senem/Gabes/El Maoui/Bou Goubrine/Ben Gardane	Apr–Sep 1943	MkIID
Egypt	Heliopolis/Fayid	Sep 1943 – Feb 1944	MkIID/MkIV
Italy	Grottaglie/Foggia/Canne	Feb 1944 – Jul 1945	MkIV
Palestine	Megiddo/Petah Tiqva/Ein Shemer/Ramat David	Jul 1945 – Oct 1946	MkIV
Cyprus	Nicosia	Oct 1946 – Jan 1947	MkIV

11 Squadron

India/Burma	Ranchi/Cholavarum/Lalmai/Ramu/Sapam/Tulihal	Sep 1943 – Apr 1944	MkIIC
India/Burma	Lanka/Dimapur/Imphal/Tamu	Apr 1944 – Jan 1945	MkIIC
India/Burma	Kan/Sinthe/Magwe/Feni/Chettinad/Tanjore	Jan – Jul 1945	MkIIC

17 Squadron

UK	North Weald/Croydon/Debden/Hawkinge/Kenley	Jun 1939 – Jun 1940	MkI
UK	Le Mans/Jersey/Guernsey	Jun 1940	MkI
UK	Debden/Tangmere/Martlesham Heath/Croydon	Jun 1940 – Apr 1941	MkI/IIA
UK	Castletown/Elgin/Tain/Catterick	Apr – Nov 1941	MkI/IIB
India/Burma	Mingaladon/Magwe/Lashio/Pankham Fort	Jan – Apr 1942	MkIIA
India/Burma	Jessore/Alipore/Red Road	May 1942 – Mar 1943	MkIIB/IIC
India/Burma	Kalyanpur/Alipore/Agartala	Mar – Aug 1943	MkIIC
Ceylon	China Bay/Minneriya	Aug 1943 – Jun 1944	MkIIC

20 Squadron

India/Burma	Charra/Kalyanpur	Feb – Nov 1943	MkIID
India/Burma	Nidania/Madhaibunia/Chiringa/Kajamalai	Nov 1943 – Sep 1944	MkIID
India/Burma	St Thomas Mount/Sapam	Sep 1944 – Jan 1945	MkIID/IV
India/Burma	Thazi/Monywa/Thedaw/Toungoo/Chettinad	Jan – Jun 1945	MkIID/IV
India/Burma	St Thomas Mount/Amarda Road	Jun – Sep 1945	MkIID/IV

28 Squadron

India/Burma	Ranchi/Imphal/Dalbumgarh/Tamu	Dec 1942 – Jan 1945	MkIIB/IIC
India/Burma	Ye–U/Sadaung/Meiktila/Mingaladon	Jan – Oct 1945	MkIIC

29 Squadron

UK	Wellingore	Aug – Dec 1940	MkI

30 Squadron

Egypt	Amriya/Idku/LGs	May 1941 – Feb 1942	MkI/IIA/IIB
Ceylon	Ratmalana/Dambulla/Colombo Racecourse	Mar 1942 – Jan 1944	MkIIA/IIB/IIC
India/Burma	Feni/Fazilpur/Comilla/Yelahanka	Jan – Jul 1944	MkIIC

32 Squadron

UK	Biggin Hill/Gravesend/Manston	Oct 1938 – Jan 1940	MkI
UK	Wittering/Biggin Hill/Acklington	May – Dec 1940	MkI
UK	Middle Wallop/Ibsley/Pembrey/Angle	Dec 1940 – Nov 1941	MkI/IIB
UK	Manston/West Malling/Friston/Honiley/Baginton	Nov 1941 – Nov 1942	MkIIB/IIC
Algeria	Philippeville/Maison Blanche	Dec 1942 – May 1943	MkIIC
Tunisia	Tingley	May – Aug 1943	MkIIC

33 Squadron

Egypt	Fuka/Amriya	Sep 1940 – Feb 1941	MkI
Greece	Eleusis/Larissa/Maleme	Feb – Jun 1941	MkI
Egypt/Libya	Amriya/Gerawla/Gamil/Fuka/Sidi Haneish	Jun – Nov 1941	MkI
Egypt/Libya	Giarabub/Msus/Antelat/Mechili/Gazala/Gambut	Nov 1941 – Jun 1942	MkI/IIB
Egypt/Libya	Sidi Azeiz/Idku/LGs	Jun – Nov 1942	MkIIC
Egypt/Libya	El Adem/Benina/Bersis/Misurata West	Nov 1942 – Dec 1943	MkIIC

34 Squadron

| India/Burma | St Thomas Mount/Cholavarum/Alipore/Palel | Aug 1943 – Apr 1944 | MkIIC |
| India/Burma | Dergaon/Yazagyo/Onbauk | Apr – Dec 1944 | MkIIC |

42 Squadron

India/Burma	Yelahanka/Palel/St.Thomas Mount	Oct 1943 – May 1944	MkIIC
India/Burma	Kangla/Tulihal/Onbauk/Ondaw	May 1944 – Apr 1945	MkIIC/IV
India/Burma	Magwe/Chakulia/Dalbumgarh	May – Jun 1945	MkIV

43 Squadron

UK	Tangmere/Acklington/Wick	Nov 38 – May 1940	MkI
UK	Tangmere/Northolt	May – Aug 1940	MkI
UK	Usworth/Drem/Crail/Acklington	Sep 1940 – Jun 1942	MkI/IIA/IIB/IIC
UK	Tangmere/Kirton–in–Lindsey	Jun – Nov 1942	MkI/IIA/IIB/IIC
Gibraltar	Gibraltar	Nov 1942	MkIIC
Algeria	Maison Blanche	Nov 1942 – Apr 1943	MkIIC

46 Squadron

UK	Digby/Acklington	Feb 1939 – May 1940	MkI
Norway	Skaanland/Bardufoss	May – Jun 1940	MkI
UK	Digby/Duxford/Stapleford Tawney/North Weald	Jun – Dec 1940	MkI
UK	Digby/Church Fenton/Sherburn–in–Elmet	Dec 1940 – May 1941	MkIIA
Malta	Luqa/Hal Far	Jun – Jul 1941	MkI/IIC

56 Squadron

UK	North Weald/Martlesham Heath	May 1938 – May 1940	MkI
UK	Gravesend/North Weald/Digby/Wittering	May – Sep 1940	MkI
UK	Boscombe Down/Middle Wallop	Sep – Dec 1940	MkI
UK	North Weald/Martlesham Heath/Duxford	Dec 1940 – Jan 1942	MkI/IIB

60 Squadron

India/Burma	Yelahanka/St.Thomas Mount/Cholavarum	Aug – Nov 1943	MkIIC
India/Burma	Agartala/Silchar West/Dergaon/Kumbhirgram	Nov 1943 – Sep 1944	MkIIC
India/Burma	Kangla/Taukkyan/Monywa	Sep 1944 – Apr 1945	MkIIC
India/Burma	Thedaw/Kalewa/Mingaladon/Tanjore	Apr – Jul 1945	MkIIC

63 Squadron

UK	Turnhouse	Mar – May 1944	MkIIC/IV

67 Squadron

India/Burma	Toungoo/Magwe/Akyab/Alipore/Chittagong	Feb 1942 – Feb 1944	MkIIB/IIC

69 Squadron

Malta	Luqa	Jan 1941 – Feb 1942	MkI/IIA

71 Squadron

UK	Kirton–in–Lindsey/Martlesham Heath/North Weald	Nov 1940 – Aug 1941	MkI/IIA

73 Squadron

UK	Digby	Jul 38 – Sep 1939	MkI
France	Le Havre/Octeville/Norrent Fontes/Rouvres	Sep 1939 – Apr 1940	MkI
France	Reims/Champagne/Raudin/Nantes	Apr – Jun 1940	MkI
UK	Church Fenton/Castle Camps	Jun – Nov 1940	MkI
Egypt/Libya	Takoradi/Heliopolis/Sidi Haneish/Gazala West	Nov 1940 – Mar 1941	MkI
Egypt/Libya	Bu Amud/El Gubbi/Sidi Haneish/Amriya	Mar – Sep 1941	MkI
Egypt/Libya	Port Said/Gamil/Shandur/El Adem/Gasr–el–Arid	Sep 1941 – Mar 1942	MkI
Egypt/Libya	Gambut/Qasaba/Burg–el–Arab/El Ballah/Shandur	Mar – Nov 1942	MkI/IIA/IIB/IIC
Egypt/Libya	Gambut/Merduma/Alemel Chel	Nov 1942 – Mar 1943	MkIIC
Tunisia	Gabes/Sfax/Alem/Monastir/La Sebala	Mar – Jul 1943	MkIIC

74 Squadron

Persia	Mehrabad/Abadan	Dec 1942 – Mar 1943	MkIIB
Iraq	Shaibah/Habbaniya	Mar – May 1943	MkIIB
Palestine	Aqir	May 1943	MkIIB
Egypt	LGs/Idku	May – Sep 1943	MkIIB

79 Squadron

UK	Biggin Hill/Manston/Digby	Nov 38 – May 1940	MkI
France	Mons/Norrent Fontes/Merville	May – Jun 1940	MkI
UK	Hawkinge/Sealand/Acklington/Biggin Hill	Jul – Sep 1940	MkI
UK	Pembrey/Fairwood Common	Sep 1940 – Dec 1941	MkI
UK	Warmwell/Fairwood Common/Baginton	Dec 1941 – Apr 1942	MkIIB
India/Burma	Kanchrapara/Dohazari/Ramu/Comilla	Jun 1942 – Jul 1943	MkIIC
India/Burma	Ranchi/Alipore/Chittagong/Dohazari/Yelahanka	Jul 1943 – Jul 1944	MkIIC

80 Squadron

Egypt	Amriya/Sidi Haneish	Jun – Aug 1940	MkI
Greece	Trikkala/Larissa/Iannina/Eleusis/Argos	Nov 1940 – Apr 1941	MkI
Palestine/Cyprus	Aqir/Nicosia/Haifa	May – Sep 1941	MkI
Syria	Rayak	Sep – Oct 1941	MkI
Egypt/Libya	Gaza/El Gubbi/Gazala/El Adem/LGs/Gambut	Oct 1941 – Sep 1942	MkI/IIC
Palestine	El Bassa	Sep – Oct 1942	MkIIC
Egypt/Libya	LGs/Bu Amud	Oct 1942 – Apr 1943	MkIIC

81 Squadron

Russia	Vayenga	Sep – Nov 1941	MkIIB

85 Squadron

UK	Debden	Sep 1938 – Sep 1939	MkI
France	Rouen/Boos/Merville	Sep – Nov 1939	MkI
France	Lille/Seclin/Mons–en–Chaussee	Nov 1939 – May 1940	MkI
UK	Debden/Croydon/Castle Camps/Church Fenton	May – Oct 1940	MkI
UK	Kirton–in–Lindsey/Gravesend/Debden	Oct 1940 – May 1941	MkI
UK	Hunsdon/West Malling/Swannington	May – Jul 1941	MkI

87 Squadron

UK	Debden	Jul 38 – Sep 1939	MkI
France	Rouen/Boos/Merville	Sep – Nov 1939	MkI
France	Lille/Seclin/Le Touquet/Amiens/Merville	Nov 1939 – May 1940	MkI
UK	Debden/Church Fenton/Exeter/Colerne	May – Dec 1940	MkI
UK	Charmy Down/Colerne	Dec 1940 – Nov 1942	MkI/IIC
Algeria	Philippeville/Djidjelli/Setif/Taher	Dec 1942 – May 1943	MkIIC
Tunisia	Tingley/La Sebala	May – Sep 1943	MkIIC
Sicily	Palermo/Borizzo	Sep 1943 – Jan 1944	MkIIC

94 Squadron

Egypt/Libya	Ismailia/El Ballah/Sidi Rezegh/Gazala/Msus	May 1941 – Jan 1942	MkI/IIC
Egypt/Libya	Antelat/El Gamil/Martuba/Savoia/El Adem	Jan 1942 – Apr 1944	MkI/IIC

95 Squadron

Sierra Leone	Freetown	Jul – Oct 1941	MkI

96 Squadron

UK	Cranage/Wrexham	Dec 1940 – Mar 1942	MkI/IIC

98 Squadron

Iceland	Kaldadarnes	Jun – Jul 1941	MkI

111 Squadron

UK	Northolt/Acklington/Drem/Wick	Jan 1938 – May 1940	MkI
UK	Northolt/Digby/North Weald	May – Jun 1940	MkI
UK	Croydon/Debden/Drem/Dyce/Montrose	Jun 1940 – May 1941	MkI/IIA

113 Squadron

India/Burma	Yelahanka/Cholavarum/Manipur Road	Sep – Dec 1943	MkIIC
India/Burma	Dimapur/Tulihal/Palel/Yazagyo/Onbauk/Ondaw	Dec 1943 – May 1945	MkIIC

116 Squadron

UK	Hendon/Heston/Croydon	Nov 1941 – Jul 1944	MkI/IIA
UK	North Weald/Gatwick/Redhill/Hornchurch	Jul 1944 – May 1945	MkI/IIA

121 (Eagle) Squadron

UK	Kirton–in–Lindsey/Digby	May – Nov 1941	MkI/IIB

123 (East India) Squadron

Persia	Mehrabad/Abadan	Nov 1942 – May 1943	MkIIC
Egypt	Bu Amud	May – Nov 1943	MkIIC
Far East	Feni/Patharkundi/St.Thomas Mount	Dec 1943 – Jul 1944	MkIIC

126 Squadron

Malta	Ta Kali	Jun 1941 – Apr 1942	MkI/IIB

127 Squadron

Iraq	Haditha/T1/Tahoune Guemac	Jun – Jul 1941	MkI
Palestine	St Jean	Mar – Jun 1942	MkI
Egypt	Shandur/Amriya/LGs	Jun 1942 – Jan 1943	MkIIB/IIC
Palestine	St Jean/Ramat David	Jan 1943 – Mar 1944	MkIIB/IIC

128 Squadron

Sierra Leone	Hastings	Oct 1941 – Mar 1943	MkI/IIB

133 (Eagle) Squadron

UK	Duxford	Aug – Dec 1941	MkIIB

134 Squadron

Russia	Vayenga	Sep – Nov 1941	MkIIA/IIB
UK	Eglinton	Jan – Feb 1942	MkIIA
Egypt/Libya	Kasfareet/Helwan/Shandur/LGs/Bu Amud/Bersis	Jun 1942 – Oct 1943	MkIIB/IIC
India/Burma	Comilla/Parashuram/Fazilpur	Dec 1943 – Jul 1944	MkIIB/IIC
India/Burma	Hay/Ramu II/Arkonam/Cuttack	Jan – Aug 1944	MkIIB/IIC

135 Squadron

UK	Baginton/Honiley	Aug – Sep 1941	MkIIA
India/Burma	Zayatkwin/Mingaladon	Jan 1942	MkIIA/IIB
India/Burma	Dum Dum/George/Hove/Ramu/Reindeer/Dohazari	Mar 1942 – May 1943	MkIIB
India/Burma	St Thomas Mount/Yelahanka	May 1943 – Jan 1944	MkIIB/IIC
Ceylon	Minneriya/Amarda Road	Jan – Sep 1944	MkIIC

136 Squadron

UK	Kirton–in–Lindsey	Aug – Nov 1941	MkIIA/IIB
India/Burma	Asansol/Alipore/Red Road/Vizagapatam/Dum Dum	Mar – Dec 1942	MkIIB/IIC
India/Burma	Chittagong/Baigachi	Dec 1942 – Oct 1943	MkIIB/IIC

137 Squadron

UK	Southend/Manston/Lympne	Jun 1943 – Jan 1944	MkIV

145 Squadron

UK	Croydon/Tangmere/Westhampnett/Drem/Dyce	Mar 1940 – Feb 1941	MkI

146 Squadron

India/Burma	Dum Dum/Alipore/Chittagong/Feni	May 1942 – Jun 1943	MkIIB
India/Burma	Comilla/Baigachi/St.Thomas Mount	Jun 1943 – Jun 1944	MkIIB

151 Squadron

UK	North Weald/Martlesham Heath/Manston	Dec 38 – May 1940	MkI
France	Vitry–en–Artois	May 1940	MkI
UK	North Weald/Stapleford Tawney/Digby/Bramcote	May – Dec 1940	MkI
UK	Wittering/Coltishall	Dec 1940 – Feb 1942	MkI/IIC

153 Squadron

Algeria	Reghaia	Aug – Sep 1944	MkIIC

164 (Argentine–British) Squadron

UK	Middle Wallop/Warmwell/Manston	Feb – Sep 1943	MkIID/IV
UK	Fairlop/Twinwood Farm	Sep 1943 –Mar 1944	MkIV

173 Squadron

Egypt	Heliopolis/LGs	Jul 1942 – Feb 1944	MkI

174 (Mauritius) Squadron

UK	Manston/Fowlmere/Warmwell	Mar – Dec 1942	MkIIB
UK	Odiham/Chilbolton/Grove/Zeals	Dec 1942 – Apr 1943	MkIIB

175 Squadron

UK	Warmwell/Harrowbeer/Gatwick	Mar 1942 – Jan 1943	MkIIB
UK	Odiham/Stoney Cross/Lasham	Jan – Apr 1943	MkIIB

176 Squadron

India	Baigachi	May 1943 – Jan 1944	MkIIC

182 Squadron

UK	Martlesham Heath	Sep – Oct 1942	MkI/X

184 Squadron

UK	Colerne/Milfield/Chilbolton/Grove/Zeals	Dec 1942 – May 1943	MkIID/IV
UK	Eastchurch/Merston/Manston/Kingsnorth	May – Aug 1943	MkIID/IV
UK	Newchurch/Snailwell/Detling/Odiham/Eastchurch	Aug 1943 – Mar 1944	MkIID/IV

185 Squadron

Malta	Ta Kali/Hal Far	May 1941 – Apr 1942	MkI/IIA

193 Squadron

UK	Harrowbeer	Jan – Feb 1943	MkI/IIC

195 Squadron

UK	Hutton Cranswick	Dec 1942 – Feb 1943	MkI

208 Squadron

Egypt/Libya	Qasaba/Gambut/Barce/Heliopolis/Kazaklar	Nov 1940 – Apr 1941	MkI
Greece	Eleusis/Argos/Maleme	Apr – May 1941	MkI
Egypt	Gaza/Ramleh	May – Sep 1941	MkI
Palestine	Aqir	Sep – Oct 1941	MkI
Egypt/Libya	Gerawla/El Gubbi/Tmimi/Acroma/Sidi Azeiz	Oct 1941 – Mar 1942	MkI
Egypt/Libya	Moascar/LGs/Heliopolis/Burg el Arab	Mar – Nov 1942	MkI/IIA/IIB/IIC
Iraq	Aqsu/K1	Jan – Jul 1943	MkI/IIA/IIB/IIC
Syria	Rayak	Jul – Nov 1943	MkIIA/IIB/IIC
Palestine	El Bassa	Nov – Dec 1943	MkIIA/IIB/IIC

213 Squadron

UK	Wittering	Jan 1939 – May 1940	MkI
France	Merville	May 1940	MkI
UK	Biggin Hill/Exeter	May – Sep 1940	MkI
UK	Tangmere/Leconfield/Driffield/Castletown	Sep 1940 – May 1941	MkI
Egypt	Abu Sueir	May – Jul 1941	MkI
Palestine/Cyprus	Haifa/Nicosia	Jul – Oct 1941	MkI/IIA/IIC
Egypt/Libya	Ismailia/Idku/Shandur/LGs/Gambut/Sidi Azeiz	Oct 1941 – Jun 1942	MkI/IIA/IIC
Egypt/Libya	LGs/El Adem/Martuba/Misurata West/Idku	Jun 1942 – Sep 1943	Mk/IIA/IIC
Egypt/Libya	Lakatamia/Gamil	Sep 1943 – Mar 1944	Mk/IIA/IIC

225 Squadron

UK	Thruxton/Macmerry	Jan – Oct 1942	MkI/IIB/IIC
Algeria	Maison Blanche	Nov 1942	MkIIB/IIC
Tunisia	Tingley/Souk–el–Arba	Nov 1942 – Apr 1943	MkIIB/IIC

229 Squadron

UK	Digby/Wittering/Northolt/Speke	Mar 1940 – May 1941	MkI
Egypt/Libya	Idku/LGs/Bu Amud/Gazala/Msus/Antelat	May 1941 – Feb 1942	MkI/IIC
Egypt/Libya	LGs/El Firdan/Gambut	Feb – Mar 1942	MkIIC
Malta	Hal Far	Mar – Apr 1942	MkIIC

232 Squadron

UK	Sumburgh/Castletown/Skitten/Drem/Elgin	Jul 1940 – Apr 1941	MkI
UK	Montrose/Abbotsinch/Ouston	Apr – Nov 1941	MkI/IIB
Singapore	Seletar	Jan 1942	MkIIB

237 (Rhodesia) Squadron

Egypt/Libya	Gambut/Tmimi/Berka/Ismailia	Sep 1941 – Feb 1942	MkI
Iraq	Mosul/Qaiyara	Mar – Sep 1942	MkI
Persia	Kermanshah/Kirkuk	Sep 1942 – Feb 1943	MkI
Egypt/Libya	Shandur/LGs/Bersis/Idku	Feb – Dec 1943	MkI/IIC

238 Squadron

UK	Middle Wallop/St.Eval/Chilbolton/Pembrey	Jun 1940 – Apr 1941	MkI
Egypt/Libya	LGs/El Firdan/Bu Amud/Gazala/Msus	Jun – Dec 1941	MkI/IIC
Egypt/Libya	Antelat/El Gubbi/Gambut	Dec 1941 – May 1942	MkI/IIC
Egypt/Libya	Gambut/Sidi Azeiz/LGs/El Adem/Martuba/Gamil	May 1942 – Sep 1943	MkIIB/IIC

239 Squadron

UK	Gatwick	Jan – May 1942	MkI/IIC

241 Squadron

Algeria	Maison Blanche	Nov 1942	MkIIB
Tunisia	Souk–el–Arba/Souk–el–Khemis/Ariana/Bou Ficha	Dec 1942 – Oct 1943	MkIIB
Algeria	Philippeville	Oct – Dec 1943	MkIIB

242 (Canadian) Squadron

UK	Church Fenton/Biggin Hill/Coltishall/Duxford	Jan – Dec 1940	MkI
UK	Martlesham Heath/Stapleford Tawney	Dec 1940 – May 1941	MkI/IIB
UK	North Weald/Manston/Valley	May – Sep 1941	MkIIB
Singapore	Seletar/Kallang	Jan 1942	MkIIB
Sumatra/Java	Palembang/Tjililitan	Jan – Feb 1942	MkIIB

245 Squadron

UK	Leconfield/Drem/Hawkinge/Turnhouse	Mar – Jul 1940	MkI
UK	Aldergrove/Ballyhalbert/Chilbolton/Warmwell	Jul 1940 – Dec 1941	MkI/IIB
UK	Middle Wallop/Charmy Down	Dec 1941 – Jan 1943	MkIIB

247 (China–British) Squadron

UK	Roborough/St Eval/Portreath	Dec 1940 – Jun 1941	MkI
UK	Predannack/Exeter/High Ercall	Jun 1941 – Feb 1943	MkIIA/IIB/IIC

249 (Gold Coast) Squadron

UK	Leconfield/Church Fenton/Boscombe Down	Jun – Aug 1940	MkI
UK	North Weald	Sep 1940 – May 1941	MkI/IIA/IIB
Malta	Ta Kali	May 1941 – Apr 1942	MkI/IIA/IIB

250 (Sudan) Squadron

Egypt	Gamil	Feb – Apr 1942	MkI/IIC

253 (Hyderabad State) Squadron

UK	Northolt/Kenley/Kirton–in–Lindsey/Turnhouse	Feb – Aug 1940	MkI
UK	Prestwick/Kenley/Leconfield	Aug 1940 – Feb 1941	MkI
UK	Skeabrae/Hibaldstow/Friston	Feb 1941 – Oct 1942	MkI/IIA/IIB/IIC
Algeria	Maison Blanche/Philippeville/Setif/Jemappes	Nov 1942 – Jun 1943	MkIIC
Mediterranean	Lampedusa	Jun – Aug 1943	MkIIC
Tunisia	La Sebala I	Aug – Sep 1943	MkIIC

255 Squadron

UK	Kirton–in–Lindsey/Hibaldstow	Mar – Jul 1941	MkI

256 Squadron

UK	SquireŌs Gate	Jul 1941 – May 1942	MkI

257 (Burma) Squadron

UK	Hendon/Northolt/Debden	Jun – Sep 1940	MkI
UK	Martlesham Heath/North Weald/Coltishall	Sep 1940 – Nov 1941	MkI/IIA/IIB/IIC
UK	Honiley/High Ercall	Nov 1941 – Sep 1942	MkI/IIA/IIB/IIC

258 Squadron

UK	Acklington/Jurby/Valley/Kenley	Dec 1940 – Jun 1941	MkI
UK	Martlesham Heath/Debden	Jun – Oct 1941	MkIIA
Singapore	Seletar/Kallang	Jan 1942	MkIIA
Sumatra	Palembang	Jan – Feb 1942	MkIIA
Ceylon	Ratmalana/Colombo Racecourse	Mar 1942 – Jan 1943	MkI/IIB
India/Burma	Dum Dum/Dambulla/Comilla/Dohazari	Jan – Dec 1943	MkIIB/IIC
India/Burma	Chittagong/Hay/Hove/Reindeer/Arkonam	Dec 1943 – Jul 1944	MkIIC

260 Squadron

UK	Castletown/Skitten/Drem	Nov 1940 – May 1941	MkI
Palestine	Haifa	Aug – Oct 1941	MkI
Egypt/Libya	LGs/Sidi Rezegh/Gazala/Msus/Antelat/Benina	Oct 1941 – Feb 1942	MkI

261 Squadron

Malta	Luqa/Hal Far/Ta Kali	Aug 1940 – May 1941	MkI
Iraq	Habbaniya/Shaibah/Mosul	Jul – Dec 1941	MkI
Palestine	Haifa/St Jean	Jan 1942	MkI
India	Dum Dum	Feb – Mar 1942	MkI
Ceylon	China Bay	Mar 1942 – Jan 1943	MkIIB
India/Burma	Baigachi/Chittagong	Jan 1943 – Oct 1943	MkIIB
India/Burma	Chiringa/Baigachi/Alipore/Yelahanka	Oct 1943 – Jun 1944	MkIIB/IIC

263 Squadron

UK	Drem/Grangemouth	Jun – Nov 1940	MkI

273 Squadron

Ceylon	Katukurunda/Ratmalana/China Bay	Aug 1942 – Mar 1944	MkI/IIB/IIC

274 Squadron

Egypt/Libya	Amriya/Sidi Haneish South/Gazala	Aug 1940 – Apr 1941	MkI
Egypt/Libya	Gerawla/Amriya/Sidi Haneish North	Apr – Nov 1941	MkI/IIB/IIC
Egypt/Libya	LGs,Msus/El Adem	Nov 1941 – Feb 1942	MkIIB/IIC
Egypt/Libya	Gasr el Arid/Gambut/Sidi Haneish/LGs/Bu Amud	Feb – Nov 1942	MkIIB/IIC
Egypt/Libya	Martuba I/Benina/Misurata/Mellaha/Derna	Nov 1942 – Sep 1943	MkIIC
Cyprus	Paphos	Sep – Oct 1943	MkIIC

279 Squadron

UK	Thornaby	Apr – Jun 1945	MkIIC/IV

284 Squadron

Tunisia	Tingley/El Aouina	Sep 1944 – Mar 1945	MkIIC

285 Squadron

UK	Woodvale/Andover/North Weald	Jan 1944 – Jun 1945	MkIIC

286 Squadron

UK	Filton/Lulsgate Bottom/Colerne/Zeals/Locking	Nov 1941 – Nov 1943	MkI/IIC/IV
UK	Weston Zoyland/Culmhead/Colerne/Zeals	Nov 1943 – May 1945	MkIIC/IV

287 Squadron

UK	Croydon	Nov 1941 – Feb 1944	MkI/IIB/IV

288 Squadron

UK	Digby/Wellingore/Coleby Grange/Collyweston	Nov 1941 – Nov 1944	MkI/IIC/IV

289 Squadron

UK	Kirknewton/Turnhouse/Acklington/Eshott/Andover	Dec 1941 – Jun 1945	MkI/IIC/IV

290 Squadron

UK	Newtownards/Long Kesh/Turnhouse	Dec 1943 – Jan 1945	MkIIC

291 Squadron

UK	Hutton Cranswick	Mar 1944 – Jun 1945	MkIIC

302 (Poznanski) Squadron

UK	Leconfield/Northolt/Wethampnett/Kenley	Jul 1940 – May 1941	MkI/IIA
UK	Jurby/Churchstanton/Warmwell	May – Oct 1941	MkI/IIB

303 (Warsaw–Kosciusco) Squadron

UK	Northolt/Leconfield	Aug 1940 – Jan 1941	MkI

306 (Torunski) Squadron

UK	Church Fenton/Ternhill/Northolt	Aug 1940 – Jul 1941	MkI/IIA

308 (Krakowski) Squadron

UK	Baginton	Oct 1940 – Apr 1941	MkI

309 (Ziemia Czerwienska) Squadron

UK	Snailwell/Drem	Feb – Oct 1944	MkIIC/IV

310 (Czechoslovak) Squadron

UK	Duxford/Martlesham Heath/Dyce	Jun 1940 – Dec 1941	MkI/IIA

312 (Czechoslovak) Squadron

UK	Duxford/Speke	Aug 1940 – Mar 1941	MkI
UK	Valley/Jurby/Kenley/Martlesham Heath/Ayr	Mar – Dec 1941	MkI/IIB

315 (Deblinski) Squadron

UK	Acklington/Speke	Feb – Jul 1941	MkI

316 (Warszawski) Squadron

UK	Pembrey/Colerne/Churchstanton	Feb – Oct 1941	MkI/IIA/IIB

317 (Wilenski) Squadron

UK	Acklington/Ouston/Colerne	Feb – Jun 1941	MkI/IIA/IIB
UK	Fairwood Common/Exeter	Jun – Oct 1941	MkI/IIA/IIB

318 (Gdanskski) Squadron

UK	Detling	Apr – Aug 1943	MkI
Palestine	Muqeibila	Sep – Oct 1943	MkIIB
Egypt	Gaza/LGs	Oct 1943 – Feb 1944	Mk/IIB

331 (Norwegian) Squadron

UK	Catterick/Castletown/Skeabrae	Jul – Nov 1941	MkI/IIB

335 (Hellenic) Squadron

Palestine	Aqir/St Jean	Oct 1941 – Jan 1942	MkI
Egypt/Libya	Helwan/El Daba/Gerawla/Idku/Dekheila/LGs	Jan 1942 – Feb 1943	MkI/IIB
Egypt/Libya	Mersah Matruh/Tocra	Feb 1943 – Jan 1944	MkIIB/IIC

336 (Hellenic) Squadron

Egypt/Libya	LGs/El Adem/Bu Amud/Mersa Matruh	Feb 1943 – May 1944	MkIIC

351 (Yugoslav) Squadron

Libya	Benina	Jul – Sep 1944	MkIIC
Italy	Canne	Sep – Oct 1944	MkIV
Yugoslavia	Vis/Prkos	Oct 1944 – Jun 1945	MkIV

352 (Yugoslav) Squadron

Libya	Benina/Lete	Apr – Jul 1944	MkIIC

Auxiliary Air Forces Squadrons

501 (County of Gloucester) Squadron

UK	Filton/Tangmere	Mar 1939 – May 1940	MkI
France	Betheniville/Anglure/Le Mans/Dinard/Jersey	May – Jun 1940	MkI
UK	Croydon/Middle Wallop/Gravesend/Kenley	Jun – Dec 1940	MkI
UK	Filton/Colerne	Dec 1940 – May 1941	MkI

504 (County of Nottingham) Squadron

UK	Hucknall/Digby/Debden/Martlesham Heath	Mar 1939 – May 1940	MkI
France	Vitry–en–Artois/Lille/Norrent Fontes	May 1940	MkI
UK	Manston/Debden/Wick/Castletown	May – Aug 1940	MkI
UK	Catterick/Hendon/Filton/Exeter	Sep 1940 – Jul 1941	MkI
UK	Fairwood Common/Chilbolton/Ballyhalbert	Jul – Nov 1941	MkIIB

601 (County of London) Squadron

UK	Tangmere	Mar – May 1940	MkI
France	Merville	May 1940	MkI
UK	Middle Wallop/Tangmere/Debden	Jun – Sep 1940	MkI
UK	Exeter/Northolt/Manston/Matlask/Duxford	Sep 1940 – Jan 1942	MkI/IIB

605 (County of Warwick) Squadron

UK	Tangmere/Leuchars/Wick/Hawkinge/Drem	Aug 1939 – Sep 1940	MkI
UK	Croydon/Martlesham Heath/Ternhill	Sep 1940 – May 1941	MkI/IIA
UK	Baginton/Honiley	May – Oct 1941	MkIIA/IIB
Sumatra/Java	Palembang/Tjililitan/Tasik Masala	Jan – Feb 1942	MkIIB
Malta	Hal Far/Ta Kali (detachment)	Jan – Feb 1942	MkIIB

607 (County of Durham) Squadron

France	Vitry–en–Artois/Abbeville/Norrent Fontes	Mar – May 1940	MkI
UK	Croydon/Usworth/Tangmere/Turnhouse	May – Nov 1940	MkI
UK	Drem/Usworth/Macmerry/Skitten	Nov 1940 – Jul 1941	MkI/IIA/IIB
UK	Castletown/Martlesham Heath/Manston	Jul 1941 – Apr 1942	MkIIA/IIB
India/Burma	Alipore/Jessore/Feni/Chittagong	May 1942 – Sep 1943	MkIIB/IIC

610 (County of Chester) Squadron

UK	Hooton Park	Sep 1939	MkI

615 (County of Surrey) Squadron

France	Poix/Abbeville/Moorseele	Apr – May 1940	MkI
UK	Kenley/Prestwick/Northolt	May – Dec 1940	MkI
UK	Kenley/Valley/Manston/Angle/Fairwood Common	Dec 1940 – Apr 1942	MkI/IIA/IIB/IIC

Meteorological Units Operating the Hurricane MkIIC

518 Squadron	Aldergrove	Sep 1945 – Oct 1946
520 Squadron	Gibraltar	Jun 1944 – Apr 1946
521 Squadron	Docking/Langham/Chivenor	Aug 1944 – Feb 1946

Turbinlite Units 530 – 539 Squadrons (Sep 1942 – Jan 1943)

530 Squadron	Hunsdon	MkIIC
531 Squadron	West Malling/Debden	MkIIC
532 Squadron	Hibaldstow	MkIIB/IIC
533 Squadron	Charmy Down	MkIIC
534 Squadron	Tangmere	MkIIB/IIC/X/XI/XII
535 Squadron	High Ercall	MkIIC
536 Squadron	Predannack/Fairwood Common	MkIIC
537 Squadron	Middle Wallop	MkIIC
538 Squadron	Hibaldstow	MkIIC
539 Squadron	Acklington	MkIIC/X

Army/Anti–Aircraft Co–Operation and Calibration Units Operating the Hurricane

516 Squadron	Dundonald	Dec 1943 – Dec 1944	MkIIB/IIC
527 Squadron	Castle Camps/Snailwell/Digby	Jun 1943 – Apr 1945	MkI/IIB
567 Squadron	Detling/Hornchurch	Dec 1943 – Jun 1945	MkIV
577 Squadron	Castle Bromwich	Dec 1943 – Jul 1945	MkIIC/IV
587 Squadron	Weston Zoyland/Culmhead	Dec 1943 – Jul 1945	MkIIC/IV
595 Squadron	Aberporth	Dec 1943 – Dec 1944	MkIIC/IV
598 Squadron	Peterhead/Bircham Newton	Feb 1944 – Apr 1945	MkIIC/IV
631 Squadron	Towyn/Llanbedr	Mar 1944 – Jul 1945	MkIIC
639 Squadron	Cleave	Aug 1944 – Apr 1945	MkIV
650 Squadron	Cark/Bodorgan	Apr 1944 – Jun 1945	MkIV
667 Squadron	Gosport	Apr 1944 – Jul 1945	MkI/IIC
679 Squadron	Ipswich	Dec 1943 – Jun 1945	MkIIC/IV
691 Squadron	Roborough/Harrowbeer	Dec 1943 – Aug 1945	MkI/IIC
695 Squadron	Bircham Newton	Dec 1943 – Aug 1945	MkIIC

Photograph Reconnaissance Units

680 Squadron	Matariya	Feb 1943 – Dec 1944	MkI/IIB
681 Squadron	Dum Dum	Jan – Sep 1943	MkIIB

Commonwealth Squadrons
Royal Australian Air Force

3 Squadron RAAF

Egypt/Libya	Berka/Benina/Got–es–Sultan/Maraua	Feb – Apr 1941	MkI
Egypt/Libya	Martuba/Gazala East/Sidi Mahmoud/LG 79	Apr 1941	MkI
Egypt/Libya	Mersa Matruh/Sidi Haneish/Aboukir/Aqir	Apr – May 1941	MkI
Palestine	Lydda/Nicosia	May – Jul 1941	MkI

450 Squadron RAAF

Egypt/Libya	Aqir/Amman/Mezze	Jun – Jul 1941	MkI
Palestine	Haifa/El Bassa	Jul – Aug 1941	MkI
Syria	Rayak	Aug – Oct 1941	MkI

451 Squadron RAAF

Egypt/Libya	Qasaba/LGs/Sidi Azeiz/Maddalena/Heliopolis	Jul 1941 – Feb 1942	MkI
Syria	Rayak	Feb – Mar 1942	MkI
Cyprus	Nicosia	Mar – Jun 1942	MkI
Palestine	El Bassa/Lakatamia/St.Jean	Jun 1942 – Jan 1943	MkI
Egypt	Mersa Matruh/Idku/El Daba	Jan – Oct 1943	MkI/IIC

Royal Canadian Air Force

401 (Ram) Squadron RCAF (Formerly 1 Squadron RCAF)

UK	Middle Wallop/Croydon	Jun – Aug 1940	MkI
UK	Northolt/Prestwick/Castletown/Driffield/Digby	Aug 1940 – Sep 1941	MkI/IIB

402 (Winnipeg Bear) Squadron RCAF (Formerly 2 Squadron RCAF)

UK	Digby/Martlesham Heath	Dec 1940 – Jul 1941	MkI/IIA
UK	Ayr/Southend/Warmwell	Jul 1941 – Mar 1942	MkIIA/IIB

417 (City of Windsor) Squadron RCAF

Egypt	Shandur/Heliopolis/Idku/Kufra	Sep – Dec 1942	MkI/IIB/IIC
Cyprus	Nicosia	Dec 1942 – Jan 1943	MkI/IIB/IIC

438 (Wild Cat) Squadron RCAF

UK	Digby/Wittering/Ayr/Hurn/Funtington	Nov 1943 – May 1944	MkIV

439 (Fangs of Death) Squadron RCAF

UK	Ayr/Hurn/Funtington	Jan – Apr 1944	MkIV

440 (City of Ottawa) Squadron RCAF

UK	Ayr/Hurn	Feb – Mar 1944	MkIV

Royal Egyptian Air Force

2 Squadron REAF

Egypt	Almaza/Idku/Mersa Matruh	Jan 1944 – Jan 1945	MkIIC

Royal New Zealand Air Force

486 Squadron RNZAF

UK	Kirton-in-Lindsey/Wittering/Hibaldstow	Mar – Aug 1942	MkI/IIA/IIB

488 Squadron RNZAF

Singapore	Kallang	Jan – Feb 1942	MkI

Indian Air Force

1 Squadron IAF

India/Burma	Trichinopoly/Arkonam/Bairagarth/Chharra/Risalpur	Sep 1942 – Jun 1943	MkI/IIB/IIC
India/Burma	Kohat/Sinthe	Jun 1943 – Mar 1946	MkIIB/IIC

2 Squadron IAF

India/Burma	Arkonam/Ranchi/Imphal/Trichinopoly	Sep 1942 – Nov 1943	MkIIB
India/Burma	Kohat/Miranshah/Kalyan/CoxÕs Bazaar/Mambur	Nov 1943 – Feb 1945	MkIIB
India/Burma	Akyab/Kohat/Samungli/Willingdon/ Jodhpur/Raipur/Kohat	Feb 1945 – Feb 1946	MkIIB

3 Squadron IAF

India/Burma	Phaphamau/Bairagarh/Ranchi/Kohat/Miranshah	Nov 1943 – Jul 1944	MkIIC
India/Burma	Bawli North/Dabaing I/Alipore/ St.Thomas Mount/Risalpur	Jan – Nov 1945	MkIIC

4 Squadron IAF

India/Burma	Phaphamau/Bairagarh/Sulur/Yelahanka	Aug 1943 – Feb 1944	MkIIC
India/Burma	Ranchi/Feni/CoxÕs Bazaar/Madhaibun/ Kyaukpyu/Yelahanka	Feb 1944 – May 1945	MkIIC
Japan	Iwakuni/Mihu	Mar – Aug 1946	MkIIC

6 Squadron IAF

India/Burma	Trichinopoly/Bairagarh/Cholavarum/ Kajamalai/Kalyan	Feb – Nov 1943	MkIIB/IIC
India/Burma	Cox's Bazaar/Ratnap/Risalpur/Kohat	Nov 1943 – Nov 1945	MkIIB/IIC

7 Squadron IAF

India/Burma	Peshawar/Kohat/Imphal/Sinthe/Magwe	Nov 1944 – May 1945	MkIIC
India/Burma	Kohat/Hathazari/Samungli/Lahore/Maharajpur	May 1945 – Mar 1946	MkIIC

9 Squadron IAF

India/Burma	Lahore/Bhopal/Kulaura/Amarda Road	Jan – May 1944	MkIIC
India/Burma	Kumbhirgram/Lanka/Dergaon/Comilla	May – Jul 1944	MkIIC
India/Burma	Singarbil/Hathazari/Ramu I/Akyab/Dabaing I/Ranchi	Jul 1944 – May 1945	MkIIC

10 Squadron IAF

India/Burma	Lahore/Risalpur/Chharra	Apr – Nov 1944	MkIIC
India/Burma	Ranchi/Ramu/Ramree/Bawli/Kyaukpyu	Nov 1944 – Apr 1945	MkIIC

South African Air Force

1 Squadron SAAF

East Africa	Eritrea/Somali/Ethiopia	Dec 1940 – Apr 1941	MkI
Egypt/Libya	Amriya/Sidi Haneish South/Maaten Bagush/ Sidi Barrani/Fuka	Apr – Nov 1941	MkIIB
Egypt/Libya	LGs/Sidi Rezegh/Gazala/Derna	Nov 1941 – Jan 1942	MkIIB
Egypt/Libya	Gazala III/El Adem/Sidi Haneish/LGs/El Gamil/Idku	Jan – Nov 1942	MkIIB/IIC

3 Squadron SAAF

East Africa	Eritrea/Somali/Ethiopia	Dec 1940 – Apr 1941	MkI
Aden	Khormaksar	Jan – Apr 1943	MkI
Egypt/Libya	Helwan/Bersis/Zuara/Mellaha/Savoia/Amriya	Apr – Mar 1944	MkI/IIB/IIC

7 Squadron SAAF

Egypt/Libya	Amriya/LGs/El Bassa/K8/Shandur/Benina/ Bersis/Derna	May 1942 – Aug 1943	MkI/IIB/IIC/IID

40 Squadron SAAF

Egypt/Libya	Burg el Arab/LGs/Sidi Azeiz/Qassassin/El Firdan	Jan – Nov 1942	MkI/IIB
Egypt/Libya	Sidi Azeiz/El Adem/Gazala II/Martuba/ Tmimi/Magrun	Nov – Dec 1942	MkIIB
Egypt/Libya	Belandah/Benina/Marble Arch/ Alem el Gzina/Hamraiet	Dec 1942 – Jan 1943	MkIIB
Egypt/Libya	Sedada/Darragh West/Castel Benito/El Assa/ Nefatia/Bu Grara	Jan – Apr 1943	MkIIB
Tunisia	Gabes Town/La Fauconnerie/Goubrine	Apr – May 1943	MkIIB

41 Squadron SAAF

Egypt/Libya	Almaza/Shandur/Bu Amud/El Adem/Savoia	May 1943 – May 1944	MkIIB/IIC

Appendix C

Order of Battle 1939–45

This appendix shows the squadrons and locations of the units, at home and abroad, which operated the Hurricane during the period September 1939 to July 1945. It includes those units which operated many different types of aircraft, including the Hurricane, for various non–operational duties. It should be noted, however, that sources often vary, particularly in theatres overseas such as the Western Desert and the Far East where squadrons often changed locations (almost daily) and one squadron could often be detached to more than one location. The Appendix, therefore, offers no more than a guide but is considered to be as accurate as possible.

1 SEPTEMBER 1939

SQUADRON	LOCATION	SQUADRON	LOCATION
1 Sqn	Tangmere	85 Sqn	Debden
3 Sqn	Biggin Hill	87 Sqn	Debden
17 Sqn	North Weald	111 Sqn	Northolt
32 Sqn	Biggin Hill	151 Sqn	North Weald
43 Sqn	Henlow	213 Sqn	Wittering
46 Sqn	Digby	501 Sqn	Filton
56 Sqn	North Weald	504 Sqn	Digby
73 Sqn	Digby	605 Sqn	Tangmere
79 Sqn	Biggin Hill		

10 JULY 1940

Squadron	Location	Organization	Squadron	Location	Organization
1 Sqn	Tangmere	11 Group	238 Sqn	Middle Wallop	10 Group
3 Sqn	Wick	13 Group	242 Sqn	Coltishall	12 Group
17 Sqn	Debden	11 Group	245 Sqn	Turnhouse	13 Group
32 Sqn	Biggin Hill	11 Group	249 Sqn	Church Fenton	12 Group
43 Sqn	Tangmere	11 Group	253 Sqn	Kirton–in–Lindsey	12 Group
46 Sqn	Digby	12 Group	257 Sqn	Northolt	11 Group
56 Sqn	North Weald	11 Group	263 Sqn	Grangemouth	13 Group
73 Sqn	Church Fenton	12 Group	310 Sqn	Duxford	12 Group
79 Sqn	Hawkinge	11 Group	501 Sqn	Middle Wallop	10 Group
85 Sqn	Debden	11 Group	504 Sqn	Castletown	13 Group
87 Sqn	Exeter	10 Group	601 Sqn	Tangmere	11 Group
111 Sqn	Croydon	11 Group	605 Sqn	Drem	13 Group
145 Sqn	Tangmere	11 Group	607 Sqn	Usworth	13 Group
151 Sqn	North Weald	11 Group	615 Sqn	Kenley	11 Group
213 Sqn	Exeter	10 Group	1 (RCAF) Sqn	Croydon	11 Group
229 Sqn	Wittering	12 Group			

Overseas

80 Sqn	Amriya, Egypt	

MAY 1941

SQUADRON	LOCATION	SQUADRON	LOCATION
1 Sqn	Kenley	255 Sqn	Hibaldstow
3 Sqn	Martlesham Heath	257 Sqn	Coltishall
17 Sqn	Castletown	258 Sqn	Jurby
32 Sqn	Ibsley	260 Sqn	Skitten
43 Sqn	Drem	302 Sqn	Kenley
46 Sqn	Digby	306 Sqn	Northolt
56 Sqn	North Weald	310 Sqn	Duxford
71 Sqn	Martlesham	312 Sqn	Valley
79 Sqn	Pembrey	315 Sqn	Speke
85 Sqn	Hunsdon	316 Sqn	Pembrey
87 Sqn	Colerne	317 Sqn	Acklington
96 Sqn	Cranage	401 Sqn RCAF	Digby
111 Sqn	Dyce/Montrose	402 Sqn RCAF	Digby
121 Sqn	Kirton–in–Lindsey	501 Sqn	Colerne
151 Sqn	Wittering	504 Sqn	Colerne/Exeter
213 Sqn	Castletown/Sumburgh	601 Sqn	Northolt
229 Sqn	Speke	605 Sqn	Ternhill
232 Sqn	Montrose	607 Sqn	Drem
238 Sqn	Chilbolton	615 Sqn	Kenley
242 Sqn	Stapleford Tawney		
245 Sqn	Aldergrove	No 52 OTU	Debden
247 Sqn	Roborough	No 55 OTU	Usworth
249 Sqn	North Weald	No 56 OTU	Sutton Bridge
253 Sqn	Skaebrae	No 59 OTU	Crosby

Overseas

MALTA COMMAND

69 Sqn	Luqa
185 Sqn	Ta Kali/Hal Far
261 Sqn	Ta Kali

MIDDLE EAST COMMAND

Egypt

6 Sqn	Qasaba
73 Sqn	Sidi Haneish
80 Sqn	Aqir
94 Sqn	Ismailia
208 Sqn	Heliopolis
274 Sqn	Amriya
1 Sqn SAAF	Amriya

Greece

30 Sqn	Maleme
33 Sqn	Maleme

APRIL 1942

UK

SQUADRON	LOCATION
1 Sqn	Tangmere
3 Sqn	Hunsdon
32 Sqn	Manston
43 Sqn	Acklington
79 Sqn	Baginton
87 Sqn	Charmy Down
116 Sqn	Hendon
174 Sqn	Manston
175 Sqn	Warmwell
225 Sqn	Thruxton
239 Sqn	Gatwick
245 Sqn	Middle Wallop
247 Sqn	Exeter
253 Sqn	Hibaldstow
256 Sqn	Squire's Gate
257 Sqn	Honiley
286 Sqn	Colerne
287 Sqn	Croydon
288 Sqn	Digby
289 Sqn	Kirknewton
306 Sqn	Churchstanton
312 Sqn	Angle
486 Sqn RNZAF	Kirton–in–Lindsey
607 Sqn	Manston
615 Sqn	Fairwood Common
885 Sqn FAA	Church Fenton
1423 Flt	Ouston
1449 Flt	St Mary's
MSFU	Speke
No 52 OTU	Aston Down
No 55 OTU	Annan
No 56 OTU	Tealing
No 59 OTU	Crosby

West Africa Command

128 Sqn	Hastings, Sierra Leone
FDF	Takoradi, Gold Coast

India Command

Ceylon

30 Sqn	Ratmalana
258 Sqn	Colombo Racecourse
261 Sqn	China Bay

OVERSEAS
HQ RAF Gibraltar

MSFU	Gibraltar

MIDDLE EAST COMMAND

Egypt/Libya

33 Sqn	Gambut
73 Sqn	Shandur
80 Sqn	Sidi Haneish
208 Sqn	Sidi Azeiz/Acroma
213 Sqn	Idku
229 Sqn	El Firdan
238 Sqn	Gambut
250 Sqn	El Gamil
274 Sqn	Sidi Haneish
335 Sqn	El Daba
1 Sqn SAAF	El Gamil
40 Sqn SAAF	Sidi Azeiz

Syria

127 Sqn	St Jean
451 Sqn	Rayak

Iraq

237 Sqn	Mosul

Malta

126 Sqn	Ta Kali
185 Sqn	Hal Far
249 Sqn	Ta Kali
1435 Flt	Ta Kali

India/Burma

17 Sqn	Pankham Fort
135 Sqn	Dum Dum
136 Sqn	Alipore

APRIL 1943

UK

SQUADRON	LOCATION	SQUADRON	LOCATION
116 Sqn	Heston	1422 Flt	Heston
164 Sqn	Middle Wallop	1449 Flt	Portreath
184 Sqn	Zeals	1472 Flt	Dishforth
286 Sqn	Locking	1480 Flt	Newtownards
287 Sqn	Croydon	MSFU	Speke
288 Sqn	Digby	No 55 OTU	Annan
289 Sqn	Turnhouse	No 56 OTU	Tealing
306 Sqn	Hutton Cranswick	No 59 OTU	Millfield
318 Sqn	Detling		

OVERSEAS

Mediterranean Air Command
Cyrenaica, Libya, Tunisia

6 Sqn	Sorman
32 Sqn	Maison Blanche
33 Sqn	Bersis
43 Sqn	Maison Blanche
73 Sqn	El Assa
80 Sqn	Bu Amud
87 Sqn	Tahir
94 Sqn	Martuba
213 Sqn	Misurata
225 Sqn	Souk el Arba
241 Sqn	Souk el Khemis
253 Sqn	Jemappes
274 Sqn	Mellaha
335 Sqn	Tocra
336 Sqn	LG 121
680 Sqn	Matariya
7 Sqn SAAF	Bersis
40 Sqn SAAF	Gabes Town

Middle East Command
Egypt

134 Sqn	LG 121
173 Sqn	Heliopolis
237 Sqn	LG 106
238 Sqn	Gamil
451 Sqn	Idku
3 Sqn SAAF	Helwan

Palestine

127 Sqn	Ramat David

Iraq and Persia

74 Sqn	Shaibah
123 Sqn	Abadan
208 Sqn	Aqsu

West Africa Command

1432 Flt	Kaduna, Nigeria

India Command
India/Burma

17 Sqn	Alipore	135 Sqn	Ramu	681 Sqn	Dum Dum
20 Sqn	Chharra	136 Sqn	Chittagong	1 Sqn IAF	Risalpur
28 Sqn	Ranchi	146 Sqn	Alipore	2 Sqn IAF	Imphal
67 Sqn	Alipore	261 Sqn	Baigachi	6 Sqn IAF	Bairagarh
79 Sqn	Ramu	607 Sqn	Chittagong		

Ceylon

30 Sqn	Colombo	258 Sqn	Dambulla	273 Sqn	China Bay

JULY 1944

UK

SQUADRON	LOCATION
116 Sqn	North Weald
285 Sqn	Woodvale
286 Sqn	Colerne
288 Sqn	Collyweston
289 Sqn	Turnhouse
290 Sqn	Long Kesh
291 Sqn	Hutton Cranswick
309 Sqn	Drem
516 Sqn	Dundonald
527 Sqn	Digby
567 Sqn	Detling
577 Sqn	Castle Bromwich
587 Sqn	Culmhead
595 Sqn	Aberporth
598 Sqn	Peterhead
631 Sqn	Towyn
650 Sqn	Cark
667 Sqn	Gosport
679 Sqn	Ipswich
691 Sqn	Roborough
695 Sqn	Bircham Newton
1449 Flt	Predannack
1681 BDTF	Honeybourne
1682 BDTF	Moreton–in–Marsh
1683 BDTF	Market Harborough
1684 BDTF	Wing
1686 BDTF	Finningley
1687 BDTF	Kirmington
1688 BDTF	Mildenhall
1689 BDTF	Holme
1690 BDTF	Swinderby
1695 BDTF	Topcliffe
1696 BDTF	Graveley
3 TEU	Annan
FLS	Millfield

OVERSEAS

HQ RAF Gibraltar

520 Sqn	Gibraltar

Mediterranean Allied Air Forces

6 Sqn	Grottaglie
351 Sqn	Benina
352 Sqn	Lete
680 Sqn	Matariya
2 Sqn EAF	Mersah Matruh

Air Command South East Asia

Imphal

5 Sqn	Dergaon
11 Sqn	Imphal
20 Sqn	Chiringa
28 Sqn	Dalbumgarh
34 Sqn	Dergaon
42 Sqn	Kangla
60 Sqn	Dergaon
113 Sqn	Palel
135 Sqn	Minneriya
1 Sqn IAF	Sinthe
2 Sqn IAF	Kohat
3 Sqn IAF	Kohat
4 Sqn IAF	Cox's Bazaar
6 Sqn IAF	Ratnap
9 Sqn IAF	Singarbil
10 Sqn IAF	Chharra

JULY 1945

UK			OVERSEAS	
SQUADRON	LOCATION			
521 Sqn	Langham		520 Sqn	Gibraltar
577 Sqn	Castle Bromwich			
587 Sqn	Weston Zoyland		**Balkan Air Force**	
691 Sqn	Harrowbeer			
695 Sqn	Bircham Newton		6 Sqn	Canne/Isle of Vis
1402 Met Flt	Ballyhalbert		**Air Command South East Asia**	
1687 BDTF	Hemswell		11 Sqn	Sinthe
1688 BDTF	Feltwell		20 Sqn	Monywa
1696 BDTF	Bourn		28 Sqn	Mingaladon
			60 Sqn	Thedaw
			1 Sqn IAF	Kohat
			2 Sqn IAF	Kohat
			3 Sqn IAF	Risalpur
			6 Sqn IAF	Kohat
			7 Sqn IAF	Samungli

Appendix D

Squadron Codes

This Appendix includes only the known squadron codes of operational Hurricane squadrons and does not include training units; although as accurate as possible, it should only serve as a guide as squadron codes were often changed.

AD	113 Sqn	BF	28 Sqn	DT	257 Sqn	EF	232 Sqn
AE	402 Sqn	BQ	451 Sqn	DU	312 Sqn	EL	181 Sqn
AF	607 Sqn	BR	184 Sqn	DX	245 Sqn	EY	80 Sqn
AK	213 Sqn			DZ	151 Sqn		
AL	79 Sqn			6D	20/631 Sqn		
AN	417 Sqn						
AP	80/186 Sqn						
AV	121 Sqn						
AW	42 Sqn						
FG	335 Sqn	GG	151 Sqn	HA	261 Sqn	II	116 Sqn
FJ	164/261 Sqn	GN	249 Sqn	HB	229/239 Sqn	I4	567 Sqn
FM	257 Sqn	GO	94 Sqn	HE	263 Sqn	I8	440 Sqn
FN	331 Sqn	GQ	134 Sqn	HF	183 Sqn		
FT	43 Sqn	GV	134 Sqn	HH	175/260/273 Sqn		
FV	81 Sqn	GZ	32 Sqn	HM	136 Sqn		
F3	438 Sqn			HN	20 Sqn		
				HP	247 Sqn		
				HS	260 Sqn		
				HV	73 Sqn		
JH	317 Sqn	KC	238 Sqn	LD	250 Sqn	MD	133 Sqn
JT	256 Sqn	KT	32 Sqn	LE	242 Sqn	ML	605 Sqn
JU	111 Sqn	KW	615 Sqn	LK	87 Sqn	MR	245 Sqn
JV	6 Sqn	KZ	287 Sqn	LR	56/146 Sqn	MS	273 Sqn
JX	1 Sqn	4K	87 Sqn	LZ	66 Sqn	MU	60 Sqn
						M4	587 Sqn
						2M	520 Sqn
						3M	679 Sqn
						4M	695 Sqn
NA	1/146 Sqn	OK	450 Sqn	PD	87/450 Sqn	QO	3 Sqn
NN	310 Sqn	OP	3 Sqn	PK	315 Sqn	8Q	34 Sqn
NO	85 Sqn	5O	521 Sqn	PO	46 Sqn		
NQ	43 Sqn						
NV	79 Sqn						
NW	33/286 Sqn						
RE	229 Sqn	SA	486 Sqn	TM	111/504 Sqn	UF	601 Sqn
RF	303 Sqn	SD	501 Sqn	TP	73 Sqn	US	56 Sqn
RG	208 Sqn	SF	137 Sqn			UV	17 Sqn
RJ	46 Sqn	SO	145 Sqn			UZ	306 Sqn
RL	279 Sqn	SW	253 Sqn				
RP	288 Sqn	SZ	316 Sqn				
RS	30/33 Sqn						
VK	238 Sqn	WC	309 Sqn	XE	123 Sqn	YB	17 Sqn
VY	85 Sqn	WG	128 Sqn	XJ	261 Sqn	YE	289 Sqn
5V	439 Sqn	WN	527 Sqn	XM	182 Sqn	YK	80 Sqn
		WX	302 Sqn	XP	174 Sqn	YO	401 Sqn
ZH	401 Sqn			XR	71 Sqn		
ZY	247 Sqn						
8Z	295 Sqn						

Appendix E

Pilots Killed During the Battle of Britain

DATE	SQUADRON	AIRCRAFT	PILOT KILLED
10 July	111	P3671	F/O T.P. Higgs
	253	P3359	Sgt I.C. Clenshaw
11 July	501	N2485	Sgt F.J. Dixon
12 July	85	P2557	Sgt L. Jowitt
	151	P3275	F/O J.H. Allen
	501	P3084	Plt Off D.A. Hewitt
13 July	56	P2922	Sgt J.J. Whitfield
		N2432	Sgt J.R. Cowsill
	238	P2950	F/L J.C. Kennedy
14 July	615	L1584	Plt Off M.R. Mudie
16 July	249	P2995	Sgt A.D. Main
19 July	43	P3531	Sgt J.A. Buck
20 July	32	N2670	S/Lt G.G. Bulmer
	43	P3964	F/O J.F. Haworth
	238	P3766	Sgt C. Parkinson
	263	P2917	Plt Off A.R. Downer
	501	P3082	Plt Off E.J. Sylvester
21 July	43	P3973	Plt Off R.A. De Mancha
22 July	85	P3895	Plt Off J.L. Bickerdike
24 July	46	P2685	Plt Off A.M. Cooper–Key
	151	P3316	Plt Off J.R. Hamar
25 July	87	P3596	Sgt J.H. Culverwell
26 July	601	P2753	Plt Off P. Chaloner–Lindsey
27 July	501	P3808	F/O P.A. Cox
29 July	43	L1955	Plt Off K.C. Campbell
	56	P3879	F/S C.J. Cooney
1 August	145	P3155	S/Lt I.H. Kestin
6 August	17	N2456	Plt Off H.W. Britton
8 August	43	P3781	Plt Off J. Cruttenden
		P3468	Plt Off J.R. Oelofse
	145	P2955	Plt Off L.A. Sears
		P3381	Sgt E.D. Baker
		P2957	Plt Off E.C. Wakeham
		P3163	F/O Lord R.U. Kay–Shuttleworth
		P3545	S/Lt F.A. Smith
	238	P3823	F/L D.E. Turner
		P3617	F/O D.C. MacCaw
	257	P2981	F/L N.M. Hall
		R4094	Sgt K.B. Smith
		P3058	F/O B.W. D'Arcy–Irvine

9 August	605	L2103	Sgt R.D. Ritchie
11 August	1	P3172	Plt Off J.A. Davey
	17	P3760	Plt Off K. Manger
	56	N2667	Sgt R.D. Baker
	87	V7231	F/L R.V. Jeff
	111	P3105	Plt Off J.H. Copeman
		P3922	Plt Off J.W. McKenzie
		?	Plt Off R.R. Wilson
		P3942	Sgt R.B. Sim
	145	P2951	F/O G.R. Branch
		V7294	F/O A. Ostowicz
	213	N2650	F/L R.D. Wight
		P3789	Sgt S.L. Butterfield
	238	P2978	Sgt G. Gledhill
		R4097	F/L S.C. Walch
		P3819	F/O M.J. Steborowski
		P3222	Plt Off F.N. Cawse
	601	P3885	Plt Off J.L. Smithers
		R4092	F/O R.S. Demetriadi
		P3783	F/O J. Gillan
		L2057	Plt Off W.G. Dickie
12 August	145	R4180	Plt Off J.H. Harrison
		P3391	Sgt J. Kwiecinski
		R4176	F/L W. Pankratz
	151	P3304	Plt Off R.W. Beley
	213	P2854	Sgt G.N. Wilkes
		P2802	Sgt S.G. Stuckey
	257	P3662	Plt Off J.A. Chomley
	501	P3803	F/O K. Lukaszewicz
13 August	87	P3387	F/O R.L. Glyde
	213	P3348	Sgt P.P. Norris
	238	P3177	Sgt H.J. Marsh
14 August	43	L1739	Sgt H.F. Montgomery
	615	P3109	F/O P. Collard
		P3160	Plt Off C.R. Montgomery
15 August	1	R4075	Plt Off D.O. Browne
		P3043	Sgt M.M. Shanahan
	87	P3215	S/L T.G. Lovell–Gregg
		P2872	Plt Off P.W. Comeley
	111	P3944	F/O B.M. Fisher
	151	P3941	Plt Off J.T. Johnston
		V7410	Plt Off M. Rozwadowski
	213	V7227	Plt Off M.S. Buchin
	615	P2801	Sgt D.W. Halton
16 August	111	R4193	F/L H.M. Ferriss
	213	AK–R	Plt Off J.E. Laricheliere
	249	P3616	Plt Off M.A. King
	601	P3358	Plt Off W.M. Fiske
18 August	17	L1921	Plt Off N.D. Solomon
	85	P2923	F/O R.H. Lee
	111	R4187	F/L S.D. Connors
	151	R4181	Plt Off J.B. Ramsay
	501	P3208	Plt Off J.W. Bland
		P2549	F/L G.E. Stoney
	601	R4191	Sgt L.N. Guy
		L1990	Sgt R.P. Hawkings
	615	P2768	Sgt P.K. Walley
20 August	242	P2967	Mid. P.J. Patterson
24 August	501	P3141	Plt Off P. Zenker

25 August	17	R4199	S/L C.W. Williams
	32	N2433	Plt Off K.R. Gillman
	87	V7250	Sgt S.R. Wakeling
	213	P3200	Plt Off H.D. Atkinson
		V7226	Plt Off J.A. Philippart
26 August	1 (RCAF)	P3874	F/O R.L. Edwards
27 August	213	N2336	S/Lt W.J. Moss
29 August	85	V6623	F/L H.R. Hamilton
30 August	43	P3179	Sgt D. Noble
		V6548	S/L J.V. Badger
	151	V7369	S/L E.B. King
		R4213	Sgt F. Gmur
	253	L1965	Plt Off C.D. Francis
		P3921	Plt Off D.N. Jenkins
		P3213	Sgt J.H. Dickinson
31 August	56	V7378	F/L P.S. Weaver
	79	V7200	Sgt H.A. Bolton
	253	L1830	S/L H.M. Starr
	257	P3175	Plt Off G.H. Maffett
	310	P3159	Plt Off J. Sterbacek
	601	R4215	F/O M.D. Doulton
1 September	1	P3276	F/S F.G. Berry
	85	L2071	Sgt G.B. Booth
		P3150	F/O P.P. Woods–Scawen
		P2673	Sgt J.H. Ellis
	253	P5185	Plt Off J.K. Clifton
2 September	43	V7420	Plt Off C.A. Woods–Scawen
	46	P3067	Plt Off J.C. Bailey
	111	P3875	Sgt W.L. Dymond
	501	L1578	F/O A.T. Rose–Price
3 September	1	P3782	Plt Off R.H. Shaw
		P3044	F/L H.B. Hillcoat
	46	P3064	Sgt G.H. Edworthy
	257	P3518	Plt Off C.R. Bon Seigneur
4 September	46	P3052	F/O R.P. Plummer
	79	P3676	Sgt J. Wright
	111	R4172	F/L D.C. Bruce
		Z2309	Plt Off J. Macinski
	151	V7406	Plt Off R. Ambrose
	253	V6638	F/O A.A. Trueman
5 September	73	P3224	Sgt A.L. McNay
6 September	253	P3032	S/L W.P. Cambridge
	501	V6612	Plt Off H.C. Adams
		V6646	Sgt O.V. Houghton
		P3516	Sgt G.W. Pearson
	601	P3363	F/L C.R. Davis
		P8818	F/L W.H. Rhodes–Moorhouse
7 September	43	V6641	S/L C.B. Hull
		V7257	F/L R.C. Reynell
	73	P3234	F/L R.E. Lovett
	242	P2962	Plt Off J. Benzie
	249	R4114	Plt Off R.D. Fleming
	257	P3049	F/L H.R. Beresford
		V7254	F/O L.R. Mitchell
	504	L1615	F/O K.V. Wendel
8 September	46	P3201	S/Lt J.C. Carpenter
9 September	242	P3087	Plt Off K.M. Sclanders
	310	P3888	F/O J.E. Boulton
	605	L2059	Plt Off G.M. Forrester
	607	P3574	Plt Off S.B. Parnall

		P3117	Plt Off J.D. Lenahan
		P2728	Plt Off G.J. Drake
11 September	46	P3525	Sgt S. Andrews
		V7232	Sgt W.A. Peacock
	213	V6667	Sgt A. Wojcicki
	238	V7240	F/L D.P. Hughes
		R2682	Sgt S. Duszynski
	303	V6665	F/O A. Cebrzynski
		V7242	Sgt S. Wojtowicz
	504	P3770	Plt Off A.W. Clarke
12 September	213	V7306	W/C J.S. Dewar
14 September	73	P2542	Sgt J.J. Brimble
	253	P5184	Sgt W.B. Higgins
15 September	1 (RCAF)	P3876	F/O R. Smither
	56	P3660	Sgt T.R. Tweed
	73	P3865	Plt Off R.A. Marchand
	229	N2537	Plt Off G.L. Doutrepont
	238	P2836	Sgt L. Pidd
	302	P2954	F/L T.P. Chlopik
	303	P3577	Sgt M. Brzezowski
	501	P2760	Plt Off A.E. van den Hove d'Ertsenrijk
	504	N2481	Plt Off J.V. Gurteen
		N2705	F/O M. Jebb
17 September	501	P3820	Sgt E.J. Egan
	504	V7529	Sgt D.A. Helcke
	607	P3933	Sgt J. Lansdell
18 September	46	V7442	Sgt G.W. Jefferys
	249	V6685	F/L D.G. Parnall
20 September	56	L1595	Sgt C.V. Meeson
21 September	601	L1894	F/O J. Topolnicki
24 September	605	P3832	Plt Off W.J. Glowacki
26 September	238	P3098	Sgt V. Horsky
	253	V7470	Plt Off W.M. Samolinski
27 September	1 (RCAF)	P3647	F/O O.J. Peterson
	213	N2401	F/L L.H. Schwind
	229	V6782	F/L R.F. Rimmer
	242	?	F/O M.G. Homer
	249	V6683	F/O P.R. Burton
		P3834	Plt Off J.R. Meaker
	303	L1696	F/O L.W. Paskiewicz
		V7246	Sgt T. Andruszkow
	501	V6645	Plt Off E.M. Gunter
28 September	238	N2400	Sgt R. Little
		V6776	Sgt S.E. Bann
		P3836	Plt Off D.S. Harrison
	501	P3417	Plt Off F.C. Harrold
	605	V6699	F/O P.G. Crofts
	607	P3108	F/L W.E. Gore
		R4189	F/L M.M. Irving
29 September	79	P5177	F/O G.C. Peters
	615	V7312	Plt Off J. McGibbon
30 September	46	?	Plt Off J.D. Crossman
	229	P2815	F/O M. Ravenhill
	501	P3414	F/O J.R. Hardacre
1 October	238	P3599	Sgt F.A. Sibley
	607	P2900	F/L C.E. Bowen
		V6686	Sgt N. Brumby
5 October	303	P3892	F/O W. Januszewicz
6 October	303	P3120	Sgt A. Siudak
7 October	245	N2707	Plt Off J.J. Beedham

	501	V6800	F/O N.J. Barry
	605	P3677	Plt Off C.E. English
	607	L1728	F/O I.B. Difford
8 October	229	V6820	Sgt J.R. Farrow
	303	R4175	Sgt J. Frantisek
9 October	1	V7376	Sgt S. Warren
10 October	56	P3421	Sgt J. Hlavak
	249	V7537	Sgt E.A. Bayley
	253	L1928	Sgt H.H. Allgood
	312	L1547	Sgt O. Hanzlicek
12 October	145	V7426	Sgt J.V. Wadham
	605	P3022	Sgt P.R. McIntosh
14 October	605	P3107	F/O R. Hope
15 October	46	N2480	Plt Off P.S. Gunning
		V6550	F/S E.E. Williams
	501	V6722	Sgt S.A. Fenemore
	605	N2546	F/L I.J. Muirhead
16 October	310	P3143	Sgt S.J. Chalupa
17 October	213	P3174	Plt Off R. Atkinson
	242	V6575	Plt Off N.N. Campbell
18 October	302	P3872	Plt Off S. Wapniarek
		V6571	Plt Off A. Zukowski
		P3931	F/O P.E. Carter
		P3930	F/O J. Borowski
19 October	3	P3260	F/O G.F. McAvity
21 October	245	P3657	Sgt E.G. Greenwood
22 October	46	R4074	Sgt J.P. Morrison
	257	R4195	Plt Off N.B. Heywood
		V6851	Sgt R.H. Fraser
24 October	43	V7303	Sgt D.R. Stoodley
	87	P3404	Plt Off D.T. Jay
	303	V6807	Plt Off J. Bury–Burzymski
25 October	46	V6804	Plt Off W.B. Pattullo
	79	N2708	Plt Off S. Platkowski
	302	V7593	F/L F. Jastrzebski
	501	P2903	Plt Off V. Goth
	601	V6917	Sgt L.D. May
		P3709	Sgt F. Mills–Smith
26 October	151	V7434	Sgt D.O. Stanley
		R4184	Sgt R. Holder
	229	W6669	F/O G.M. Simpson
27 October	43	L1963	Sgt L.V. Toogood
	145	P3167	Plt Off A.R. Jottard
29 October	46	?	Sgt H.E. Black
	213	V7622	Plt Off R.R. Hutley
	257	V6852	Sgt A.G. Girdwood
	310	P3889	Plt Off E. Fechtner
30 October	249	V7536	Plt Off W.H. Millington

NB These statistics include those who died of wounds or injuries.

Appendix F

Aces

This appendix lists all the fighter pilots who achieved five or more kills while flying the Hurricane. To keep the list to a manageable number, it includes only the confirmed individual kills in air–to–air combat and does not include 'shared' kills, 'probable' kills, claims of 'damaged' or kills against aircraft on the ground. It is acknowledged that many of the pilots listed went on to achieve more kills while flying aircraft of different types, but no reference to these are made in this appendix. It is also acknowledged that different sources may vary in the number of kills attributed to an individual. This appendix should, therefore, be treated as a guide and not necessarily definitive.

The tables below show the name of the pilot, the highest rank that he went on to achieve, and any decorations he received. It shows the squadron (or squadrons) with which he achieved his kills, and the mark (or marks) of Hurricane he flew during the period in which he achieved those kills. It also shows the period during which the kills were achieved, the dates showing the first and last kills, and the theatre (or theatres) in which he served during that same period. Finally and, sadly, inevitably, not all pilots survived the war; dates of death during the war are shown in the final column.

Top–Scoring Hurricane Pilots

NAME	RANK/DEC	KILLS	SQN	MK	PERIOD	THEATRE	REMARKS
Pattle MT St J	S/L DFC*	35	80/33	I	Feb – Apr 41	Greece	KIA 20 Apr 41
Carey FR	G/C CBE DFC* AFC DFM	25	43/3/135/267	I/IIB	May 40 – Feb 42	France/BoB/Far East	–
Lacey JH	S/L DFM*	23	501	I	May – Oct 40	France/BoB	–
Crossley MN	W/C DSO OBE DFC	20	32	I	May – Aug 40	France/BoB	–
Vale W	S/L DFC* AFC	20	80	I	Mar – Jun 41	Greece	–
Edge GR	G/C OBE DFC	18	605/253	I	May – Sep 40	BoB	–
Kuttelwascher KM	F/L DFC*	18	1	IIA/C	Apr 41 – Jul 42	UK	–
Lewis AG	S/L DFC*	18	85/249	I	May – Sep 40	France/BoB	–
Frantisek J	Sgt DFM*	17	303	I	Sep 40	BoB	KIA 8 Oct 40
McKellar AA	S/L DSO DFC*	17	605	I	Aug – Oct 40	BoB	KIA 1 Nov 40
McKnight WL	F/O DFC*	17	615/242	I	May – Sep 40	France/BoB	KIA 12 Jan 41
Clisby LR	F/O DFC	16	1	I	Apr – May 40	France	KIA 14 May 40
Hallowes HJL	W/C DFC DFM*	16	43	I	Apr – Aug 40	BoB	–
Kain EJ	F/O DFC	16	73	I	Nov 39 – May 40	France	Killed 6 Jun 40
Rabagliati AC	W/C DFC*	16	46/126	I/IIA	Aug 40 – Feb 42	BoB/Malta	KIA 6 Jul 43
Brown MH	W/C DFC*	15	1	I	Apr – Aug 40	France/BoB/Malta	KIA 12 Nov 41
David WD	G/C CBE DFC* AFC	15	87/213	I	May – Oct 40	France/BoB	–
Mason EM	S/L DFC	15	274/261	I/IIA	Dec 40 – Aug 41	N.Africa	KIA 15 Feb 42
Orton N	S/L DFC*	15	73	I	Nov 39 – May 40	France	KIA 17 Sep 41
Tuck RRS	W/C DSO DFC**	15	257	I/IIC	Sep 40 – Aug 41	BoB/UK	–
Urbanowicz W	W/C DFC	15	145/303	I	Aug – Sep 40	BoB	–
Dodds J	Sgt DFM	14	274	IIB/C	Dec 41 – Jun 42	N.Africa	–
Stevens RP	F/L DSO DFC*	14	151	I/IIC	Jan – Oct 41	UK	KIA 16 Dec 41

Woodward VC	W/C DFC*	14	33	I	Oct 40 – Jun 41	N.Africa/Greece	–
Czernin CMB	S/L DSO MC DFC	13	85/17	I	May – Sep 40	France/BoB	–
Dalton–Morgan TF	G/C DSO OBE DFC*	13	43	I/IIB	Jul 40 – Oct 41	BoB	–
Hewett EWF	F/L AFC DFM	13	80	I	Feb – Apr 41	Greece	–
Kilmartin JI	W/C DFC	13	1/43	I	Apr – Sep 40	France	–
Llewellyn RT	F/L DFM	13	213	I	May – Sep 40	BoB	–
Machlachlan JAF	S/L DSO DFC**	13	261/1	I/IIC	Jan 41 – Jun 42	Malta/UK	KIA 18 Jul 43
Barton RA	W/C OBE DFC*	12	249	I/IIA	Aug 40 – Nov 41	BoB/Malta	–
Boyd AH	G/C DSO DFC*	12	145	I	May – Oct 40	BoB	
Brothers PM	A/Cdre CBE DSO DFC*	12	32/257	I	May – Sep 40	France/BoB	–
Connors SDP	F/L DFC*	12	111	I	May – Aug 40	France/BoB	KIA 18 Aug 40
Higginson FW	F/L OBE DFC DFM	12	56	I	May – Sep 40	France/BoB	–
Marshall AE	F/L DFC DFM	12	73	I	Jun 40 – Apr 41	N.Africa	KIA 27 Nov 44
Neil TF	W/C DFC* AFC	12	249	I/IIA	Sep 40 – Jun 41	BoB/Malta	–
Scouler JE	S/L DFC AFC	12	73	I	Apr – May 40	France	–
Wade LC	W/C DSO DFC**	12	33	I/IIB/C	Nov 41 – Sep 42	N.Africa	Killed 12 Jan 44
Allard G	F/L DFC DFM*	11	85	I	May – Sep 40	France/BoB	Killed 13 Mar 41
Bader DRS	G/C KBE DSO* DFC*	11	242	I	Jul – Sep 40	BoB	–
Gibson JAA	S/L DSO DFC	11	501	I	May – Sep 40	France/BoB	–
Howes HN	Sgt DFM	11	85/605	I	May – Nov 40	France/BoB	Killed 22 Dec 40
Lapsley JH	AM KBE DFC AFC	11	80/274	I	Aug – Dec 40	N.Africa	–
Stephens MM	W/C DSO DFC**	11	3/232/80	I/IIA	May 40 – Dec 41	Fr/Turkey/N.Africa	–
Bazin JM	W/C DSO DFC	10	607	I	May – Sep 40	France/BoB	–
Cock JR	S/L DFC	10	87	I	Apr – Sep 40	France/BoB	–
Currant CF	W/C DSO DFC*	10	605	I	Aug – Dec 40	BoB	–
Driver KW	Maj DFC	10	1 SAAF	I	Dec 40 – May 41	Eritrea	–
Dymond WL	Sgt DFM	10	111	I	May – Aug 40	France/BoB	KIA 2 Sep 40
Gleed IR	W/C DSO DFC	10	87	I	May 40 – May 41	France/BoB	KIA 16 Apr 43
Goodman GE	F/O DFC	10	1/73	I	May 40 – Apr 41	Fr/BoB/N.Africa	KIA 14 Jun 41
MacKenzie KW	F/L DFC	10	501/247	I/IIC	Oct 40 – Sep 41	UK	–
Robertson FN	F/O DFM	10	261	I	Nov 40 – Mar 41	Malta	KIA 31 Aug 43
Soper FJ	S/L DFC DFM	10	1/257	I/IIC	May 40 – Sep 41	France/UK	KIA 5 Oct 41
Storrar JE	W/C DFC* AFC	10	145/73	I	May 40 – Apr 41	BoB/N.Africa	–
Upton HC	F/L DFC	10	43	I	Aug – Sep 40	BoB	–
Woods–Scawen PP	F/O DFC	10	85	I	May – Aug 40	BoB	KIA 1 Sep 40

Pilots with Nine Confirmed Hurricane Kills

NAME	RANK/DEC	SQN	MK	PERIOD	THEATRE	REMARKS
Atkinson HD	Plt Off DFC	213	I	May – Aug 40	France/BoB	KIA 25 Aug 40
Clowes AV	S/L DFC DFM	1	I	Nov 39 – Sep 40	France	
Clyde WP	G/C DFC	601	I	May – Oct 40	BoB	–

Cooper–Slipper TPM	S/L DFC	605/232	I/IIB	May 40 – Feb 42	BoB	–
Cork RJ	Lt Cdr DSO DSC	242/880	I/SH I	Aug 40 – Aug 42	BoB/Malta	Killed 14 Apr 44
Cullen RN	F/L DFC	80	I	Feb – Mar 41	Greece	KIA 4 Mar 41
Davis CR	F/O DFC	601	I	Jul – Sep 40	BoB	KIA 6 Sep 40
Dyson CH	F/L DFC*	33	I	Dec 40	N.Africa	–
Ferriss HM	F/O DFC	111	I	May – Aug 40	BoB	KIA 16 Aug 40
Joyce EL	S/L DFM	73	I/IIC	May – Dec 42	N.Africa	KIA 18 Jun 44
Lee RHA	F/L DSO DFC	85	I	Nov 39 – May 40	France	KIA 18 Aug 40
Millington WH	Plt Off DFC	79/249	I	Jul – Sep 40	BoB	KIA 30 Oct 40
Proctor JE	S/L DFC*	501/32	I	May – Aug 40	France	–
Simpson JWC	G/C DFC*	43	I	Feb 40 – May 41	UK	–
Talbot RH	Lt	274	I	Dec 40 – May 41	N.Africa	KIA 3 Jun 41
Townsend PW	G/C CVO DSO DFC*	43/85	I	Feb 40 – Feb 41	BoB	–
Turner PS	G/C DSO DFC*	242	I	May – Sep 40	BoB	–
Westlake GM	W/C DSO DFC	213/80	I/IIC	Nov 40 – Jul 42	N.Africa	–
Wykeham–Barnes PGAM KCB DSO* OBE DFC*		274/73	I	Dec 40 – Apr 41	N.Africa	–

Pilots with Eight Confirmed Hurricane Kills

NAME	RANK/DEC	SQN	MK	PERIOD	THEATRE	REMARKS
Badger JVC	S/L DFC	43	I	Jul – Aug 40	BoB	DOW 30 Jun 41
Denis J	Cmdt DFC	73	I	Apr – May 41	N.Africa	–
Eyre A	W/C DFC	615	I	Jun – Aug 40	BoB	–
Glowacki A	S/L DFC DFM	501	I	Aug 40	BoB	–
Grier T	S/L DFC	601	I	Aug – Sep 40	BoB	KIA 5 Dec 41
Henneberg ZK	S/L DFC	303	I	Aug – Oct 40	BoB	KIA 12 Apr 41
Kayll JR	W/C DSO OBE DFC	615	I	May – Aug 40	France/BoB	–
Mayers HC	W/C DSO DFC*	601	I	Aug – Sep 40	BoB	KIA 20 Jul 41
Mould PWO	S/L DFC*	1/185	I/IIA	Oct 39 – Jul 41	France/Malta	KIA 1 Oct 41
Nowell GL	F/L DFM*	87/32	I	May 40	France	–
Richey PHM	W/C DFC*	1	I	Mar – May 40	France	–
Storey WJ	S/L DFC	135	IIB	Jan – May 42	Far East	–
Szaposznikow E	F/L DFM	303	I	Aug – Oct 40	BoB	–
Urwin–Mann JR	S/L DSO DFC*	238	I	Aug – Oct 40	BoB	–
Zumbach JEL	S/L DFC*	303	I	Sep 40	BoB	–

Pilots with Seven Confirmed Hurricane Kills

NAME	RANK	SQN	MK	PERIOD	THEATRE	REMARKS
Aitken JWM, The Hon	G/C DSO DFC	601	I	May – Sep 40	France	–
Allen JAS	F/O DFM	232/242	IIB	Feb – Mar 42	Far East	–

Bayne AWA	W/C DFC	17/136	I/IIB/C	Aug 40 – Mar 43	BoB/Far East	–
Beard JMB	S/L DFM	249	I	Sep 40	BoB	–
Brooker REP	W/C DSO* DFC*	56/232/242	I/IIB	Jul 40 – Mar 42	BoB/Far East	KIA 16 Apr 45
Cleaver GNS	S/L DFC	601	I	May – Aug 40	France	–
Cottingham L	F/O DFC	33	I	Feb – Apr 41	Greece	–
Eckford AF	S/L DFC	32/242/253	I	May – Nov 40	France/BoB	–
Edghill DFK	Plt Off DFC	229	I	May 40 – Jul 41	BoB/N.Africa	–
Farnes PCP	S/L DFM	501	I	May – Sep 40	France/BoB	–
Feric M	F/O DFC	303	I	Aug – Oct 40	BoB	Killed 14 Feb 42
Forbes AS	G/C OBE DFC	303	I	Sep 40	BoB	–
Frost JE	Maj DFC*	3 SAAF	I	Feb – Apr 41	Somali/Ethiopia	KIA 16 Jun 42
Gardner PM	F/L DFC	3/32	I	May – Aug 40	France/BoB	–
Genders GEC	F/L AFC DFM	33	IIA	Apr – Jun 41	Greece/N.Africa	–
Godden S	Plt Off	274	I	Dec 40 – Apr 41	N.Africa	KIA 1 May 41
Grassick RD	F/L DFC	607/242	I/IIA	May 40 – Jun 41	France/UK	–
Hanks PP	G/C DSO DFC AFC	1	I	Apr – May 40	France	–
Holden E	W/C DFC	501	I	May – Oct 40	France/BoB	–
Jay DT	F/O DFC	607/87	I	May – Aug 40	France/BoB	KIA 24 Oct 40
Latta JB	Plt Off DFC	242	I	May – Sep 40	France/BoB	KIA 12 Jan 41
Mackie JF	F/O	33	I	Dec 40 – Apr 41	N.Africa	KIA 15 Apr 41
Meaker JRB	Plt Off DFC	249	I	Aug – Sep 40	BoB	KIA 27 Sep 40
Milne RM	W/C DFC*	151	I	May – Aug 40	BoB	–
Olser MS	Lt Col DFC*	1 SAAF	I	Jun – Dec 41	N.Africa	–
Pain JF	F/L	32/261/73	I/IIC	Aug 40 – Jul 42	BoB/Malta	–
Patterson TL	F/O	274	I	Dec 40 – Jan 41	N.Africa	KIA 25 Apr 41
Rayner RMS	W/C DFC	87	I	May – Aug 40	France	–
St Quintin PR	S/L	33	I	Oct – Dec 40	N.Africa	–
Satchell WAJ	W/C DSO	302	I/IIA	Aug 40 – Apr 41	BoB/Malta	–
Sing JEJ	S/L DFC	213	I	Aug 40	BoB	–
Skalski S	W/C DSO DFC**	501	I	Aug – Sep 40	BoB	–
Smith JD	F/L	73	I	Sep 40 – Apr 41	BoB/N.Africa	KIA 14 Apr 41
Stones DWA	S/L DFC*	79/605	I/IIA	May 40 – Mar 42	France/Far East	–
Taylor FF	F/O DFC	261	I	Jul 40 – Jan 41	Malta	KIA 26 Feb 41
Tweedale GR	Plt Off DFM	126/185	IIB	Mar – May 42	Malta	KIA 9 May 42
Weaver PS	F/L DFC	56	I	Jul – Aug 40	BoB	KIA 31 Aug 40
Wilkimson RC	W/C OBE DFM**	3	I	May 40	France	–
Wilson FAWJ	F/L DFC	80/213	I/IIC	Jun 41 – Jun 42	France	–
Woods–Scawen CA	Plt Off DFC	43	I	Jun – Aug 40	BoB	KIA 2 Sep 40

Pilots with Six Confirmed Hurricane Kills

NAME	RANK	SQN	MK	PERIOD	THEATRE	REMARKS
Barclay RGA	S/L DFC	249/238	I/IIB	Sep 40 – Jul 42	BoB/N.Africa	KIA 17 Apr 42
Beamish FV	G/C DSO* DFC AFC	151	I	Jun 40 – Jan 41	BoB	KIA 22 Mar 42
Blair KH	W/C DFC*	85/151	I	May – Aug 40	France/BoB	–
Boot PV	F/L DFC	1	I	May – Sep 40	France/BoB	–
Bruce DC	F/L DFC	111	I	May – Aug 40	BoB	KIA 4 Sep 40
Dafforn RC	S/L DFC	501	I	May – Oct 40	France/BoB	Killed 9 Sep 43
Daw VG	S/L DFC AFC	32	I	May – Jun 40	France	–
Dovell RL	Sgt DFM	232	IIB	Jan 42	Far East	–
Friendship AHB	S/L DFM*	3	I	May 40	France	–
Hamilton CE	Plt Off	261	I	Jan – Mar 41	Malta	DoW 14 May 41
Honor DSG	G/C DFC*	274	I/IIB	May – Dec 41	N.Africa	–
Jeka J	S/L DFM	238/306	I/IIA	Sep 40 – Jun 41	BoB	–
Karubin S	Sgt DFM	303	I	Aug – Oct 40	BoB	Killed 12 Aug 41
King GJ	F/L DFC	232/242	IIB	Feb – Mar 42	Far East	–
Laricheliere JEP	Plt Off	213	I	Aug 40	BoB	KIA 16 Aug 40
Lee KNT	S/L DFC	501	I	May – Aug 40	France/BoB	–
Lofts KT	W/C DFC*	615/249	I	Aug – Sep 40	France/BoB	–
Mitchell HT	S/L DFC	87	I	May – Aug 40	France/BoB	–
Morfill PF	F/L DFM	501	I	May – Sep 40	France/BoB	–
Nicholls HT	Plt Off	232	I	Jan – Feb 42	Far East	–
Pasziewicz LW	S/L DFC	303	I	Aug – Sep 40	BoB	KIA 27 Sep 40
Peacock–Edwards SR	S/L DFC	253/261/258	I/IIB	Oct 40 – Apr 41	UK/Malta/Far East	–
Philippart JAL	Plt Off	213	I	Aug 40	BoB	KIA 25 Aug 40
Powell RPR	G/C DFC*	111	I	May – Jun 40	France	–
Sanders JG	W/C DFC	615	I	May – Sep 40	France/BoB	Maybe 16 kills
Scott DS	S/L DFC	73	I	Apr – Sep 40	France/BoB	–
Shaw JT	G/C DSO DFC AFC	3/32	IIA/C	Aug 41 – Apr 43	UK/N.Africa	–
Sizer WM	W/C DFC*	213	I	May – Aug 40	BoB	–
Smythe RF	F/L DFC	32	I	Jun – Aug 40	BoB	–
Taylor EM	F/L DFC	232	IIB	Jan – Feb 42	Far East	KIA 8 Feb 42
Taylor N	F/L DFC DFM	601	I/IIB	Aug 40 – Jan 42	BoB	–
Thompson JM	G/C DSO DFC*	111	I	May – Aug 40	BoB	–
Tracey OV	F/L DFC	79/274	I	Aug 40 – May 41	N.Africa	KIA 8 Dec 41
Walker JA	F/L DFC	111	I	May – Aug 40	BoB	KIA 8 Feb 44
Wallace TY	S/L DFM	111	I	Aug – Sep 40	BoB	KIA 11 Nov 44
Ward DH	S/L DFC*	87/73	I/IIC	May 40 – May 42	France/N.Africa	KIA 17 Jun 42
Waugh LRS	Capt DFC	1 SAAF	I/IIA	Oct 41 – Jul 42	N.Africa	–
Whittaker RC	Plt Off DFC	17	I	May 40	France	KIA 7 Jun 40

Pilots with Five Confirmed Hurricane Kills

NAME	RANK	SQN	MK	PERIOD	THEATRE	REMARKS
Angus AB	F/O DFC	85	I	May 40	France	KIA 16 May 40
Ayre HW	F/L	261	I	Sep 40 – Mar 41	Malta	–
Barnwell DU	Plt Off DFC	185/MNFU	IIA	Jul – Oct 41	Malta	KIA 14 Oct 41
Barrick JF	F/L DFM	17	IIB	Feb – Apr 42	Far East	–
Barton ARH	S/L DFC*	32	I	Aug – Sep 40	BoB	–
Beard DR	F/S DFM	73	IIB/C	Oct 42 – May 43	N.Africa	–
Berry FG	F/S DFM	1	I	Apr – Aug 40	France/BoB	KIA 1 Sep 40
Botha AJ	Lt	1 SAAF	IIA	May – Jun 41	N.Africa	KIA 14 Jun 41
Bowes RRH	F/L DFC	79	IIC	Dec 42 – Apr 43	Far East	KIA 21 May 43
Burnell–Phillips PA	Plt Off DFM	607	I	Aug – Sep 40	BoB	KIA 9 Feb 41
Butterfield SL	Sgt DFM	213	I	May 40	France	KIA 11 Aug 40
Carpenter JMV	S/L DFC*	46/126	IIA	Jun – Dec 41	Malta	–
Cartwright H	Sgt DFM	79	I	May 40	France	KIA 4 Jul 40
Comely PW	Plt Off	87	I	May – Aug 40	France/BoB	KIA 15 Aug 40
Craig JT	Sgt DFM	111	I	May – Aug 40	BoB	Killed 2 Jun 41
Dahl R	W/C	80	I	Apr – Jun 41	Greece	Author
Demozay JF	W/C DSO DFC*	1/242	I/IIB	Mar – Jun 41	UK	–
Dini AS	Plt Off	607	I	May 40	France	Killed 31 May 40
Donaldson EM	Air Cdre CB CBE DSO AFC*	151	I	May – Jul 40	France/BoB	–
Dygryn–Ligoticky JD	W/O DFM	1	IIA/B	May – Jun 41	UK	KIA 4 Jun 42
Flinders JL	F/L	32	I	May – Aug 40	BoB	–
Foskett RG	S/L DFC	80	I/IIB/C	Nov 41 – Nov 42	N.Africa	KIA 31 Oct 44
Gaunce LM	S/L DFC	615/46	I	Jul – Nov 40	BoB	KIA 19 Nov 41
Gracie EJ	W/C DFC	56	I	Jul – Aug 40	BoB	KIA 15 Feb 44
Grice DH	W/C MBE DFC	32	I	May – Aug 40	BoB	–
Griffiths G	F/L DFM	17	I	Jul – Nov 40	BoB	–
Hardacre JR	F/O	504	I	May – Sep 40	France/BoB	KIA 30 Sep 40
Haw C	S/L DFC DFM	504/81	I/IIB	Sep 40 – Sep 41	Russia	–
Haysom GDL	G/C DSO DFC	79	I	Jun 40 – Apr 41	BoB	–
Hodgson WH	Plt Off DFC	85	I	Aug 40	BoB	Killed 13 Mar 41
Hogan HAV	AVM CB DFC	501	I	Jul – Oct 40	BoB	–
Horricks GE	F/L DFM	185	IIA/C	Jan – Apr 42	Malta	–
Hughes DP	F/L DFC	238	I	Aug 40	BoB	KIA 11 Sep 40
Humpherson JBW	F/L DFC	607/32	I	May – Aug 40	France/BoB	Killed 22 Jun 41
Hyde RJ	S/L AFC	261	I	Sep 40 – Apr 41	Malta	–
Julian I	S/L DFC	232/242	IIB	Feb – Mar 42	Far East	–
Kellett RG	W/C DSO DFC	303	I	Aug – Sep 40	BoB	–
Lardner–Burke HP	W/C DFC*	126	IIA/C	Aug – Nov 41	Malta	–

Latimer J	S/L DFC	17/310/312	I	May – Sep 40	BoB	KIA 15 Apr 43
Leary DC	Plt Off DFC	17	I	Jun – Nov 40	BoB	Killed 28 Dec 40
Littolf A	Capt	73/274	I	Apr – May 41	N.Africa	KIA 16 Jul 43
Maciejowski MM	F/O DFC DFM	249	I	Oct 40 – Feb 41	UK	–
Manger K	Plt Off DFC	17	I	May – Jun 40	France	KIA 11 Aug 40
Mason F	F/L DFC	80	I/IIC	Dec 41 – Jul 42	N.Africa	–
McGrath JKUB	S/L DFC	601	I	May – Aug 40	BoB	–
McGregor GR	G/C OBE DFC	1 RCAF	I	Aug – Oct 40	BoB	–
McKay DAS	F/L DFM*	501	I	May – Aug 40	France/BoB	–
Muirhead IJ	Plt Off DFC	605	I	May 40	France	KIA 15 Oct 40
Parker BJ	F/L DFC	232/242	IIB	Jan – Mar 42	Far East	–
Parrott PL	S/L DFC*	607/145	I	May – Aug 40	France/BoB	–
Payne AD	F/S	501	I	May – Jun 40	France	–
Perrin JR	W/C DFC	3 RAAF	I	Feb – Apr 41	N.Africa	–
Plinston GHF	S/L DFC	607/242	I	May 40	France	–
Pniak K	S/L DFC	32/257	I	Aug – Nov 40	BoB	–
Rhodes–Moorhouse WH	F/L DFC	601	I	May – Sep 40	France/BoB	KIA 6 Sep 40
Smith IS	W/C OBE DFC*	151	I	Aug – Oct 40	BoB	–
Smith WA	W/C DFC	229	I/IIC	Sep 40 – Dec 41	BoB/N.Africa	–
Smythe G	W/C DFM	56	I	May – Aug 40	BoB	–
Snowdon EG	F/L	213	I	Aug – Oct 40	BoB	–
Soden IS	F/L	56	I	May 40	France	KIA 18 May 40
Sowrey JA	Air Cdre DFC AFC	73/213/80	I/IIC	Jun – Jul 41	N.Africa	–
Stansfeld NK	S/L DFC	242	I	May – Sep 40	BoB	–
Stone CAC	W/C DFC*	3/17	I/IIA	May 40 – Jan 42	France/Far East	–
Strickland JM	F/L DFC	213	I	Aug 40	BoB	Killed 14 Aug 41
Tait KW	F/LDFC	87	I	May – Aug 40	France/BoB	KIA 4 Aug 41
Theron S van B	Lt Col DSO* DFC AFC	3 SAAF	I	Feb – Apr 41	Somali/Ethiopia	–
Whitehead C	Fg Off DFM	56	I	May – Aug 40	BoB	Killed 4 Jul 42
Wight RDG	Flt Lt DFC	213	I	May 40	France	KIA 11 Aug 40
Witorzenc S	G/C DFC	501/302	I/IIC	Aug 40 – Sep 41	BoB	–

Bibliography

Air Ministry combat reports (various)
Air Ministry log books (various)
Air Ministry, Squadron History, Forms F540 (various)
Air Ministry, Squadron History, Forms F541 (various)
Ashworth, Chris, *Action Stations 5* (PSL, 1982)
Ashworth, Chris, *Action Stations 9* (PSL, 1985)
Barrymore Halfpenny, Bruce, *Action Stations 8* (PSL, 1984)
Bowyer, Chaz, *History of the RAF* (Hamlyn Publishing, 1979)
Bowyer, Chaz, *Hurricane at War 1* (Ian Allan, 1974)
Clarke R.M., *Hawker Hurricane Portfolio* (Brooklands Books, 1986)
Cotton, DFC, Sqn Ldr M.C., *Hurricanes over Burma* (Grub Street, 1995)
Cull, Brian, Lander, Bruce, and Weiss, Heinrich, *Twelve Days in May* (Grub Street, 1995)
Deighton, Len, *Battle of Britain* (Book Club Associates, 1980)
Delve, Ken, and Jacobs, Peter, *Six Year Offensive* (Arms and Armour, 1992)
Delve, Ken, *Source Book of the RAF* (Airlife, 1994)
Dibbs, John, and Holmes, Tony, *Hurricane, A Fighting Legend* (Osprey, 1995)
Franks, Norman, *The Greatest Air Battle* (Grub Street, 1992)
Franks, Norman, *Hurricane at War 2* (Ian Allan, 1986)
Gelb, Norman, Scramble, *A Narrative History* (Michael Joseph Ltd, 1986)
Golley, John, *Hurricanes over Murmansk* (PSL, 1987)
Golley, John, and Gunston, Bill, *So Few* (W H Smith, 1992)
RAF in Russia, *From the Diary of Hubert Griffith* (Hammond, 1942)
Halley, James J., *Squadrons of the RAF and Commonwealth* (Air Britain, 1988)
Hough, Richard, and Richards, Denis, *The Battle of Britain* (Guild Publishing, 1990)
James, Derek N., *Hawker Aircraft Limited* (Chalford Publishers, 1996)
Kaplan, Richard, and Collier, Richard, *The Few* (Blandford, 1989)
Koniarek, Dr Jan, *Polish Air Force* (Squadron/Signal Pubs, 1994)
Longyard, William H., *Who's Who in Aviation* (Airlife, 1994)
Mason, Francis K., *The Hawker Hurricane* (Aston, 1987)
Mason ,Peter D., *Nicolson VC* (Geerings, 1991)
Personal memoirs (various)
Pilot's Notes, Hurricane MkII & MkIV, Air Ministry Publication 1564B and D (Air Ministry, 1941)
Price, Alfred, *The Hardest Day* (Arms & Armour Press, 1988)
Ramsey, Winston G., Ed., *Battle of Britain, Then and Now* (Battle of Britain Prints Int, 1989)
Rawlings, John, *Fighter Squadrons of the RAF* (MacDonald & Co, 1969)
Rawlings, John, *History of the RAF* (Temple Press, 1984)
Shores, Christopher, and Williams, Clive, *Aces High* (Grub Street, 1994)
Spooner, DSO DFC, Tony, Faith, *Hope and Malta GC* (Newton Publishers, 1992)
Stones, Donald, *Dimsie* (Wingham Press, 1991)
Tavender, I .T., *The Distinguished Flying Medal* (J B Hayward & Son, 1990)
Townsend Bickers, Richard, *The Battle of Britain* (Salamander Books, 1990)
Wallace Clarke, R., *British Aircraft Armament* (PSL, 1994)
Wynn, Kenneth G., *Men of the Battle of Britain* (Gliddon Books, 1989)

Index

Acworth, Plt Off 121

Advanced Air Striking Force (AASF) 20-1, 25-6, 30-1

Air Component (France) 20-1, 25-6, 31

Aircraft & Armament Experimental Establishment 12, 64

Aircraft controls/systems/handling 14-17, 53-56

Air intercept (AI) radar 120-1, 130

Aitken, the Hon Max 28

Arakan, The 110-11

Armament 60-5

Bader, S/L Douglas 37, 48

Badger, S/L 'Tubby' 42

Baines, F/S GI 106-7

Balden, S/L Denys 68

Balkan Air Force (BAF) 128-9, 133-4

Barbarossa, Operation 76

Barclay, Plt Off George 37, 97

Barnwell, Plt Off David 73

Barratt, AM AS 20

Barton, S/L 'Butch' 70

Battle of Britain 33-50

Battle of Britain Memorial Flight (BBMF) 71, 133, 135, 137-43

Baumann, Sgt 115

Beamont, F/O Roly 27

Beard, F/S Don 99

Beazley, F/L John 72

Benedict Force 76-87

Berry, S/L Alex 130

Beyts, F/O NM 106-7

Blount, AVM CHB 20

Bodman, S/L 93

Bombs, general-purpose 63

Boothby, F/L Bob 24

Boyd, F/L 'Ginger' 38

Boyens, F/S R 102, 106-7

British Commonwealth Occupation Force 112

British Expeditionary Force (BEF) 20-1

Brooker, F/O Richard 33, 45

Brothers, F/L Peter 44

Brown, F/O 'Hilly' 28

Browning 0.303in machine gun 60

Brzezina, S/L Stanislaw 114

Bulman, 'George' 9, 12, 19, 136

Burma 100-12

Burton, Plt Off Percy 37

Butterfield, Sgt Sam 39

Cameron, MRAF Sir Neil 77, 81

Camm, Sir Sydney 8, 10-11

Canadian Car & Foundary Co. 19, 58-9

Cap, Sgt 115

Carey, F/L Frank 28, 45, 111

Carter, W.George 8

Case, Sgt BP 106-7

Cassidy, F/L 'Cass' 73

Catapult Aircraft Merchantmen (CAM) ships 66

Ceylon 101

Chancellor, F/O Paddy 104

Chelmecki, Plt Off Marian 43

Chindwin River 101, 109, 111

Chocolate, Operation 99

Churchill, Winston 33, 50, 76, 80, 87

Clisby, F/O Leslie 27-8

Clowes, Sgt Arthur 28

Cock, F/O John 36, 39, 46

Coghlan, F/L 24, 33

Connors, F/L Stanley 41

Coope, S/L W 23

Cork, Lt 'Dickie' 67

Cottingham, W/O Leonard 124

Courtney-Clarke, F/L CS 106

Crete 123 ,125, 131

Crossley, S/L Mike 44-5

Crusader, Operation 94-5, 97

Cullen, F/O 'Ape' 121, 123

Currant, Plt Off 'Bunny' 41

Dahl, F/O Roald 24

Darween, W/C Johnny 99

David, Plt Off Dennis 28, 31, 39

Day, S/L Paul 137-8

Denis, Lt James 94

Desert Air Force (DAF) 94, 99

Desert war 90-9

Dewar, S/L JS 21, 29, 41

Dieppe Raid 127

Dodds, Sgt James 97

Donne, F/L Michael 25

Dowding, Sir Hugh 13, 29, 33, 35

Drake, S/L Billy 94

Driver, Capt Ken 92

Dryden, Plt Off 24-6, 33

Dunn, S/L Patrick 89

Dymond, Sgt Bill 41

Dynamo, Operation 31

Dyson, F/O Charles 91

East Africa 91-3

Eckford, Plt Off Alan 45

Edge, S/L Gerry 47

Egypt 90-9

El Alamein 98

Engine, performance/figures 51-52

Europe 113-35

Everett, Lt Bob 66

Far East 100-12

Farnes, Sgt Paul 41

Fayolle, S/L Emile 130

Ferguson, W/O BA 106

Ferris, F/O Henry 36

Fighter catapult ships 66

Fighter Flight (Hastings) 94

First Libyan Campaign 90-1

France 20-33

Frantisek, Sgt Josef 46, 48

Frost, Capt 'Jack' 92-3

Fury, Hawker 9, 20

Fury Monoplane 9-10

Garland, F/O Donald 27

Garnett, Plt Off WSS 106

Genders, Sgt 'Jumbo' 124

Gibson, F/L Johnny 41

Gillan, S/L John 18

Gittins, F/L 80

Gleed, F/L Ian 'The Widge' 35-6, 38, 46, 50, 117

Gloster Aircraft Co. 13, 18-9
Glowacki, Sgt Toni 41, 46
Godden, Plt Off Stan 90
Goodman, Plt Off George 44, 94
Gore, Sgt FA 106
Gracie, F/L 'Jumbo' 36, 40, 44
Grant, Plt Off Jackie 74
Gray, Sgt Thomas 27
Greece 117, 121-4, 131, 133
Gunsights 62
Hal Far Fighter Flight 68
Halahan, S/L 'Bull' 20, 27-8
Hallowes, Sgt 'Darkie' 42, 45
Hamilton, F/L 'Hammy' 45
Hancock, F/L Pat 71
Hanks, F/L Prosser 24, 28
Haw, Sgt 'Wag' 49, 76, 78, 81-4, 86-7
Hawker Aircraft/Engineering Ltd. 7-8, 13, 136
Hawker, Harry 7
Hewett, Sgt Ted 124
Higgs, F/O Tom 36
Hispano-Suiza 20mm cannon 60
Hogan, S/L GJC 106-7, 109
Holmes, Plt Off 'Artie' 76
Home front 125-7
Howell, Sgt 'Dinky' 22
Humpherson, F/O John 35
Imphal 110-11
India 100-12
Indian Air Force (IAF) 104-12
Iran 132
Iraq 93
Irish Air Corps 135
Italy 131
Java 101-2
Jay, Plt Off Dudley 42, 46
Jeffries, F/O Jerrard 25
Jones, S/L EG 121
Joyce, F/S Ernest 97
Kain, F/O 'Cobber' 21-2, 24, 28, 30
Kay-Shuttleworth, F/O Lord 38
Kilmartin, F/O 'Iggy' 28
Kuharienko, Kapt 83, 85
Lacey, Sgt 'Ginger' 28, 48
Lapsley, F/O John 89-90
Laricheliere, Plt Off Joseph 41
Lawrence, Plt Off R 102 ,106-7
Lea-Cox, S/L Charles 18
Lee, F/L Dickie 22, 45
Lee, F/O Johnny 102, 104, 106-7, 109

Lester, S/L Hugh 18
Lewis, Plt Off Albert 'Day' 25, 28, 49
Llewellyn, Sgt Reg 39, 41
Lloyd, AVM Hugh Pughe 71
Lockhart, S/L 95
Lovell-Gregg, S/L Terence 38, 42
MacEwan, F/O Keith 104
Mackie, Plt Off AS 74
Mackie, F/O John 91, 124
Malengreau, Plt Off Roger 41
Malta 68-75
Malta Fighter Flight 68
Malta Night Fighting Unit (MNFU) 70, 72-4
Marsden, S/L JW 94
Marshall, F/O Alfred 91
Mason, F/O 'Imshi' 90, 99
McClure, Plt Off Andrew 35
McGregor, F/O Alan 76
McKay, Sgt Donald 41
McKellar, F/L Archie 41, 47, 50
McKeown, S/L Des 64
McLauchlan, W/O R 106
Meaker, Plt Off Bryan 37
Mendizabel, F/O Rudy 102, 104, 106
Merchant Ship Fighter Unit (MSFU) 66
Meredith, F/O Dickie 25
Middle East 90-9
Miller, S/L Tony 77-8, 84, 87
Millington, Plt Off Bill 41
Mitchell, F/O Harry 24
More, S/L JWC 20, 24
Morgan, F/S 106
Mould, Plt Off 'Boy' 21, 28, 70
Moulton-Barrett, W/C Edward 66
Mounsdon, Plt Off Maurice 44
Munro, Plt Off RH 114
Nicolson, F/L James 43
Night fighter 115-21
North Africa 90-9
Nowell, Sgt Gareth 24, 26, 28
Observer Corps 47
Oliver, S/L JO 21
Operational Training Units (OTUs) 127, 132
Origins 7-12
Orton, F/O 'Fanny' 22, 28
Overlord, Operation 132
Overseas contracts 19
Palmer, Plt Off FR 74
Parrott, Plt Off Peter 38
Parsons, Sgt David 102, 106, 109

Patterson, F/O Tom 90
Pattle, S/L Pat 123-4, 135
Paul, F/O 'Ginger' 22
Pavey, Sgt Charles 25
Pedestal, Operation 67, 74
Persia 131, 135
Philippart, Plt Off Jacques 39, 41
Photo-Reconnaissance 67
Pickup, F/O Derrick 25
Playfair, AVM PHB 20
Pniak, Plt Off Karol 45
Portal, ACM Sir Charles 81
Porteous, W/C Roger 97
Portugal 135
Powell-Shedden, S/L George 'Polly' 72-5
Prototype 9-12
Ramsbottom-Isherwood, W/C Henry 76, 87
Rashleigh, F/O 102, 106
Rayner, F/O Roddy 28, 35, 41
Richey, F/O Paul 28
Rocket projectiles 64
Rook, Plt Off Michael 49, 76-7
Rook, F/L Tony 49, 76, 87
Roscoe, F/L Geoffrey 121
Ross, F/L Jack 77, 81, 83
Rowley, S/L Clive 138-43
Russia 76-87
Ryde, F/O 106
Safanov, Lt Col Boris 83, 85
Scoular, F/L John 28
Sea Hurricane 65-7
Sector Operations Centres 47
Seifert, Plt Off 106
Sharpe, F/L 109
Sicily 131
Simpson, S/L John 119
Sing, F/L Jackie 41
Singapore 100-2, 111
Sizer, Plt Off Bill 39, 41
Skidmore, Plt Off AB 106
Slee, Plt Off George 25
Smallwood, S/L Denis 121, 123
Smith, F/L James Duncan 91
Smith, F/O Michael 27
Smith, Sgt 'Nudger' 81-2
Smith, F/L Rod 40
Snowball, F/O 102, 106
Solomon, Plt Off Neville 44
Soper, Sgt Frank 27-8
Sopwith Aviation Co. 7
Sopwith, Thomas 7

Souter, F/O 102, 104, 106
South African Air Force (SAAF) 89-99
South East Asia Command (SEAC) 110
Spirlet, Plt Off Francois Xavier de 34
Srom, Sgt 115
St Quintin, F/O Peter 91
Stafford, F/S 106
Stephens, S/L Mike 94
Stone, S/L 'Bunny' 103
Stones, F/L Donald 73
Storrar, Plt Off 'Jas' 38, 91
Strange, Plt Off Louis 31-2
Strickland, F/O James 39, 41
Sumatra 101-2
Sutton, Plt Off 24
Sweeting, Sgt 106
Syria 93
Szczesny, F/L Henryk 114-5 ,134
Tait, Plt Off Ken 27, 35
Talbot, Lt Bob 90
Theron, Capt Servaas 92
Thomas, F/O LD 106-7, 109
Thompson, Plt Off AR 114
Thompson, S/L John 36, 41
Thompson, Captain 'Tommy' 8
Thorogood, Sgt 'Rubber' 35, 107
Tomlinson, S/L George 25
Torch, Operation 67, 98-9
Townsend, S/L Peter 39, 45, 75, 136
Trials & Development 12, 127
Tuck, S/L Bob Stanford 47
Turbinlite squadrons 130
Upton, Plt Off Hamilton 42
Urbanowicz, F/O Witold 38, 49
Vale, F/O William 'Cherry' 93, 123-4
Variants 56-60
Vickers 'S' gun/40mm cannon 61
Wade, F/L Lance 97
Walker, Plt Off Jimmy 81
Wallace, Sgt Tom 41
Ward, F/L Derek 43, 97
Watson, Plt Off 'Watty' 28, 35
Watt, Sgt 106
Waud, Sgt 'Ibby' 81, 86
Weapon switches 64-5
Weaver, F/O Percy 44
Wells, F/O Pat 37, 59, 71-2, 113-4
Western desert 90-9
Westlake, F/L George 97
Westmacott, F/O Innes 44, 73
Whitehead, Sgt Clifford 36, 44

Whitney, F/O 95
Wicks, Plt Off Bryan 24, 73
Wight, F/L Ron 39
Williams, S/L Cedric 44
Winton, F/O Denis 74
Witorzenc, F/O Stefan 41, 45
Wlasnowolski, Plt Off Boleslaw 44
Wood, Sgt JE 74
Woodward, F/O 'Woody' 90-1, 124
Worts, F/S 102, 106-7
Wykeham-Barnes, F/O Peter 89-90
Wynn, Sgt 25
Yacobenko, Kapt 83, 85
Yapp, F/L Derek 130
Yugoslavia 123, 131, 133-5
Zenker, Plt Off Pawel 45

Squadrons

1   19-24, 27-32, 35, 40-1, 44, 48, 50, 57,
     77, 94, 127, 146
3   18-9, 25, 29, 35, 40, 50, 57, 94, 103,
     120, 127-8, 146
5   57, 102-3, 105-6, 109, 111, 146
6   57, 61, 93-4, 97-99, 129, 134, 146
11   57, 147
17   19, 25, 29, 31-2, 35, 40-1, 43-4, 48, 50,
     57, 77, 101, 103-4, 147
20   57, 111, 147
28   57, 111, 147
30   57, 94, 98, 101, 104, 147
32   19, 25, 29, 35, 40-1, 43-5, 50, 57, 89,
     98, 127-8, 148
33   57, 89-92, 94-5, 97-8, 121, 123-5,
     135, 148
34   57, 148
42   57, 148
43   19, 28, 35, 38, 40, 42, 45, 50, 57,
     98-9, 127-8, 148
46   19, 32, 35, 40, 45, 48, 50, 71-2, 74, 149
56   17-9, 24-5, 29-30, 33-6, 40, 43-5,
     50, 57, 73, 113, 149
60   57, 149
63   149
67   57, 104, 149
69   74-5, 149
71   115-6, 149
73   19-24, 29-32, 34-5, 40, 48, 57, 89-94,

          97-9, 131, 150
74   57, 150
79   19, 25, 29, 35, 40-1, 50, 57, 73, 150
80   57, 89, 93-5, 98, 117, 121, 123-5, 150
81   76, 78-82, 84, 86-7, 150
85   19-25, 28-9, 35, 39-40, 45, 50, 130, 151
87   18-26, 28-9, 31, 34-43, 46, 50, 57, 60,
     116-7, 121-3, 127-8, 151
94   57, 94, 98, 151
95   94, 151
96   57, 117, 151
98   151
111 18-9, 29-30, 35-7, 39-41, 44, 50, 152
113 57, 152
116 126, 152
121 57, 115, 152
123 57, 152
126 57, 72-4, 152
127 57, 93-4, 98, 152
128 57, 94-5, 98, 153
133 57, 115, 153
134 57, 76-78, 81, 83-4, 87, 153
135 57, 101, 104, 153
136 57, 101, 104, 153
137 58, 64, 153
145 29, 35, 38, 40, 50, 153
146 57, 154
151 19, 26, 29-30, 35, 40-1, 45, 50-1,
     57, 154
153 154
164 58, 64, 131, 154
173 98, 154
174 57, 127-8, 130, 154
175 57, 127-8, 154
176 57, 154
182 155
184 57-8, 64, 131, 155
185 69-74, 155
186 155
193 155
195 155
208 57, 94, 98, 121, 124-5, 155
213 19, 26, 29-30, 35, 38-41, 45, 50, 57,
     93, 95, 97-9, 156
225 57, 127, 156
229 35, 40, 48, 50, 57, 74, 94, 98, 156
232 37, 40, 50, 94, 101-2, 156
237 57, 94, 98, 156
238 35, 38-40, 50, 57, 71, 74, 94, 97-9, 156
239 157
241 57, 157

242	31-2, 35, 37, 40, 48, 50, 57, 72, 102, 157	317	114-5, 134, 161	567	164
245	27, 35, 40, 50, 54, 57, 59, 103, 115, 118-20, 122-3, 126-8, 130, 157	318	162	577	164
247	57, 124, 127, 157	331	162	587	164
249	35, 37, 40, 42-3, 48-50, 57, 59, 70-4, 97, 113-4, 118, 157	335	57, 98, 162	595	164
250	157	336	162	598	164
253	29, 35, 40, 47-8, 50, 57, 127-8, 158	351	128, 133, 162	601	26, 28-30, 35, 38-40, 45, 50, 57, 163
255	158	352	133, 162	605	19, 24, 35, 40-1, 47-8, 50, 57, 74-5, 101-2, 163
256	158	401/1(RCAF)	35, 40, 48, 50, 57, 115, 165	607	24, 27, 29, 35, 40, 50, 56-7, 163
257	35, 38, 40, 45, 47, 50, 57, 127, 158	402/2(RCAF)	57, 115, 125, 165	610	163
258	57, 72, 104, 158	417 (RCAF)	166	615	29, 35, 40-1, 43-4, 50, 57, 72, 163
260	94, 98, 158	438 (RCAF)	131, 166	631	164
261	57, 68, 70, 73-4, 94, 98, 104, 159	439 (RCAF)	166	639	164
263	35, 40, 50, 103, 159	440 (RCAF)	166	650	164
273	57, 159	450(RAAF)	94, 98, 165	667	164
274	57, 89-90, 92, 94, 97-9, 159	451(RAAF)	57, 94, 98, 165	679	132
279	159	486 (RNZAF)	57, 166	680	67
284	159	488 (RNZAF)	166	681	164
285	159	501	19, 25, 27-32, 35, 40-1, 43-5, 48, 50, 162	691	127, 164
286	132, 160	504	19, 26, 29, 35, 40, 48-9, 50, 57, 76, 163	695	164
287	160	516	132, 164	3 (RAAF)	165
288	132, 160	518	130, 134, 164	1 (SAAF)	90, 92, 94, 98, 168
289	126, 160	520	133, 164	3 (SAAF)	92, 168
290	160	521	132, 134, 164	7 (SAAF)	57, 98-9, 168
291	160	527	132, 164	40 (SAAF)	98, 168
302	37, 40, 48, 50, 114-5, 160	530	130, 164	41 (SAAF)	168
303	37, 40, 46, 48-50, 114, 160	531	130, 164	1 (IAF)	105, 111, 166
306	161	532	130, 164	2 (IAF)	105, 111, 167
308	114, 161	533	130, 164	3 (IAF)	111, 167
309	57, 132, 161	534	130, 164	4 (IAF)	111-2, 167
310	35, 40, 48, 50, 161	535	130, 164	6 (IAF)	111, 167
312	46, 50, 57, 161	536	130, 164	7 (IAF)	111, 167
315	114, 161	537	130, 164	9 (IAF)	167
316	114-5, 161	538	130, 164	10 (IAF)	111, 167
		539	130, 164	2 (REAF)	166
				1 Russian Sqn	85